The Queen's Eyes:
Sir Nicholas Throckmorton

THE QUEEN'S EYES: SIR NICHOLAS THROCKMORTON

KNIGHT, WARRIOR, AMBASSADOR AND DIPLOMAT, 1513–1570

Edited and Annotated by

James D. Taylor Jr., AF-RHS, UCL

Algora Publishing
New York

Library of Congress Cataloging-in-Publication Data

Names: Taylor, James D., 1958– author.
Title: The queen's eyes : Sir Nicholas Throckmorton : knight, warrior,
    ambassador and diplomat 1513–1570 / James D. Taylor Jr., AS, RHS, UCL.
Description: New York : Algora Publishing, [2023] | Includes
    bibliographical references and index. | Summary: "Queen Elizabeth's
    ambassador in France and Scotland, Throckmorton threaded his path
    through skirmishes of all sorts. At the apex of the Reformation, his
    refined skills and those of his spies saved hundreds of lives and
    prevented conflicts. Painstaking research corrects some errors in the
    accepted history; letters, maps and illustrations bring the story to
    life"— Provided by publisher.
Identifiers: LCCN 2023035696 (print) | LCCN 2023035697 (ebook) | ISBN
    9781628945256 (hardcover) | ISBN 9781628945249 (trade paperback) | ISBN
    9781628945263 (pdf)
Subjects: LCSH: Throckmorton, Nicholas, Sir, 1513–1570. |
    Ambassadors—Great Britain—Biography. | Great
    Britain—History—Elizabeth, 1558–1603.
Classification: LCC DA317.8.T76 T38 2023 (print) | LCC DA317.8.T76
    (ebook) | DDC 327.41092 [B]—dc23/eng/20230821
LC record available at https://lccn.loc.gov/2023035696
LC ebook record available at https://lccn.loc.gov/2023035697

Cover image: Portrait of Sir Nicholas Throckmorton (1515–71) from *Memoirs of the Court
of Queen Elizabeth*, published in 1825.

Printed in the United States

Table of Contents

Introduction

Sir Nicholas Throckmorton, an English diplomat, soldier, and politician, served as an ambassador to France and then Scotland during the turbulent Tudor era. He played a crucial role in managing the interactions between Elizabeth I of England, Mary Queen of Scots, and the French monarchy. During the apex of the English Reformation, which involved France and Scotland as well, he had to call upon not only his own refined skills but also on liaisons, informants and spies who would save hundreds of lives and prevent conflicts.

Throckmorton skillfully balanced his allegiance to the Crown with the potential risk of treason by diligently supplying Queen Elizabeth with precise and up-to-date intelligence. This invaluable knowledge enabled the Queen to make crucial decisions in safeguarding her kingdom and potentially preventing the outbreak of war. Despite receiving commendations from Queen Elizabeth herself, his acts frequently garnered disapproval from others, resulting in his imprisonment, alternating between the two sides of the channel.

When Mary Tudor, a Roman Catholic, seized the throne from the young and innocent Protestant Jane Grey and subsequently declared her intention to wed Philip of Spain, also a Catholic, discontent spread throughout the kingdom. This led to the formation of coalitions aiming to forcibly dethrone her. This culminated in the Wyatt rebellion. Its leader, Thomas Wyatt Jr., and hundreds of others were ruthlessly put to death due to their involvement in the uprising, resulting in the widespread adoption of the infamous moniker "Bloody Mary."

Sir Nicholas Throckmorton, too, faced charges of treason and conspiracy against the Crown. In a well-documented trial, he had to mount his own defense (as was standard at the time). Throckmorton's vigorous and adept defense against his accusers resulted in a complete acquittal, a rare outcome in Tudor treason trials.

Like many powerful individuals, his eventual death as well as the disappearance of important documents and correspondence raised suspicions of poisoning. This biography will delve into these mysterious circumstances.

Ambassador Sir Nicholas Throckmorton was a prolific writer during his tenure. This fact, in conjunction with the improvement of Elizabeth I's record archives from the middle to the end of her reign, provides multiple volumes and hundreds of sources of correspondence. Throckmorton's copious writings provide a mirror in which his life and that of Queen Elizabeth I are reflected. The selections presented here help today's readers focus on his outstanding personality and the drama of his life.

When Sir Nicholas Throckmorton served as Chamberlain of the Exchequer during the reign of Queen Elizabeth, he was in possession of vast quantities of State Papers. Nicholas entrusted these papers to his son Arthur, who in turn gave them to Sir Henry Wotton, who in turn gave them to King Charles I with the intention of preserving them in the State Paper Office. As indicated in the introduction to Russell Prendergast's State Papers, this did not occur until 1857. Numerous valuable letters between Queen Elizabeth, Cecil, Randolph, and Sir Nicholas did survive. In fact, it is reasonable to assume that some of the correspondence was lost or destroyed before the collection was set aside for preservation.

Sir Henry Wotton, diplomat and poet (uncle of Sir Thomas Wotton, second Baron Wotton, who married Sir Nicholas Throckmorton's granddaughter) bequeathed the majority of Throckmorton's correspondence to Charles I, but the bequest did not take effect. After many tribulations, the papers were acquired by Francis Seymour Conway, the first Marquess of Hertford (1719–1794), whose descendant, the third Marquess of Hertford, donated them to the public record office on John Wilson Croker's recommendation prior to 1842. Since that time, the letters have been divided into separate collections.

I have endeavored to review as many as I could locate. Between 1559 and 1563, these letters reflect his time as Queen Elizabeth's ambassador in France during numerous battles, skirmishes, war, political and religious upheavals, and express his dread of the epidemic.

Immediate Ancestral Tree for Sir Nicholas Throckmorton

Assembled from information contained in A Genelogical and Historical Account of the Throckmorton Family

Sir George Throckmorton ——— Anne Katherine Vaux

Sir Robert Throckmorton—— First- Murial Berkely ——— Second-Elizabeth Hussey

Deodatus Throckmorton

Clement Throckmorton —— Catherine Neville

Sir Nicholas Throckmorton ——— Anne Carew

Kellemn Throckmorton — Edward Throckmorton

Thomas Throckmorton — William Throckmorton

Sir John Throckmorton
Died 1580 —— DeMargaret Puttenham — Sir Arthur Throckmorton

Sir George Throckmorton
1520-1612 — Mary Brydes — Robert Throckmorton

Anthony Throckmorton — Catherine Willington — Sir Nicholas Throckmorton
called Carew

Mary Throckmorton
Died 1558 — Thomas Throckmorton

Anne Throckmorton ——— John Digby of Coleshill — Henry Throckmorton

Elizabeth Throckmorton
Married Sir Walter Raleigh

CHAPTER 1: TURBULENCE

Recent historians date Nicholas Throckmorton's birth to 1515 or 1516, but the author of *A Genealogical and Historical Account of the Throckmorton Family*, Charles Wickliffe Throckmorton, places his birth in Coughton (a small village in the county of Warwickshire) in 1513. Furthermore, as previously mentioned, the fact that his tomb still exists indicates that he died 'in stone' at the age of 57 and that there should be no doubt that he died in 1570, making his birth year 1513.

In 1513, Juan Ponce de Leon became the first known European to visit Florida, and Vasco Nunez de Balboa was the first European to see the Pacific Ocean after crossing the Panama Isthmus.

Fig. 1. Throckmorton, Charles W. A Genealogical and Historical Account of the Throckmorton Family. Front piece.

Nicholas was born into a noble family with a lengthy history. The name Throckmorton, like the majority of surnames with three or four syllables, has witnessed numerous spelling variations over the centuries, making it difficult to track Nicholas and his ancestors through recorded history. The principle examples of the name spelling variances are as follows: de Trokemardtune, de Throkemortor, de Throkemertone, de Throkemerton, de Throckmertone, de Throckemerton, de Throgemerton, Throkmorton, Throckmerton, Throkmorton, Throckmarton, Throkmortone, Throgmorton, Throcmorton, Throkemerton, Throlmerton, and Throckmorton. Frogmorton has also been mentioned multiple times in accounts of Nicholas's father's participation in the 1513 Battle of Flodden.

The example of his signature on a 1559 document is provided below. His use of Throckmorton will serve as my reference point.

Since approximately 1500, the name has been spelled either Throckmorton or Throgmorton; in fact, it is frequently spelled both ways in the same document or letter. After the tenure of John de Throckmorton, son of Thomas, in 1445, the prefix 'de' was no longer used.

The manor of Throckmorton, or Throkemorton (the Rock-Moor-Town), from which the Throckmorton family derives its surname, is located in the Vale of Evesham, in the parish of Fladbury, formerly spelled Flandenburgn, in the hundred of Oswaldslawe, Worcestershire, England.

I had the privilege of reviewing an ancient catalogue of charters from the monastery of Worcester, in which there is mention of a charter by Wulfstan, the Archbishop of Worcester from 1062 to 1095, relating to four 'mansae' at Throckmorton (Throcmortune XI century, Throkemardtune XII century, Throckmerton XIII century, and Throkmarton XIV century), but the nature of the charter is not known; there is no additional information other than the same catalogue mentioning the number and size of the lands owned at that time and how much John de Throkemerton and Joscelin de Throkemerton paid in taxes.

Furthermore, it appears that the Throckmorton families were the primary landowners as early as 1175, if not much earlier. However, there are no known surviving documents that could help determine John de Throkemerton's progenitors.

The Domesday Book provided the majority of this early information. This ancient and valuable manuscript is a chronicle of King William the Conqueror's 1086 'Great Survey' of a large portion of England and sections of Wales. The objective of this survey, written in medieval Latin, was to ascertain what taxes were owed during the reign of King Edward the Confessor. Henry de Throkemerton was the son of John de Throkemerton, son of John de Throkemerton, who was taxed two marks in 1175, according to this survey. Adam was the son of Robert, son of Henry de Throkemerton, but it is presumed that William was the son of Joscelin, son of Edwardus, son of Gervase, who held land in 1086 in the town of Throckmorton, as indicated by the record.

Through these land records, much of the early history of the Throckmorton family is known, but as the centuries passed, records of daily events became more prevalent than records of transactions.

Nicholas Throckmorton was the fourth child of George Throckmorton and Anne Katherine Vaux. George, son of Robert, was born around 1489 in Worcestershire and would have claimed the majority of his inheritance in that shire, but it appears that his father had made Coughton the family seat, and George was the first of his line to serve as a knight of the shire for Warwickshire in Parliament. His grandfather and great-grandfather served as knights for the shire of Worcestershire in Parliament.

Sir Robert Throckmorton was a soldier and courtier who advised King Henry VII. Shortly before Sir Robert's demise while on a pilgrimage to the Holy Land, he sent his son George to the Middle Temple (the Honourable Society of the Middle Temple) and joined the society on the same day as his relative Edmund Knightley.

George Throckmorton was soon recognized in court and promoted to various positions. A recent biographer attributes this to his marriage to the daughter of Sir Nicholas Vaux, whose stepson Sir Thomas Parr subsequently served as King Henry VIII's comptroller.

Nicholas was born on 13 May 1513, when his father and grandfather were serving as commanders on royal supply ships for an expedition to Brittany. The crew manifest indicates that Sir Robert Throckmorton commanded the 350-ton The Great New Spanyard and that George commanded the Erasmus (Herasmus). By 27 May, approximately 132 ships had conveyed King Henry VIII and his army of approximately ten thousand men, artillery, horses, and provisions from England to France. The historical record does not indicate whether George was present on 22 April, when a squadron of

French galleys attacked the English fleet off Brest, scuttling one vessel and severely damaging another.

On the basis of payment records made to George Throckmorton as commander of the Erasymus, the last of which was dated 25 September 1513, it is reasonable to assume that he participated in the Battle of Flodden. The Battle of Flodden occurred on 9 September 1513, between the kingdoms of England and Scotland during the War of the League of Cambrai. The conflict took place between an invading Scots army led by King James IV and an English army led by the Earl of Surrey near Branxton in the county of Northumberland in northern England, and resulted in a triumphant English victory.

According to archival records, George returned home in early October after the conflict. It is unknown when Robert, his father, returned, but it would have likely been around the same time.

Nicholas lost his grandfather, Robert, who passed away on 12 August 1518, around the time he would have begun primary education. The postmortem examination reveals that he accumulated a large amount of land (approximately 6,000 acres) and several residences, the majority of which George inherited.

In the early to mid-1520s, Sir George Throckmorton and Cardinal Wolsey were involved in numerous events, including land transactions. On 14 February 1525, Wolsey leased land to George Throckmorton, which would later become part of the foundation of St. Fresworth's College, which was located in Oxford. Perhaps in part, Wolsey's contributions to Oxford facilitated George's admission to the university, where he earned multiple degrees prior to 1530. This would have ensured that George would have provided his children with an exceptional secondary education, supervised in whole or in part by Cardinal Wolsey.

Thomas Wolsey was a Catholic bishop and English statesman. In 1509, when Henry VIII became king of England, Wolsey was appointed as the king's almoner. Wolsey's affairs flourished, and by 1514, he was the dominant figure in virtually all state affairs. Furthermore, he held significant ecclesiastical positions.

Nicholas Throckmorton entered the service of Henry Fitzroy, the Duke of Richmond, who was and is regarded as a bastard son of King Henry VIII, in a year not recorded by history. However, it is likely that his uncle Sir William Parr, who served as the duke's chamberlain, helped him secure a position in his household.

Henry Fitzroy, Duke of Richmond and Somerset, was the only child conceived out of wedlock that Henry VIII acknowledged. He was the son of King Henry VIII of England and his mistress, Elizabeth Blount. He was Queen Mary I's junior half-brother and the elder half-brother of Queen Elizabeth I and King Edward VI.

Nicholas Throckmorton accompanied the duke to France at the end of 1532, according to a solitary document. The most prevalent explanation for the duke's trip to France is that he was serving his father's personal interests. It is possible that he was sent to university to further his education and to learn the manners and customs of the French; in fact, most likely it was a combination of all three. This period in France would also have exposed Nicholas Throckmorton to French court life, experience which would rove invaluable later in his career.

In the spring of 1532, preparations were made for King Henry VIII to meet with King Francis I of France, and by the summer, food and furnishings were being shipped across the channel. The two monarchs convened on 20 October between Calais and Boulogne. The festival meeting was as extravagant as could be expected, with trumpets, feats of strength, food, and drink, surrounded by gold cloths draped over regal seating for viewing jousts and tournaments and gilding opulent banquets and entertainment, all of which took place in ideal weather. There are numerous accounts of each monarch endeavoring to outdo the other in various activities. According to history, Henry's activities were extremely costly, and Francis had to borrow money to compete. There were fundamental political motives that brought the two monarchs together and produced positive results, despite the extravagant nature of the event. Rome was informed that Anglo-French relations were favorable.

King Henry returned to England in the second week of November after assuring that everything was to his satisfaction and determining that it was "safe" to dispatch his son. On 5 December 1532, the Duke of Richmond, accompanied by a retinue of an estimated sixty people, was warmly welcomed by King Francis I of France.

Anne's pregnancy was among the multitude of events circulating around King Henry when he learned of it in mid-January 1533. This would have been considered favorable information. Early in September, the king and queen awaited the birth of their child at Greenwich, where physicians and astrologers assured him that Anne would give birth to a son. On 7 September, Anne gave birth to a daughter who would later become one of the most celebrated women in English history, despite being the least-wanted royal daughter. Before returning to England to see his new half-sister, the duke remained in France until approximately mid-November 1533.

Nicholas was likely a close friend of the Duke of Richmond, who married Mary Howard at Hampton Court, England, on 26 November.

In Chapter 5, The Legend of Sir Nicholas Throckmorton, which has been passed down through the Throckmorton family, there is a passage describing Nicholas's time in France with the young Duke of Richmond between autumn 1532 and September 1533. It is unclear whether this passage was written by Nicholas or his son Andrew. The entire poem will be examined in greater depth at a later time.

> A brother fourth, and far from hope of land,
> By parents' hest I served as a page
> To Richmond's duke, and waited still at hand,
> For fear of blows that happen's in his rage.
> In France with him I lived most carelessly,
> And learned the tongue, though nothing readily.

Almack, *Papers Relating to Proceedings in the County of Kent*, pg. XCV.

Nicholas remained with the Duke of Richmond while his voyage to Ireland was planned. With rumors that King Henry VIII would declare the duke the king of Ireland, an early source states that the duke "is soon to depart for Wales at the head of a large force." There are no records indicating that the duke was in Ireland, and an early historian suggests that this was due to ailing health; however, I was unable to find evidence to support this claim. When serving as host for a St. Andrew's Day feast, it is apparent that King Henry VIII wished to keep his young son near and at court. According to court records, he was present at the New Year's celebration, where he received gifts from his father.

The fifteen-year-old Duke of Richmond began to assume more responsibilities from his father at the start of 1536, which kept him at court and increased his popularity. According to historical records, a number of his subordinates received quite valuable gifts. Nicholas Throckmorton received a doublet of silver cloth, a crimson riding coat, a robe of black velvet, and a riding coat 'of new colored cloth,' from the duke.

The issue of the succession to the English throne, exacerbated by the legitimate births of Mary in 1516 and Elizabeth in 1533, began to compound the young duke's problems early in the same year. The duke realized he was not in the line of succession as a result of the two legitimate births. Henry was injured during a jousting battle in the tilt yard at Greenwich on 24 January 1536 and rendered unconscious for two hours when he tumbled off his horse during the match. Who would succeed the king if he died became an issue of paramount importance. The law plainly stated that the king's illegitimate son had no claim to the throne, yet Henry attempted to place his son on the throne by any means possible.

The trial and execution of Anne Boleyn in May 1536 greatly troubled the young duke, whose circumstances continued to deteriorate and became more difficult. The Duke of Richmond died on 22 July 1536, despite suspicions that he was poisoned by the late queen before she passed away, according to early historical accounts. Another tale for a different volume.

King Henry was devastated by the news of his son's death, which was compounded by the fact that he was 'left only with daughters.' At this time Nicholas Throckmorton would have been approximately 23 years old; the duke was 17 years old, so it is reasonable to assume that Nicholas lost a close companion.

On 25 July 1536, a report of the dissolution of the Duke of Richmond's household was recorded, detailing the duration of the servants' stay and the order of their departure. Nicholas Throckmorton's name occurs on the relatively brief list of unmarried servants. The document mentions whether the king will accept newly enlisted men into his security. Nicholas could have been included in that decision, but no known inventory of names exists.

Sir George Throckmorton supplied two hundred men from Warwickshire on 7 October 1536, in response to the king's request for a list of all those who would provide men against the northern separatists during the Lincolnshire Rebellion. Nicholas, who was twenty-two at the time, does not appear on the roster, but this does not imply that he and his siblings did not assist their father in suppressing the uprising.

The first of the uprisings in the Pilgrimage of Grace began on 2 October and lasted until 18 October, posing a serious threat to King Henry VIII as it involved not only 'common people' but also a number of nobles who opposed Henry's rule and his desire to separate from the Catholic church.

By the 5th of October, an estimated forty-thousand men had participated in the suppression of the rebellion commanded by Charles Brandon, Duke of Suffolk, whose display of force dispersed a large number of rebels. But as swiftly as the uprising was crushed, a more serious revolt headed by numerous nobles broke out in Yorkshire. By 21 October, an estimated thirty-five thousand insurgents had amassed, prompting King Henry to request additional support from the Duke of Norfolk and the Earl of Shrewsbury, who could only muster eight thousand men.

Robert Aske, a lawyer who came from a prominent Yorkshire family, became the recognized leader of the Yorkshire separatists and made it plain that he did not desire conflict or violence and favored settlement negotiations. King Henry received the insurgents' demands but withheld a response for several weeks, recognizing that it would be difficult for Aske to feed and supply thirty-five thousand men.

Twenty-four articles were presented to Norfolk on 6 December, and if the insurgents disbanded, they would be presented to the king. The king continued to delay his response, and by the end of January, the tactic was effective as the rebels were in disarray and the king's army was poised to strike. In May of 1537, fifteen of the most prominent leaders were arrested, and all were found guilty of treason and executed. Aske was executed in Yorkshire at his own request.

Sir George Throckmorton was apprehended on suspicion of rebellion participation because he possessed a copy of the rebels' demands and it was presumed that he played a role in the rebellion. His three-page confession contains multiple references to his offspring, but he does not specify who they are or how they are related to him. Sir George Throckmorton was exonerated because the allegations against him and his sons could not be proven due to the lack of tangible evidence.

The most difficult aspect of compiling this biography was determining which Throckmorton or Throgmorton did what. References to a Throckmorton or Throgmorton without their given names are confusing to historians of any era, and although the various Calendars of State Papers attempt to elucidate, they are not conclusive if the surviving correspondence was not obvious to begin with.

Several references by early historians to Sir Nicholas' impact on the fate of Thomas Cromwell only serve to exacerbate the difficulty.

> It is a puzzle to learn that Sir Nicholas Throckmorton was one of the Star Chamber witnesses against Lord Cromwell. He must have been a spy in early life. Perhaps in the service of Cromwell himself. Nothing more likely.
>
> Burke, S. Hubert. *Historical Portraits of the Tudor Dynasty and the Reformation Period*, pg. 475.

According to references cited by Mr. Merriman in *The Life and Letters of Thomas Cromwell* and confirmed in the *State Papers*, Michael Throgmorton frequently met with King Henry VIII regarding Thomas Cromwell. I was unable to link Nicholas Throckmorton to the incident involving King Henry VIII and Thomas Cromwell. Nor was I able to locate Nicholas Throckmorton as being present during the attainder or trial of Thomas Cromwell, which was first recorded in Letters and Papers, Foreign and Domestic of the Reign of Henry VIII on 12 April 1540 as a representative in Parliament records, despite the attainder not being printed in 'Statutes at Large.' However, 'Sir' Nicholas Throckmorton was not knighted until many years later, possibly for semantic reasons.

Political and territorial tensions between Scotland and England were not new, and by the middle of 1542, Scotland was pursuing an alliance with France, which did not set well with King Henry VIII. The 12 November 1542 Battle of Solway Moss appears to have been caused by a multitude of factors that are often debated by scholars, but it appears that following his break from the Roman Catholic church, King Henry VIII requested that his nephew James V of Scotland do the same, but James refused and the Scots began raiding towns on the English side of the border. Obviously, King Henry VIII prepared for war with Scotland, and he assembled and dispatched forces to meet the Scottish army in the north.

The size of the Scottish army that invaded England varies between twelve and eighteen thousand, while the size of the English army ranges between four and eight thousand. On 12 November, the two forces met at Solway Moss near the river Esk on the English side of the border. The English were led by an experienced military commander who quickly dispersed the Scottish army, whose leaders lacked cohesion. Although history only records a small number of deaths, a large number of Scottish prisoners (approximately 1,200) were taken to London and were treated very well. Nicholas could not be found in the muster nor was he mentioned during the battle, which does not indicate he was excluded.

On 14 December, King James V died of natural causes and the juvenile Mary, Queen of Scots, assumed the throne, leaving Scotland vulnerable. On 25 August 1543, both kingdoms agreed to the Treaties of Greenwich, which contained two fundamental parts: the first was to unite both kingdoms in peace, as developed by King Henry VIII, and the second was a marriage between Edward VI of England and Mary, Queen of Scots. Additionally, the treaty allowed Scotland to maintain its laws and customs.

The proposed treaty did not sit well with the majority of Scots, and as the spring and summer weather improved, minor flare-ups and assaults started to occur along the border from both sides. Nicholas Throckmorton may or may not have participated in the battle of Solway Moss (24 November 1542), but he is documented in the north in October 1543 as a commander in the king's army.

Three letters from the period have survived, which vividly depict not only his involvement but also the tensions he encountered along the English-Scottish border.

The first letter is addressed to William Parr by Nicholas. Before Elizabeth's reign, there is scant correspondence from or to Nicholas. In my opinion as a historian, one of the finest aspects of Elizabeth's reign is how much the recorded archives improved, thereby providing more information for subsequent scholars.

In his conference on the 22nd instruction with Walter Carr of Cesforthe, Sir Walter Scott of Bowclowghe and Mark Carr, at Carram, found much less conformity than he expected. When they began by declaring that they would procure any means to have the king surcease the rigor of the sword against them, he supposed that they would proffer something, or else condescend to what he (by Parr's command) should propone; but the effect of their long prattling was that they did not impugn the treaties and would induce the chosen council of Scotland (with whom they boasted that they did much prevail) to perform them, if Parr would meanwhile make abstinence on the borders. Answered that the treaties concluded by their ambassadors were (notwithstanding sundry ratifications) not accomplished in time, and Parr, not knowing whether the king would accept them again, would intromit with no private person touching such a matter; but, if they, with humble submission to the king, relinquished the perverse factions which they adhered to, would become the king's servants and combine with his friends, Parr would desist from annoying them, and would so prefer them to the king that they should be able to resist the malice of the greatest in Scotland. 'The larde of Bowclowghe very furiously answered that they would rather be hanged than so disgrade their houses,' swearing that they would be true Scottish men and marveling that Parr 'would so will them to stain their honors' told them how they were forfeiting Parr's pity and procuring their own destruction, and that the assurance granted at their suit would hereupon cease. They, with idle suggestions, extolling the cardinal and his adherents, protracted the time till night; when the writer departed towards Norham, devising, by the way, with the captain of Warke to show them some fruits of their obstinacy at Kelso where they all lodged; who, having no convenient number to encounter the Scots assembled with those chieftains, approached in the dark within half a mile of Kelso, with 60 men, and burnt a grange and took prisoner Dan Carte's horsekeeper. The above declares all proceedings on the 22nd Oct., save that the laird of Sessforthe claimed the benefit of Parr's assurance, within which time Robert of Colyngwoode attempted a raid at Hounam and exploited certain cattle. Thinks restitution should be made 'that no proud neither perverse Scot, being your enemy, may have cause to exclaim against your promise.' Told him that Parr would see to it, if he would send a certificate of the goods taken and make like redress if any Englishman during the said five days was plaintiff; whereunto he condescended.

Also Lord Hume sent a servant to ask the writer if he would convoy a man of his with credit to Parr. Answered that, unless the messenger were a man of estimation, fully instructed and bringing Hume's determination in writing, Parr would not hear him. Hume replied that he could not, without conference with his friends, send his mind so precisely. Has intelligence that he sought this delay in expectation of man and money from the cardinal; and intends, tonight, with the captain of Norham, to attempt a raid against him in the Marse, entering by Berwick, as the Tweed is here not passable. Norham, 23 Oct.

Gairdner, James. *Letters and Papers Foreign and Domestic*, Henry VIII, V.18, Part-2, pg. 166.

Nicholas Throkemorton to Parr:

The captain of Norham, being hurt at the raid, desires him to certify their success against lord Hume. The captain of Norham, with Mr. Harry Evers and the garrison of Berwick, Mr. Clyfforthe, the captain of Warke, the writer's brother Kellan and forty of Parr's gentlemen and yeoman, with 50 of the garrison at Alnwick, burnt lord Hume's house of Kello, on 24 October, as a sequel of his obstinacy, and to try those in the Marse to whom Parr, upon Mr. Douglasse motion, granted assurance. Found these assured persons their first and most continual enemies. Douglas's dearest friends were among them, and his household servants burned beacons whereby their enterprise was described and they often skirmished with than they expected. Save the slaughter of one of the captain of Norham's servants and his own hurt, at the first assault by the laird of Blakerter, all returned safe to Berwick, at 1 p.m., having done the greatest exploit since Parr's coming. Burned 1,500 gr. of grain, besides taking horse, cattle and prisoners, and that in open day. Will declare the circumstances at his coming. Begs him to license Mr. Clyfforde of Asperden to go, for three weeks or a month, into Yorkshire to receive livery and seisin of certain land. Berwick, 24 Oct.

Gairdner, James. *Letters and Papers Foreign and Domestic*, Henry VIII, V.18, Part-2, pg. 167.

Nicholas Throkemorton to Suffolk:

This morning, on arriving from Berwick, received a letter to the lord Warden from Mr. Dowglas (enclosed). As he omitted on the 24th to write all occurrents at the last exploit in the Marshe, and now finds the lord Warden gone to court, this is to advertise Suffolk that John of Blakerter, after his first onset, before daylight, continued during their abode in Scotland to pursue them. By the captain of Norham's advice (considering that this was contrary to Mr. Douglas's promise when he received the lord Warden's assurance) sent George Selbie to him with a message warning him to desist. On coming to Blaketor's company, further off, but declared the message to one of Mr. Douglas's household servants; who answered that they could not find in their hearts to see their neighbors spoiled and not defend them adding 'that England might well fill their bellies, but the same should not daunt their hearts.' One of Blakettor's servants among the prisoners taken said, at Berwick that the Douglasses would ere long manifestly abandon England, or else Angus would be appointed a ruler in Scotland and George Douglasse would get him committed to prison, as though for his constancy to the king. Will repair to Suffolk with diligence. Warkeworthe, 26 Oct.

Gairdner, James. *Letters and Papers Foreign and Domestic*, Henry VIII, V.18, Part-2, pg. 174.

The Scottish parliament rejected the Greenwich treaties on 11 December 1543, escalating hostilities, while the English proceeded to demolish everything they could on land, leaving the region incapable of supporting a possible French landing in 1544.

On 31 December 1543, King Henry VIII and Charles V, the Holy Roman Emperor, signed a treaty committing to invade France by 20 June 1544 with an army of at least 34,000 infantry and 7,000 mounted troops. Both parties understood that the campaign could not commence until their disputes with Scotland were resolved. With France now in his sights, Henry VIII escalated his aggression in Scotland on 3 May 1544, launching an assault on Edinburgh.

A single account of the attack has survived and is reprinted in Tudor Tracts (1903) under the title "The Late Expedition in Scotland conducted by the King's army under the command of the right honorable Earl of Hertford in 1544," by Reynold Wolf, London, printed in 1544.

Nicholas Throckmorton's involvement in the assault on Edinburgh is unclear, as no records exist that might place him there. As there is no correspondence from him at the time, he may have still been in the north.

Had he been there, he would have had to sail on one of the supply ships returning to England or directly to France, where records indicate he was at the start of July 1544.

THE SIEGE OF BOULOGNE BY KING HENRY VIII MDXLIV.

Fig. 2. Public Domain usage. After an 18th century engraving after a coeval painting in the Cowdray House. The original was destroyed in a fire in 1793.

Henry VIII's affairs with Scotland were largely resolved, and it was time for the planned invasion of France. On 19 July 1544, a large English force led by Charles Brandon, Duke of Suffolk, lay siege to the city of Boulogne. A fleeting mention in a single document indicates that Nicholas Throckmorton served as a captain under the command of Charles Brandon, but I have been unable to locate a roster.

The second party, commanded by the Duke of Norfolk Thomas Howard, captured Montreuil on the Canche River.

The English confronted approximately 1,800 French soldiers, 500 Italian mercenaries, and the town's militia, which had garrisoned the city. A few weeks later, King Henry VIII arrived and assumed command, and the town's lower section succumbed swiftly to heavy, repetitive bombardment that lasted until August. The rest of the settlement, excluding the central citadel, was captured. The French firepower prevented an easy approach by foot soldiers, so the English excavated passages beneath the castle walls, and on 13 September 1544, the French capitulated.

Nicholas Throckmorton's arrival in France is obscured by history, but the following is the only known document that places him there during the siege.

Warrants to Sir Richard Southwell, as vice-treasurer of the middle ward, or battle, of the king's army in France, at sundry dates.

Like request of Nicholas Throkmarton, captain of 100 light horsemen, 'Northenstaves', wages from 1 to 22 July 36 Henry VIII for

40 men levied from the Earl of Essex, 20 from Sir Henry Knevet, 3 from Robert Barwick and 1 from John Baker; and wages from 19 to 22 July of 13 levied from Sir Richard Long and 20 from Sir William Willoughbye; also of 2 footmen attendants from 1 to 22 July. Signed; Nicoles Throkemorton, 23 July.

Letters and Papers, Foreign and Domestic, of the Reign of Henry VIII. Volume 19, pt. 2, pg. 307.

There was an additional request for wages for himself, his commanders, and his men from 23 July to 14 August, so it is fair to assume that he remained there until then or at least until the date of the French capitulation. This experience would have influenced his decision to serve as ambassador to France in the future.

Sir George Throckmorton was released from the Tower of London in 1543 upon the marriage of King Henry VIII and Catherine Parr, because Catherine Parr was Lady Throckmorton's niece. Sir George Throckmorton gained significant favor with the monarch, and several members of his family, including Nicholas, obtained lucrative positions within the court.

Nicholas Throckmorton, who had served his monarch and country with distinction and was now without a conflict to fight, was appointed sewer to Queen Catherine between January and July 1545. A sewer was an officer who arranged the dishes on the regal table, a position typically bestowed upon a person of distinction.

On 17 June 1546, Nicholas Throckmorton presented King Henry VIII with a gift, but it is unknown what it was. On the same date, he continued to serve as a sewer for Queen Catherine and received a generous grant for his efforts. He was granted the Ben Jowe *alias* Ben Jowehall, Panssanger, Magdaleyn Bury, and Westington Herts manors, farms, and other lands. Nicholas received the lands as a result of the attainder of Gertrude Courtenay, Henry Marquis of Exeter's wife. Nicholas received a recompense for his service to the monarch and nation.

Anne Askew was questioned and tortured on the rack in the Tower of London at the end of June 1546. Anne was charged with heresy, tortured to disclose the identities of fellow Protestants, and ultimately stretched so far that her arms and shoulders were dislocated and her screams were audible from a considerable distance. On 16 July 1546, she was transported from the Tower to Smithfield, London, to be burned at the stake before a large crowd that included Nicholas. She was bound to the stake with chains, and the reeds were ignited. The duration of the execution was approximately one hour. As her cries diminished, so too did the crowd.

John Loud, an educated man who narrowly escaped the same fate, commented on the execution as follows:

> I must needs confess of her, now departed to the lord, that the day before her execution, and the same day also, she had an angel's countenance and a smiling face. For I was with Lascals, Sir George Blage and the other (Belenian the priest, then burned) and with me were three of the Throckmortons, Sir Nicholas, being one, and Mr. Kellum the other. By the same token, one unknown to me said 'ye are all marked that come to them, take heed of your lives.'

Writings of Edward the Sixth, pg. 35-36.

Nicholas would have remained in London due to his obligations as queen's sewer. An early historian suggested that Nicholas had frequent opportunities to visit and associate with Princess Elizabeth around this time, which would later award him numerous titles of distinction during Elizabeth's reign as queen.

Nicholas also married Anne Carew, daughter of Sir Nicholas Carew, around this period. Sir Nicholas Carew was executed on Tower Hill on 3 March 1539 for his alleged participation in the Exeter conspiracy, a plot to overthrow King Henry VIII and replace him with Henry Courtenay, First Marquess of Exeter, father of Edward Courtenay, a fascinating subject of one of my biographies.

Nicholas married into the Carew family, but it appears he had little to no knowledge of Sir Peter Carew, son of William Carew, prior to the 1544 siege of Boulogne. Also serving under the command of Charles Brandon, Duke of Suffolk, was Peter Carew. Later in life, Nicholas would encounter Peter Carew again.

As 1546 came to a close, King Henry VIII's health continued to deteriorate, causing concern in the court. Perhaps he was confined to bed by a combination of gluttony and inactivity due in part to an ulcerated leg. In mid-January 1547, he had a brief opportunity to meet with the French and Imperial ambassadors, and the French noted that he was well and gracious, and that he remained in command throughout their conversation.

This was short-lived, and he relapsed shortly thereafter. On 27 January, he was overheard gently whispering in bed, "Yet, Christ's mercy is able to pardon me all my sins, though they were greater than they be." Henry then fell unconscious and died peacefully in the early hours of 28 January 1547. As with many royal deaths, Henry's was kept secret for a brief period to allow for preparations for his funeral and private discussions regarding the succession of his heir.

On 12 February, King Henry VIII's coffin arrived at the Bridgetine monastery of Syon Abbey in Isleworth, Middlesex, carried by sixteen yeomen of the guard with 'great stamina.' As the enormous coffin was being moved into position, it exploded open, releasing 'offensive matter' and flooding the chapel with a 'most offensive and obnoxious odor.' Later, dogs were discovered licking the remains. The king of England was interred at Windsor's St. George's Chapel.

Son of King Henry VIII and Jane Seymour, Edward VI ascended the throne. Several years prior to the young king's ninth birthday, his father established a hierarchy that designated individuals to make decisions on his behalf, with a guardian overseeing these decisions. Edward Seymour, 1st Duke of Somerset, was confronted with a number of issues, the first of which was the possibility of war with Scotland. Despite his best efforts to prevent it, conflict did occur later that year.

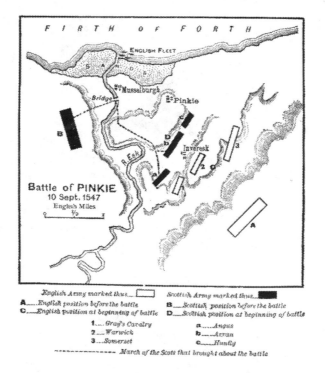

Fig. 3. *Historical Portraits, Richard II to Henry Wriothesley, 1400–1600*, pg. 426.

The Battle of Musselburgh, or as some modern historians refer to it, the Battle of Pinkey, occurred on 10 September 1547 on the banks of the River Esk near Musselburgh, Scotland. Considered the first modern conflict in the British Isles, it was the final pitched battle between the Scottish and English armies. It was a devastating loss for Scotland, often referred to as 'Black Saturday.' According to accounts of the Battle of Pinkey, 10,000 Scottish soldiers were killed, 1,500 were taken prisoner, and 500 English soldiers were killed.

The precise date and role of Nicholas Throckmorton's participation in the Battle of Musselburgh have not been documented in history. During this campaign, it is highly likely that Nicholas came into contact with Thomas Wyatt the Younger, with whom he would later serve.

Nicholas Throckmorton was recommended for commendation by the protector, Edward Seymour, for his conduct during that campaign. This is one of several pieces of evidence indicating Nicholas's participation in that conflict.

On 3 May 1551, King Edward VI held a tournament at Greenwich in the same grand form as his father. The king and his entire entourage, including his footmen and trumpeters, wore hats and cloaks, carried black and white banners, and had black and white streamers wrapped around their spears. Earl of Hertford and a large group of lords and knights, including Sir Nicholas Throckmorton, Sir Peter Carew, and Sir William Cobham, fought against the king, their young men, trumpeters, and footmen donning yellow hats and carrying yellow banners. King Edward recorded the events of that day in his personal journal: 'Finally, the yellow band took it twice in 120 courses, while my band never did, which seemed very odd, and so the prize was lost by my side.' After the tournament, there was a feast with abundant entertainment that was enjoyed by all.

Nicholas served as a member of Parliament for the county of Northampton during the reign of King Edward VI, according to a single record in the Throckmorton family's annals. As the young king only held two sessions of Parliament during his reign, locating this information should have been straightforward. However, I was unable to locate his name in either of the sessions recorded in The Parliamentary History of England, volume 1, 1066-1625, or The Parliaments and Councils of England Chronologically Arranged from the Reign of William I to the Revolution of 1688. Nicholas may have attended a session in place of a member who was absent, though this is not conclusive evidence.

Nicholas hid his wife, Lady Anne, from the court, and when the king expressed a desire to meet her, she disguised herself as a peasant to meet him. The king informed her that her spouse was poor because he had poorly attired her, which she excused on the grounds of poverty. Nicholas responded, "It was a poor decision to wear clothing for which you still owed merchants." The king accused him of 'bashfulness' and informed him that he was not entitled to anything unless he specifically requested it. Nicholas was quick-witted enough to request the manor of Paulperspury, and the king granted his request.

On 22 October 1551, King Edward VI learned that Mary of Lorraine, the Queen Regent of Scotland, was forced to land at Portsmouth due to a tempest at sea. The king immediately made preparations to receive the royal guest at his Hampton Court palace. King Edward VI noted in his journal that the queen dined at the home of the Earl of Arundel on October 29 before being transported to Guildford on 30 October. The next day, she arrived in a valley along the Thames approximately two miles from Hampton Court, where she was greeted by knights and nobles clad in formal court attire, including Nicholas Throckmorton, despite the typically foul late-October weather. Mary of Lorraine left Hampton Court the next day via the Thames River and landed at Baynard Castle, where she was greeted by John Dudley, the Duke of Northumberland, and other peers, and given another lavish feast.

The next day, King Edward VI dispatched Henry Grey, the Duke of Suffolk, and several other nobles to greet the royal party and deliver a message from the king: 'if she lacked anything, she should have it for her better furniture, and I would gladly see her the next day.' The king left St. Paul's in a chariot, accompanied by Lady Frances, Duchess of Suffolk, and Lady Jane Grey, two English princesses.

During the queen's short journey, all the spectators' eyes were drawn to their chariot as they passed, followed by approximately one hundred nobles and their spouses. The Dukes of Suffolk and Northumberland greeted and escorted the royal visitor to the young king at the palace's entrance. Mary of Lorraine curtsied as Edward approached, and the king took her hand, kissed it, embraced her, and then welcomed her. This is the final entry in the king's journal for the day. It is safe to assume that the royal guest was entertained and served dinner before leaving.

On 6 November, Mary of Lorraine departed London for an eighteen-day journey to Edinburgh, Scotland. Long retinue of English nobility, including the Duchess of Suffolk and Lady Jane Grey, escorted her through London's streets to Shoreditch Church. Mary of Lorraine held a favorable opinion of the young king, and both she and Edward relished the visit, despite the queen's recent loss of her son, who was only one year older than Edward.

There is debate regarding whether Nicholas was knighted. After conducting additional investigation, I uncovered several gems that helped clarify this matter. Within *The Knights of England, Volume II of A Complete Record from the Earliest Times to the Present*, the following entry appears verbatim: '18 September 1547, Nicholas Throckmorton (by the (?) king in London)'. This is an extremely useful piece of information.

In addition, I examined letters sent by the king to various high sheriffs in January 1552 announcing the election of certain individuals as knights. Northamptonshire's magistrate received notices for Nicholas Throckmorton and Robert Lane, among the few named.

King Edward held Nicholas in high regard and regarded him as a trusted servant and confidential agent who carried documents between the king and the clerk of the council. Nicholas's service to his father undoubtedly earned him the rank. There is no additional information regarding the exact date Nicholas was knighted or whether a ceremony took place. In an unrelated document from May 1552 that lists all the gentlemen of the king's privy chamber, 'Sir' Nicholas Throckmorton is among the distinguished men named. Since this is the first mention of 'Sir' Nicholas Throckmorton, the ceremony could have taken place between late January and April 1552.

> An annuity of 100£ to Sir Nicholas Throckmorton, in consideration as well of the surrender of his office of one of the treasurers of the coin of the mint in the Tower, as for his faithful service, during life: granted Jan. 28. (1553)'

> *Strype, Ecclesiastical Memorials, vol. II, pt. 223–230*

Despite the assertions of a few recent historians that Nicholas was never knighted, and the fact that one of them still disputes the date of his birth, I believe the information I have presented will rectify this misconception.

Nicholas and Lady Anne traveled to Coughton, Warwick, to see his parents. Shortly before their arrival, he informed his father of his visit so that he could prepare for it. Apparently, the message offended his father.

> He thumpt me on the breast and thus began,
> Sir Knight! Sir Knave! A foolish boy you are:
> And yet thou thinkest thyself a goodly man!
> Why shouldst thou scorn they father's daily fare?
> Or send me word when I should see you here,

As who should say, I should provide good cheer.
Too base for thee thou though'st thy father's food
But say tis so, I tell you in good sooth
My Carter's meat I think is far too good
For such an one who brings so dainty tooth
I see your grow'st into distain of me,
Wherefore, know this, I careless am of thee.

Throckmorton, Wickliffe. *A Genealogical and Historical Account of the Throckmorton Family, pg.* 178.

Nicholas received this treatment, presumably because George was a devout Catholic and Nicholas was advancing within a Protestant court and was knighted before his older brother Robert.

George Throckmorton died on 6 August 1552, and was interred in the tomb he had constructed for himself out of marble in Coughton Church. At the time of his demise, George Throckmorton was said to have 116 living descendants, including Job Throckmorton, William Gifford, Archbishop of Rheims, and the first Peer of France, among others.

As the New Year's celebrations concluded, King Edward VI was compelled to deal with his deteriorating health. First, he contracted measles, from which he quickly recovered, but then he was afflicted with a persistent cough that could not be treated with medication. The rapid onset of symptoms of consumption alarmed not only his physicians but also those closest to the throne.

On 1 March, he was compelled to inaugurate a new session of Parliament in Whitehall's great hall instead of Westminster. Later, he was unable to attend Easter in Greenwich because he continued to suffer from catarrh and a persistent cough. The kingdom soon learned of Edward's illness, which was now more severe than his previous ailments. Many, including his own physicians, feared that the young king would not survive much longer, and he was confined to his bed, where he grew weaker with each passing day.

Nicholas, who was a Protestant and adhered to the 'New Doctrine,' believed that Mary was the rightful heir to the throne and departed promptly for a family estate in London, where he met three of his brothers. After consulting with them, he determined that it was appropriate to send Mary's goldsmith to deliver the news of the king's death.

JOHN DUDLEY, DUKE OF NORTHUMBERLAND, K.G.

From a portrait in the possession of Lord Sackville

Fig. 4. John Dudley. Historical Portraits, Richard II to Henry Wriothesley, 1400–1600, pg. 55.

The poem *The Legend of Nicholas Throckmorton* contains a description of Nicholas's actions and how he was responsible for informing Mary of her brother's death. According to some recent authors, there are several contradictory descriptions of how Mary was informed; perhaps the information in the poem can clarify. The entire poem is contained in chapter 5.

> Mourning, from Greenwich I did stray depart
> To London, to a house which bore our name.
> My brethren guessed by my heavy heart
> The king was dead, and I confessed the same:

> The hushing of his death I did unfold,
> Their meaning to proclaim queen Jane I told.
>
> And, though I liked not the religion
> Which all her life queen Mary had professed,
>   Yet in my mind that wicked motion
>   Right heirs for to displace I did detest.
>   Causeless to proffer any injury,
>   I meant it not, but sought for remedy.
>
> Wherefore from four of us the news was sent,
> How that her brother he was dead and gone;
>   In post her goldsmith then from London went,
>   By whom the message was dispatched anon.
>   She asked,' 'If we knew it certainly?'
>   Who said, 'Sir Nicholas knew it verily.'
>
> The author bred the errand's great mistrust:
>   She feared a train to lead her to a trap.
>   She said, 'If Robert had been there she durst
>   Have gauged her life, and hazarded the hap.'
>   Her letters made, she knew not what to do:
>   She sent them out, but not subscribed thereto."

Nichols, John. *The Chronicle of Queen Jane and of Two Years of Queen Mary*, pg. 2.

Mary's constitution dictated that she remain suspicious of the information as a potential plot to capture and imprison her in the Tower of London. When she questioned the goldsmith about the source of his information, he stated that Nicholas Throckmorton had provided it. That did not dispel her suspicions, and she stated that if the information had come from Sir Robert, his eldest brother and a Papist, she "would have staked her head on it."

Even though this information was obtained from *A Genealogical and Historical Account of the Throckmorton Family*, the conversation between Mary and the goldsmith appears to be described in a variety of ways.

Mary responded swiftly to the news of her brother's death by writing a letter to the lords of the council on 9 July asserting her claim to the throne. She remarked how odd it was that they had not informed her of the tragic news themselves. The council replied that she should remain silent and serve the new queen with obedience. The council, at this point thoroughly subjugated and terrorized by Northumberland, chose to crown Lady Jane queen. Not all council members readily adhered to Northumberland's scheme.

Secretary Cecil

Fig. 5. . Cust, Lionel. The National Portrait Gallery. London, 1901.

Secretary Cecil was one of the council members who declined to issue a proclamation crowning Jane and he sought counsel from Nicholas Throckmorton. Cecil refused to write the letters announcing Jane's coronation because he would not write "Queen Mary, bastard," so the Duke of Northumberland penned the letters himself.

Mary Sidney was then instructed to bring Jane Grey to Syon House to wait.

The Duke of Northumberland led the councilors into the room where Lady Jane and Mary Sidney were waiting before requesting that they accompany him and the lords to the state chamber. The 15-year-old girl discovered her parents, spouse, mother-in-law, and Lady Northampton, who all showed her respect.

LADY JANE GREY.

Jane Grey

Fig. 6. Davey, Richard. *The Nine Days Queen, Lady Jane Grey and her Times.* London, 1909.

Following Northumberland's speech, Lady Jane was in a state of great confusion, not knowing whether to mourn the king's demise or celebrate her adoption of the kingdom. After thoroughly considering the situation, she responded with tears:

"That the laws of the kingdom, and natural right, standing for the king's sister, she would beware of burthening her weak conscience with a yoke, which did belong to them; that she understood the infamy of those, who had permitted the violation of right to gain a scepter; that it were to mock God, and deride justice, to scruple at the stealing of a shilling, and not at the usurpation of a crown. Besides I am not so young, nor so little read in the guiles of fortune, to suffer myself to be taken by them. If she enrich any, it is but to make them the subject of her spoil, if she raise others, it is but to pleasure herself with their ruins. What she adored yesterday, is today her pastime. And, if I now permit her to adorn, and crown me, I must tomorrow suffer her to crush, and tear me in pieces. Nay with what crown doth she present me. A crown, which hath been violently and shamefully wrestled from Katherine of Aragon; made more unfortunately by the punishment of Ann Boleyn, and others, that wore it after her. And why then would you have me add my blood to theirs, and to be the third victim, from whom this fatal crown may be ravished with the head that wears it? But in case it should not prove fatal unto me, and that all its venom were consumed; if fortune should give me warranties of her constancy: should I be well advised to take upon me these thorns, which would dilacerate, though not kill me outright; to burthen myself with a yoke, which would not fail to torment me, though I were assured not to be strangled with it? My liberty is better, then the chain you proffer me, with what precious stones so ever it be adorned, or of what gold so ever framed. I will not exchange my peace for honorable and precious jealousies, for magnificent and glorious letters. And, if you love me sincerely, and in good earnest, you will rather wish me a secure, and quiet fortune, though mean, then an exalted conditions exposed to the wind, and followed by some dismal fall."

Heylyn, *Ecclesia Restaurata*, or *The History of the Reformation*, pg. 159-160.

Jane questioned the legality of the changes made to King Henry VIII's will, which enraged Northumberland and altered his course of persuasion. However, Jane did not readily succumb to his intimidating tactics, and only after a lengthy delay did she give in. "If what hath been given to me is lawfully mine, may Thy Divine Majesty grant me such spirit and grace that I may govern to Thy glory and service, to the advantage of this realm,"

Jane was proclaimed Queen of England with the usual formalities in a relatively brief and modest ceremony, in contrast to previous monarchs. All relevant parties were sent letters announcing the new queen and requesting their allegiance. Jane Grey was not well-known in the kingdom, and the Duke of Northumberland's unfavorable reputation exacerbated the kingdom's lack of enthusiasm for their new queen.

As Jane assumed the role and responsibilities of queen, she spent the majority of her time reviewing and signing documents, oblivious to Mary's actions as she began to accumulate large numbers of loyal supporters and assert her rightful claim to the throne. This caused great concern within Jane's council.

Northumberland realized by 12 of July that military operations would be required to capture the Princess Mary. Despite being the most accomplished military commander, he did not trust the resolve of some of his colleagues and wished to remain in London to safeguard his interests. Queen Jane refused to dispatch her father because she feared being left alone with the duke, despite the fact that the Duke of Suffolk possessed comparable qualifications. Therefore, the queen commanded Northumberland to personally head the forces.

As he left the Tower of London, he declared, "In a few days I will bring the Lady Mary captive, ordered like a rebel as she is." Jane's decision not to send her father proved disastrous to Northumberland's plans, as the Council was no longer under his control and the peers began to form alliances. Nicholas appears to have chosen neutrality in this matter, as neither he nor his brothers are mentioned in the records.

The next morning, the Duke of Northumberland left London with between 1,500 and 8,000 foot soldiers, 2,000 mounted soldiers, and a small train of ordnance. As they rode out of London, the Duke of Northumberland reportedly remarked to Lord Gray of Wilton, who accompanied him, "Do you see, my lord, what a conflux of people here is drawn to see us march? And yet of all this multitude, you hear not so much as one that wisheth us success."

Mary relocated her expanding army from Kenninghall because Kenninghall was difficult to defend and a significant battle was expected. The Duke of Northumberland reached the outskirts of Cambridge on the morning of 16 July, and as he proceeded toward Bury St. Edmunds, he received word from Yarmouth that eight ships had switched allegiance to support Mary. This was yet another setback to the duke's plans, as he had counted on their support.

The next day, the Duke of Northumberland retreated from Bury St. Edmunds to Cambridge, and many of his soldiers deserted out of fear of treason charges should Mary ascend to the throne. By the time Northumberland reached Cambridge, he had lost roughly half of his forces to desertion, but none in combat because there had been no fighting.

Queen Jane penned a letter that was sent to a number of her officers, commanding them to promptly muster forces and then march to Buckinghamshire to put down the rebellion as soon as possible. At this time, it was reported that Mary's forces numbered approximately 30,000, and additional guards were set in the tower to safeguard Jane. Without

Northumberland's presence, the council continued to divide, and several councilors met at the residence of the Earl of Pembroke to denounce Northumberland as a 'bloodthirsty tyrant, and Mary had the strongest claim to the throne.'

A proclamation was sent to Northumberland, and if he did not respond immediately, the Earl of Arundel would travel to Cambridge to apprehend the villain who had led so many against the throne's legitimate heir.

Fig. 8. Lady Anne Throckmorton, *Charles W. A Genealogical and Historical Account of the Throckmorton Family*, pg. 33.

Lady Anne Throckmorton (Nicholas's wife) served as godmother to Edward Underhill's son at his christening at the Tower of London on 19 July, acting on behalf of Queen Jane. The child was given the surname of Jane's spouse, Guildford. Earl of Pembroke and Duke of Suffolk agreed to serve as proxy sponsors. Lady Throckmorton, in accordance with etiquette, received orders from Lady Jane following the ceremony and relayed them to specific individuals. She then returned to the Tower, where she discovered that the canopy of state and all other regal emblems had been removed in such a short period of time. Lady Throckmorton was then informed by one of the new officers-in-charge that Lady Jane had been dethroned and that she must attend to her, 'but under the weight of a similar charge.'

Mary was crowned queen the following day. The council altered its allegiance publicly and officially, then sent two councilors to Suffolk to inform him that his daughter's reign had ended and that Mary had been crowned queen. When the Duke of Suffolk learned that his daughter's reign was over, he instructed her to be content with her return to private life and forbade her from using any further royal ceremonies. She calmly responded that she would "relinquish the crown." There are differing accounts of Jane's reaction, ranging from relief to disappointment because she desired to be queen.

On 18 July, a proclamation was made in Northamptonshire, a county in the east midlands, proclaiming Mary as queen. The letter's unknown author noted that Nicholas was present:

> Great stir was in Northamptonshire about proclaiming of her. Yesterday at Northampton sir Thomas Tresham proclaimed her with the aid and help of the town, being born amongst them, whether he would or not; Sir Nicholas Throgmorton being present, withstanding him to his power, was driven for safety of his life to take a horse, and so being born amongst divers gentlemen escaped with much ado; the inhabitants would have killed him very fine.
>
> Nichols, John. *The Chronicle of Queen Jane and of Two Years of Queen Mary*, pg. 12.

It is unclear why his life would have been in peril other than because of his Protestant beliefs, which differed from those of the new monarch and could have been the author's opinion. The following letter, also by an unknown author, could be interpreted in a variety of ways, though Nicholas's name does not appear in the records of prisoners at the Tower of London at that time. As the conclusion of the following letter suggests, it is reasonable to assume that Nicolas was not incarcerated but rather summoned to duty.

> Since the 24 of July, 6 of your men on horseback like soldiers, in coats of red and white, at your cost and charges, have waited on sir Thomas Tresham and sir Nicholas Throgmorton, to guard the queen to London.
>
> Nichols, John. *The Chronicle of Queen Jane and of Two Years of Queen Mary*, pg. 13.

Mary had ordered the Earl of Arundel to apprehend and bring to justice the traitorous Duke of Northumberland because she had received no response to the proclamation sent to Northumberland. The Duke of Northumberland and his army surrendered at Cambridge on 24 July. The next day, at dusk, they arrived in London and rode through the massive crowds that had congregated on the streets. Stones, rotten eggs, and filth from the sewers were flung at the Duke, and according to one witness, a deceased cat was also thrown. The crowd cried out, "Death! Death to the traitor!" The once-confident, powerful, and arrogant Duke of Northumberland rode slowly past the crowd with his head bowed in shame, and a solitary record indicates that tears flowed from his eyes as he passed. Later, the Duke of Northumberland was prosecuted, found guilty of treason, and executed on Tower Hill.

Mary rapidly adjusted to her duties as queen, and the court began to speculate about her future marriage. Many believed that she would not be able to rule without a spouse, and several candidates, including the recently released Edward Courtenay, Earl of Devonshire, were considered.

The greatest concern for many in the realm was the change in religion, as Mary was Catholic. Although many accepted the sermons, some feared the harsher methods of punishment for non-conformity, such as confiscation of personal property, imprisonment, and even execution for their beliefs that differed from the new queen's. Nicholas Throckmorton was evidently not afraid to express his opinion to a friend, Sir Edward Warner, the late lieutenant of the tower, whose daughter his brother had married, about the tyranny of the time, according to a record that has survived.

> "I wish it were lawful for all of each religion to live safely according to their conscience. For the law ex officio, would be intolerable, and the clergy discipline now might rather be resembled to the Turkish tyranny, than to the teaching of Christian religion."

> Strype, *Ecclesiastical Memorials; Relating Chiefly to Religion and its Reformation*. V.4, 1816 edition, pg. 129.

The coronation of Queen Mary took place on 1 October 1553. According to early accounts, Mary rode in a lavishly decorated chariot drawn by six horses, wore a purple velvet gown draped with powdered ermine furs, and sported a tinsel headpiece embellished with pearls and precious stones. The height of her headdress required her to support her head with one hand, and the canopy had to be elevated to accommodate the added height. Several nobles, knights, and members of the privy council rode in front of Mary's chariot, and Sir Nicholas Throckmorton was almost certainly among them.

Mary's coronation by the Bishop of Winchester was witnessed by hundreds of onlookers in a magnificently decorated Westminster Abbey. During the procession, Edward Courtenay and the Earl of Westmoreland carried swords, while the Earl of Shrewsbury carried the crown. Following the ceremony, an extravagant banquet was held, during which Mary was offered 312 dishes and over 7,000 dishes were offered to those in attendance, of which 4,900 were declared waste and given to the impoverished citizens.

Queen Mary's ever-increasing debts compelled her to turn outside of her domain for financial assistance, as she was informed that no one in her realm could help, but that Prince Philip of Spain could. By late October, Mary was contemplating a union with Spain, despite the opinion of many in her council that the kingdom would not support such a union with an outsider. Mary, despite the reservations of her council, instructed her ambassador to request the terms of an alliance from the emperor on 31 October, making her preference obvious. Mary had indicated that her decision was made for the sake of her dominion rather than for personal reasons.

Edward Courtenay fell out of favor with the queen as rumors circulated that he was seen more frequently with Princess Elizabeth for unknown reasons. Despite allegations that Elizabeth had lent her ear to certain French heretics, those close to Mary advised Edward Courtenay to marry Elizabeth. The frequency of Nicholas Throckmorton's visits with Princess Elizabeth was also reported to have increased, though the reasons were unknown.

Mary withdrew from court for a few days under the guise of being ill so she could consider all of her options without interruptions, possibly to help her manage with the increased stress she was experiencing.

Lady Jane and her spouse were removed from the Tower of London and brought to trial on 13 November 1553. Several accounts exist, with the following perhaps being the most vivid:

> Lady Jane appeared before her judges in all her wonted loveliness: her fortitude and composer never forsook her; nor did the throng and bustle of the court, the awful appearance of the seat of judgment, or the passing of the solemn sentence of the law, seem to disturb her mind: of their native bloom her cheeks were never robbed, nor did her voice seem once to falter: on the beauteous traitress every eye was fixed; and the grief that reigned throughout the whole assembly bespoke a general interest in her fate: indeed.
>
> > Her very judges wrung their hands for pity:
> > Their old hearts melted in 'em as she spoke,
> > And tears ran down upon their silver beards.
> > E'en her enemies were moved, and for a moment
> > Felt wrath suspended in their doubtful breasts,
> > And questioned if the voice they heard were mortal.
>
> Bayley, *The History and Antiquities of the Tower of London*, pg. 428.

Lady Jane and *Guildford Dudley* were convicted and sentenced to execution for treason. Lady Jane believed they would serve a brief period of incarceration, be released to lead a private life, and then recommence her studies. If her father had not subsequently participated in a rebellion, it is probable that this would have occurred.

Despite the secrecy surrounding Mary's choice of husband, reports of possible uprisings over her union with a foreigner reached court. If this occurred, the queen would be deposed and be replaced by Elizabeth and Courtenay. The tense relationship between Mary and Elizabeth was made even worse by these reports.

Mary responded to the allegations by ordering the two to be closely monitored and their activities reported to her, including Nicholas Throckmorton's frequent visits, whom she continued to mistrust. Certainly, trouble was developing.

Thomas Wyatt, William Pickering, George Harper, and several unidentified men devised a plan to prevent the marriage of Mary and Philip of Spain on 26 November 1553, which is the earliest date for which a meeting of conspirators is documented. I cannot find any evidence that Nicholas was present at the meeting, but it is reasonable to assume that he was aware of it.

The plan involved the Duke of Suffolk, who would recruit men in the northern counties, Thomas Wyatt in the eastern counties, Edward Courtenay and Peter Carew in the western counties, march into London, seize the Tower of London, imprison Mary, and replace her with Lady Jane on 18 March 1554.

Fig. 9.   Portraits of Peter Carew and Thomas Wyatt by Hans Holbein, in Chamberlain, Arthur. *Hans Holbein the Younger*. London, 1913.

Sir Nicholas Throckmorton was among the principal rebel commanders, according to a confession disclosed at a later court trial, but there is no conclusive evidence to support this claim. However, Thomas Wyatt is recorded in history as the primary leader. In addition, two separate disclosures made during the trial indicated that Nicholas was not only aware of the conspiracy but also a participant in it, including the taking of the Tower of London. Nicholas does not appear in any other incident-related archival records besides those just mentioned.

Queen Mary was informed that unidentified conspirators had convened to deliberate ways to thwart the English and Spanish alliance. The conspirators were unaware that as they convened, the council was drafting a treaty, which was concluded by early January 1554. Nicholas was an active member of the council during the reign of Edward VI, but his name does not appear in or on council records at that time. However, it is subsequently revealed that he was cognizant of parliamentary proceedings at the time, possibly through a close friend or relative.

Queen Mary continued to receive information that Elizabeth may be 'lending an ear' to certain French dissidents, and of Sir Nicholas Throckmorton's continued visits, resulting in the princess being questioned. This suspicion grew when a French ambassador indicated in a letter that Elizabeth would joyfully marry Edward Courtenay and then lead a rebellion against Mary in the east if given the opportunity. Elizabeth denied the claim and relocated to her childhood residence to avoid further suspicion. Nicholas was observed attentively for any adverse actions or reactions.

The treaty between England and Spain was finalized on 1 January 1554, and preparations were made for the arrival of the emperor's ambassadors. On 2 January 1554, they arrived at Tower Wharf on the Thames River to be greeted by an impressive display of canon fire. The emperor's envoys met with Mary, and they all agreed with the terms of the treaty. Mary indicated her approval with a ring on her finger.

On the same day, the council received word that Peter Carew was organizing an army. On 7 January, the council sent Carew a summons to appear before them, with the intention of placing him in the Tower of London as a heretic. The following day, Peter Carew launched the rebellion prematurely and sent word to his allies. Nicholas Throckmorton, who was close to the council and may have informed Carew that Philip was coming to England prior to the Feast of Purification on 2 February, is one of the earliest hypotheses regarding why Carew acted prematurely. Edward Courtenay may have confessed during interrogation about the activities of Wyatt, Carew, and Nicholas Throckmorton, motivating him to act before the queen's forces could respond.

Peter Carew relied significantly on the support of Edward Courtenay and Nicholas Throckmorton, who were to meet the Duke of Suffolk and Wyatt and then march into London, but neither Courtenay nor Throckmorton arrived. There is no record of the precise motives, but it is reasonable to assume that neither of them viewed it as a risk-free venture and therefore decided not to participate.

Wyatt learned of Carew's actions in the third or fourth week of January and responded by initiating a full campaign, with plans to enter Maidstone on 25 January and issue his proclamations. Wyatt and his small force of well-armed men secured the Rochester bridge, as the other confederates had issued proclamations in other areas without encountering opposition.

On the 28 January, Wyatt's forces encountered approximately 600 members of the queen's army. Both sides exchanged shots and arrows, wounding men on both sides before the queen's army dispersed Wyatt's forces. There were no reported fatalities, but several subjects were captured.

Queen Mary dispatched a few members of her council, accompanied by a small number of officers, to transport Elizabeth back to London and imprison her in the Tower of London as the rebellion gained momentum. Wyatt acquired an additional 500 soldiers who deserted from the queen's army and joined him at Rochester as a result. A report stated that the two leaders exchanged a hand salute upon meeting. Wyatt began his march to London with a formidable army that included three ships captured at Rochester after gaining confidence and support.

The queen swiftly issued her own counter-proclamations, responding to the uprising with the same command of the situation as her father.

The Duke of Suffolk, who was initially reluctant to join the rebellion, attempted to initiate the rebellion in the north. However, after several days of receiving no support, he broke off and was later discovered by the Earl of Huntington hiding in a hollow tree.

Wyatt continued his march to London, unaware of Suffolk's failure. The queen was advised to abandon Westminster for the protection of the Tower of London, but she refused, remaining confident that she would crush the rebellion. She then delivered a lengthy speech to a very large audience that appeared to have a positive effect on morale, as many began to prepare to defend London if necessary.

The arrival of Wyatt in London caused alarm and even a degree of pandemonium. Thomas Wyatt found a portion of the London Bridge removed and a large number of the queen's forces on the London side when he arrived at the foot of the bridge. The next day, Wyatt decided to travel west along the Thames to another location, only to discover that every bridge had been removed, preventing him from traversing. In the end, Wyatt seized a few barges and painstakingly moved his soldiers and ordnance across the river toward London in the cold and rain. After a protracted march toward London, most of Wyatt's soldiers deserted, but he eventually arrived in a field near Saint James Park to face a large and well-equipped queen's army led by the Earl of Pembroke.

While Wyatt attempted to avoid Pembroke, his forces dispersed and fled as artillery rumbled and shots were exchanged between the opposing forces. Wyatt continued to avoid Pembroke's forces, and each time he attempted to advance toward the Tower of London, he not only encountered resistance but also failed to receive the additional support he had hoped for; by the time they arrived at Temple Bar, he had fewer than one hundred men and realized his campaign had failed. Wyatt reportedly hopped on a passing knight's horse and surrendered before arriving in London as a prisoner.

Wyatt, Suffolk, and numerous Confederates were incarcerated. There were so many dissidents imprisoned that the prisons were at capacity, so other facilities had to be utilized to house them. The queen expedited Wyatt's trial, and he was judged guilty of treason and sentenced to death.

Lady Jane and Guildford were executed on the 12th of February, 1554, on a bitterly chilly morning. Their fate was secured by her father's participation in Wyatt's rebellion, and Mary did not want to take any chances. John Strype's 1721 edition of the Historical Memorials, Ecclesiastical and Civil, of events during the reign of Queen Mary I included a chronicle of the events that occurred on 'Black Monday.'

> Thus, this Black Monday began, with the execution of this most noble and virtuous lady and her husband. On the same day, for a terrifying sight, were many new pairs of gallows set up in London. As at every gate one, two pair in Cheapside, one in Fleet Street, one in Smithfield, one in Holborn, one at Leadenhall, one at St. Magnus, one at Billings-gate, one at Pepper Alley Gate, one at St. George's, one in Barnsby Street, one on Tower Hill, one at Charing Cross, and one at Hide Park Corner. These gallows remained standing until Wednesday when men were hanged on every gibbet, and some quartered also. In Cheap-side six; at Aldgate one, hanged and quartered; at Leadenhall three; at Bishopgate one, and was quartered; at Moorgate one, and he was quartered; at Ludgate one and he was quartered; at Billingsgate three hanged; at St. Magnus three hanged; at Tower Hill three hanged; at Holborn three hanged; at Fleet Street three hanged; at Paul's Church-yard four; at Pepper Alley Corner three; at Barneby Street three; at St.

George's three; at Charing Cross four; whereof two belonged to the court; at Hidepark Corner three, one of them named Pollard, a water bearer. Those three were hanged in chains. But seven were quartered, and their bodies and heads set upon the gates of London.

Strype, John. *Historical Memorials, Ecclesiastical and Civil, of Events Under the Reign of Queen Mary I. XX.*

During the preceding weeks, several hundred brutal executions occurred, and London was filled with the overwhelming odor of rotting carcasses. Mary acquired the nickname 'Bloody Mary' due to the high number of executions she carried out.

On 14 February 1554, additional insurgents were executed; the following is an account of that day.

Both, one of the queen's footmen, one vicars, a yeoman of the guard, great John Norton, and one king, were hanged at Charring Crosse. And three of the rebels, one called Pollard, were hanged at the park pale by Hide Parke, three also in Fleet Street, one at Ludgate, one at Bishopgate, one at Newgate, one at Aldgate, three at the Crosse in Cheape, three at Soper Lane end in Cheape, and therein Smithfield, which persons hanged still all that day and night till the next morning, and then cut down. And the bodies of them that were hanged at the gates were quartered at Newgate, and the heads and bodies hanged over the gates where they suffered.

Hamilton, *A Chronicle of England, during the Reigns of the Tudors*, pg. 112.

The next day, ten more dissidents were brought to Westminster to face trial for their crimes. Additional executions comprised:

Three of the rebels were hanged against St. Magnus Church, three at Billingsgate, three at Ledenhall, one at Moregate, one at Creplegate, one at Aldrigegate, two at Paules, three in Holborne, three at Tower Hill, two at Tyburne, and at four places in Sowthwerke fourteen were executed and divers others were executed at Kingston and other places.

Hamilton, *A Chronicle of England, during the Reigns of the Tudors*, pg. 112.

CHAPTER 2: BLOODY MARY

William Thomas, clerk of the council, and Mr. Winter were carried as captives to the Tower of London on 20 February. Nicholas Throckmorton was also apprehended and brought to the tower, although no charges were submitted, in order for the queen to keep a close watch on him.

Duke of Suffolk was executed on February 23 for his participation in Wyatt's rebellion and was decapitated on the exact location where his daughter Jane lost her head as a result of his actions.

Many early historians place the prosecution of Wyatt on 15 March 1554, despite conflicting dates. Thomas Wyatt the Younger was transported to Westminster from the Tower of London to stand prosecution for high treason. He was found culpable and sentenced to be executed by hanging, drawing, and quartering on Tower Hill on 11 April 1554.

The ambassador Simon Renard wrote to the emperor on 24 February 1554, including the names of all the dissidents held captive in the Tower of London. Sir Nicholas Throckmorton was not among the forty-five names, which included Thomas Wyatt and Edward Courtenay. By 9 March, however, Sir Nicholas is listed as a prisoner alongside others awaiting indictments and executions. There are indications in the archives that Nicholas was released after a brief detention.

An early source indicates that Nicholas fled England as quickly as possible after the rebellion to avoid prosecution. Although there is no evidence to corroborate the claim I discovered in the archives, his sibling John Throckmorton may have fled to France with Peter Carew. John was charged with 'complicity participation' in Wyatt's rebellion and sentenced to death; however, he was later pardoned, released, and welcomed into Mary's court in good standing due to his belief in the 'old religion.' Nicholas most likely went into seclusion in order to enable the situation to calm down and give him time to plan his defense for the inevitable trial. A warrant appears to have been issued for his arrest, possibly after Wyatt's 'deathbed confession' implicating Nicholas in the rebellion. Nicholas surrendered himself to the council at some point in late February or early March. According to the evidence presented at his prosecution, he was incarcerated for 58 days.

During the morning of 11 April, the day of Wyatt's execution, Wyatt was permitted to confront Edward Courtenay prior to his execution in a one-hour meeting conducted in the Tower. Wyatt entered Courtenay's chamber, fell to his knees in front of Courtenay, and pleaded for forgiveness because he had falsely accused Courtenay and the princess Elizabeth of conspiring with him upon his capture.

Wyatt was escorted to the Tower Hill platform and addressed the audience as follows:

> "Good people, I am come presently here to die, being thereunto lawfully and worthily condemned, for I have sorely offended against God and the queen's majesty, and am sorry therefore. I trust God hath forgiven and taken his mercy upon me. I beseech the queen's majesty also of forgiveness."

Weston interjected, "She hath forgiven you already."

> Wyatt continued, "And let every man beware how he takes anything in hand against the higher powers. Unless God be prosper able to his purpose, it will never take good effect or success, and thereof ye may now learn at me. And I pray God I may be the last example in this place for that or any other like. And whereas it is said and wised abroad, that I should accuse my lady Elizabeth's grace, and my lord Courtenay, it is not so, good people, for I assure you neither they nor any other now yonder in hold or durance was privy of my rising or commotion before I began; as I have declared no less to the queen counsel. And this is most true."

> Weston again interrupted Wyatt, "Mark this, my masters, he said that that which he hath showed to the counsel in writing of my lady Elizabeth and Courtenay is true."

Nichols, *The Chronicle of Queen Jane and of Two Years of Queen Mary*, pg. 73-74.

The executioner removed Wyatt's head with a single stroke after Wyatt placed his head down on the block. His corpse was then dismembered and hung from gibbets by chains at various city locations. The head of Wyatt was hung on the gallows on Hay Hill near Hyde Park for six days before it was taken. It is unknown what happened to his body and head, but it is conceivable that a member of his family claimed his remains for burial beside his father in the Sherborne church.

Sir Nicholas Throckmorton appeared before the bar at Guildhall, London, on 17 April 1554, on the allegation of high treason. His trial is quite renowned because it offers a rare view into a Tudor-era court proceeding. It has been republished numerous times in various formats. The oldest known copy was first published in 1586 in *The First and Second Volumes of Chronicles*, compiled by Raphael Holinshed. This transcript was compared to the version in

Cobbett's Complete Collection of State Trials, London, 1809, and to the version in *The Lives and Criminal Trials of Celebrated Men*, Philadelphia, 1839, and a number of discrepancies were discovered in comparison to the Holinshed version. It was a difficult choice, but I chose to present the earliest known version of the transcript, despite the fact that its publication 32 years after the trial does not guarantee its accuracy. It is exceedingly likely that all subsequent versions were based on Raphael Holinshed's transcription.

A solitary record indicates that the trial began at 7:00 a.m. on 17 April 1554 and lasted until almost 5:00 p.m.

The trial of Throckmorton did not utilize a stenographer or court reporter to record every word spoken, as is the case in modern court proceedings. It is likely a recounting of the events from memory, possibly by Sir Nicholas himself. It may never be known what source Raphael Holinshed used originally, but this is the closest we have to the actual trial date.

> The order of the arraignment of Nicholas Throckmorton, knight, in the Guildhall of London on the seventeenth day of April (Tuesday) 1554, expressed in a dialog for the better understanding of every man's part.
>
> The names of the commissioners. Sir Thomas White knight lord mayor of London, the Earl of Shrewsbury, the Earl of Derby, Sir Thomas Bromley, knight, Lord Chief Justice of England, Sir Nicholas Hare, knight, Master of the Rolls, Sir Francis Englefield, knight, Master of the Court of Wards and Liberties, Sir Richard Southwell, knight, one of the Privy Council, Sir Edward Waldegrave, knight, one of the Privy Council, Sir Roger Cholmley, knight, Sir William Portman, knight, one of the justices of the King's Bench, Sir Edward Sanders, knight, one of the justices of the Common Pleas; Master Stanford and Master Dyer sergeants, Master Edward Griffin, Attorney General, Master Sendall and Peter Tichbourne, clerks of the Crown.
>
> First after proclamation made and the commission read, the lieutenant of the Tower, Master Thomas Bridges, brought the prisoner to the bar; then silence was commanded, and Sendall said to the prisoner as follows:
>
> Sendall. Nicholas Throckmorton knight hold up thy hand, thou art before this time indicted of high treason, and that thou then and there didst falsely and traitorously and conspire and imagine the death of the queens majesty, and falsely and traitorously did levy war against the queen with her realm and also thou was adherent to the queen's enemies within her realm, giving to them aid and comfort, and also falsely and traitorously did conspire and intend to depose and deprive

the queen of her royal estate and so finally dethrone her, and also thou did falsely and traitorously devise and conclude to take violently the tower of London, of all which treasons and every of them in manner, form art thou guilty or not guilty?

Throckmorton. May it please you my lords and masters, which be authorized by the queens commission to be judges this day, to give me leave to speak a few words, which do both concern you and me, before I answer to the indictment, and not altogether impertinent to the matter, and then plead to the indictment.

Bromley. No, the order is not so, you must first plead whether you be guilty or no.

Throckmorton. If that be your order and law, judge accordingly to it.

Hare. You must first answer to the matter where with you are charged, and then you may talk at your pleasure.

Throckmorton. But things spoken out of place, were as good not spoken.

Bromley. These be but delays to spend time, therefore answer as the law will you.

Throckmorton. My lords I pray you make not too much hast with me, neither think not long for your dinner, for my case requires leisure, and you have well dined when you have done justice truly. Christ said, blessed are they that hunger and thirst for righteousness.

Bromley. I can forbear my dinner as well as you, and care as little as you peradventure.

Shrewsbury. Come you hither to check us Throckmorton; we will not be so used, no no, I for mine own part have forborne my breakfast, dinner, and supper to serve the queen.

Throckmorton. Yea my good lord I know it right well, I meant not to touch your lordship, for your service and pains is evidently known to all men.

Southwell. Master Throckmorton, this talk need not, we know what we have to do, and you would teach us our duties, you hurt your matter: go to, go to.

Throckmorton. Master Southwell, you mistake me, I meant not to teach you, nor none of you, but to remember you of that I trust you all be well instructed in; and so I satisfy myself, with [?] I shall not speak, thinking you all know what you have to do, or ought to know: so I will answer to the indictment, and do plead not guilty to the whole, and to every part thereof.

Sendall. How wilt thou be tried?

Throckmorton. Shall I be tried as I would, or as I should?

Bromley. You shall be tried as the law will, and therefore you must say by God and by the country.

Throckmorton. Is that your law for me? It is not as I would, but with you will have it so. I am pleased with it, and do desire to be tried by faithful just men, which more fear God that the world.

Then the entire was called. The names of the jurors. Lucar, Low, Young, Whetston, Martin, Painter, Bestwick, Banks, Barscarfeld, Calthrop, Knightley, Cater.

What time the attorney went forthwith to master Cholmley, and showed him the sheriff's return, who being acquainted with the citizens, knowing the corruptions and dexterities of them in such cases, noted certain to be challenged for the queen (a rare case) and the same men being known to be sufficient and indifferent, that no exceptions were to be taken to them, but only for their upright honesties: notwithstanding, the attorney prompting Sergeant Dyer, the said sergeant challenged one Bacon, and an other citizen peremptorily for the queen. Then the prisoner demanded the cause of the challenge; the sergeant answered; we need not to show you the cause of the challenge for the queen. Then the inquest was furnished with other honest men, that is to say, Whetston and Lucar, so the prisoner used these words:

Throckmorton. I trust you have not provided for me this day, as in times past I knew another gentleman occupying this woeful place was provided for. It chanced one of the justices upon jealousy of the prisoners acquittal, for the goodness of his cause, said to an other of his companions a justice, when the jury did appear: I like not this jury for our purpose, they seem to be too pitiful and to charitable to condemn the prisoner. No, said the other judge, I warrant you, they be picked fellows for the nonce, he shall drink of the same cup his fellows have done. I was then a looker one of the pageant as others be now here: but now woe is me, I am a player in that woeful tragedy. Well, for these and such other like the black ox has of late trodden on some of their feet: but my trust is, I shall not be so used. Whilst this talk was, Cholmley consulted with the attorney about the jury, which the prisoner espied, and then said as here ensues; Ah, ah, Master Cholmley, will this foul packing never be lest?

Cholmley. Why, what do I, I pray you Mr. Throckmorton? I did nothing, I am sure, you do pick quarrels to me.

Throckmorton. Well, Master Cholmley if you do well, it is better for you, God help you.

The jury then was sworn, and proclamation made, that whosoever would give evidence against Sir Nicholas Throckmorton knight, should come in and be heard, for the prisoner stood upon his deliverance, whereupon Sergeant Stanford presented himself to speak.

Throckmorton. And it may please you Master Sergeant and the others my masters of the queen's learned counsel, like as I was minded to have said a few words to the commissioners, if I might have had leave for their better remembrance of their duties in this place of justice, and concerning direct indifference to be used towards me this day: so by your patience I do think good to say some what to you, and to the rest of the queen's learned counsel, appointed to give evidence against me. And albeit you and the rest by order be appointed to give evidence against me, and entertained to set forth the depositions and matter against me; yet I pray you remember I am not alienate from you, but that I am your Christian brother; neither you so charged, but you ought to consider equity; nor yet so privileged, but that you have a duty of God appointed you how you shall do your office; which if you exceed, will be grievously required at your hands. It is lawful for you to use your gifts which I know god has largely given you, as your learning art and eloquence, so as thereby you do not seduce the minds of the simple and unlearned jury, to credit matters otherwise than they be.

For Master Sergeant, I know how by persuasions, enforcements, presumptions, applying, implying, inferring, conjecturing, deducing of arguments, wresting and exceeding the law. The circumstances, the depositions and confessions that unlearned men may be enchanted to think and judge those that be things indifferent, of at the worst but oversights to be great treasons; such power orators have and such ignorance the unlearned have. Almighty God by the mouth of his prophet does conclude such advocates be cursed, speaking these words: Cursed be he that does his office craftily, corruptly, and maliciously. And consider also, that my blood shall be required at your hands and punished in you and yours, to the third and fourth generation. Notwithstanding, you and the justices excuse always such erroneous doings, when they be after called in question by the verdict of the twelve men: but I assure you the purgation serves you as it did Pilate, and you wash your hands of the bloodshed, as Pilate did of Christ's, and now to your matter.

Stanford. And it please you my lords, I doubt not to prove evidently and manifestly, that Throckmorton is worthy and rightly indicted and arraigned of these treasons, and that he was a principal deviser, procurer, and contriver of the late rebellion; and that Wyatt was but his minister. Now say you Throckmorton, did not you send Winter to Wyatt into Kent, and did devise that the tower of London should be taken, with other instructions concerning Wyatt's rebellion.

Throckmorton. May it please you that I shall answer particularly to the matters objected against me, in as much as my memory is not good, and the same much decayed since my grievous disquietness: I confess I did say to Winter that Wyatt was desirous to speak with him, as I understand.

Stanford. Yea sir, and you devised together of the taking of the Tower of London, and of the other great treasons.

Throckmorton. No, I did not so, prove it.

Stanford. Yes sir, you met with Winter sundry times as shall appear, and sundry places.

Throckmorton. That granted, prove no such matter as is supposed in the indictment.

Stanford read Winters confession, which was of this effect, that Throckmorton met with Winter one day in the tower street and told him, that Sir Thomas Wyatt was desirous to speak with him, and Winter demanded where Wyatt was, Throckmorton answered at his house in Kent, not far from Gillingham, as I heard say, where the ships lie, then they parted at that time, and shortly after, Throck-morton met with Winter, to whom Winter said; "Master Wyatt does much as daily he hears thereof, does see daily divers of them arrive here, scattered like soldiers; and therefore he thinks good the Tower of London should be taken by a flight, before the prince came, least that piece be delivered to the Spaniards. How say you Throckmorton to it?" Throckmorton answered; "I dislike it for diverse respects." "Even so do I" said Winter. At another time Throckmorton met me the said Winter in Paul's, when he had sent one to my house, to seek me before, and he said to me, you are admiral of the fleet that now goes into Spain.

I answered "Yea." Throckmorton said, "When will your ships be ready?" I said "within ten days." Throckmorton said, "I understand you are appointed to conduct and carried the Lord Privy Seale into Spain, and considering the danger of the Frenchmen, which you say arm them to the sea apace, me think it well done, you put my said lord and his train on land in the West Country to avoid all dangers". Throckmorton said also, that Wyatt changed his purpose for taking the tower of London. I said I was glad of it, as for the Frenchmen, I care not much for them. I will so handle the matter, that the queens ships shall be (I warrant you) in safeguard. Another time I met with Master Throckmorton, when I came from the emperor's ambassadors, to whom I declared that the emperor had sent me a fair chain, and showed it to Throckmorton, who said; "for this chain you have sold your country". I said "It is neither French king nor emperor that can make me sell my country, but I will be a true Englishman". Then they parted. This is the sum of the talk between Throckmorton and Winter.

Stanford. Now my masters of the jury, you have heard my saying confirmed with Winter's confession. Now say you Throckmorton, can you deny this. If you will, you shall have Winter say it to your face.

Throckmorton. My lords, shall it please you that I shall answer.

Bromley. Yea, say your mind.

Throckmorton. I may truly deny some part of this confession, but because there is nothing material greatly, I suppose the whole be true, and what is herein deposed, sufficient to bring me within the compass of the indictment.

Stanford. It appears that you were of counsel with Wyatt, in as much as you sent Winter down to him, who uttered to him diverse traitorous devises.

Throckmorton. This is but conjectural, yet with you will construe it so maliciously, I will recount how I sent Winter to Wyatt, and then I pray you of the jury judge better than master sergeant do. I met by chance a servant of Master Wyatt, who demanded of me from Winter, and showed me, that his master should gladly speak with him: and so without any further declaration, desired me if I met Winter to tell him Master Wyatt's mind, and where he was. Thus much for the sending down of Winter.

Attorney. Yea sir, but now say you to the taking of the Tower of London, which is treason?

Throckmorton. I answer, though Wyatt thought meet to attempt so dangerous an enterprise, and that Winter informed me of it, you cannot pretend Wyatt's devise to be mine, and to bring me within the compass of treason. For what manner of reasoning or proof is this, Wyatt would have taken the tower, ergo, Throckmorton is a traitor? Winter does make my purgation in his own confession, even now read as it was by Master Sergeant, though I say nothing: for Winter does avow there, that I did much dislike it. And because you shall the better understand that I did always not allow these master Wyatt's devises, I had there words to Winter, when he informed me of it; I think Master Wyatt would no Englishman hurt and this enterprise cannot be done without the hurt and slaughter of both parties.

For I know him that has the charge of the peace, and his brother, both men of good service, the one had in charge a peace of great importance, Bulloingne I mean, which was stoutly assailed, and notwithstanding he made a good account of it for him time: the like I am sure he will do by this his charge. Moreover, to account the taking of the Tower, is very dangerous by the law. These were my words to Winter. And besides, it is very unlike that I of all men would confederate in such a matter against the lieutenant of the tower, whose daughter my brother has married, and his house and mine allied together by marriage sundry times within these few years.

Hare. But how say you to this, that Wyatt and you had conference together sundry times at Warner's house and in other places?

Throckmorton. This is a very general charge to have conference, but why was it not as lawful for me to confer with Wyatt as with you, or any other man? I then knew no more by Wyatt, than by any other. And to prove to talk with Wyatt was lawful and indifferent, the last die that I did talk with Wyatt, I saw my lord of Arundel, with other noble men and gentlemen, talk with him familiarly in the chamber of presence.

Hare. But they did not conspire nor talk of any stir against the Spaniards as you did pretend, and meant it against the queen, for you, Crofts, Rogers, and Warner did oftentimes devise in Warner's house about your traitorous purposes, or else what did you so often there?

Throckmorton. I confess I did dislike the queen's marriage with Spain, and also the coming of the Spaniards here, and then me thought I had reason to do so: for I did learn the reasons of my disliking of you Master Hare, Master Southwell, and other in the parliament house, there I did see the whole consent of the realm against it; and I a hearer, but no speaker, did learn my disliking of those matters, confirmed by many sundry reasons amongst you: but as concerning any stir or uproar against the Spaniards, I never made any, neither procured any to be made and for my much resort to Master Wyatt, but to show my friendship to my very good lord the marquise of Northampton, who was lodged there when he was enlarged.

Stanford. Did not you Throckmorton tell Winter that Wyatt had changed his mind for the taking of the tower, whereby it appeared evidently that you knew of his doings?

Throckmorton. Truly I did not tell him so. But I care not greatly to give you that weapon to play you withal, now let us see what you can make of it.

Stanford. Yea sir, that proves that you were privy to Wyatt's mind in all his devised and treasons, and that there was sending between you and Wyatt from time to time.

Throckmorton. What Master Sergeant? Does this prove against me, that I knew Wyatt did repent him of an evil devised enterprise? Is it to know Wyatt's repentance sin? No, it is but a venial sin, if it be any it is not deadly. But where is the messenger of message that Wyatt sent to me touching his alteration, and yet it was lawful enough for me to hear from Wyatt at that time, as from any other man, for any act that I knew he had done.

Dyer. And it may please you my lords, and you my masters of the jury, to prove that Throckmorton is a principal doer in this rebellion, there is yet many other things to be declared: among other, there is Crofts confession, who said, that he and you, and your accomplices, did many times devise to all his determinations, and you showed him that you would go into the west country with the Earl of Devon, to Sir Peter Carew, accompanied with others.

Throckmorton. Master Crofts is yet living, and is here this day, how happens it he is not brought face to face to justify this matter, neither has been of all this time? Will you know the truth? Either he said not so, or he will not abide by it, but honestly has reformed himself. And as for knowing his devises, I was so well acquainted with them, that I can name none of them, nor you neither as matter known to me.

Attorney. But why did you advise Winter to land my Lord Privy Seal in the west country?

Throckmorton. He that told you that my mind was to land him there, does partly tell you a reason why I said so, if you would remember as well the one as the other: but because you are so forgetful, I will recite wherefore. In communication between Winter and me, as he declared to me that the Spaniards provided to bring their prince hither, so the Frenchmen prepared to interrupt his arrival: for they began to arm to the sea, and had already certain ships on the west coast (as he heard). Into who, I said, that peradventure not only the queens ships under his charge might be in jeopardy, but also my Lord Privy Seal, and all his train; the Frenchmen being well prepared to meet with them, and therefore for all events it were good you should put my said lord in the west country in case you espy any jeopardy. But what does this prove to the treasons, if I were not able to give convenient reasons to my talk?

Stanford. Marry sir, now comes the proof of your treasons, you shall hear what Cuthbert Vaughan said against you.

Vaughan's confession was read by Stanford. Then Sergeant Stanford did read Vaughan's confessions, tending to this effect. That Vaughan coming out of Kent, met with Throckmorton at Master Warner's house, who after had had done commendations from Wyatt to him, desired to know where Crofts was. Throckmorton answered "Either at Arundel house where he lodged, or in Paul's". Then Vaughan desired to know how things went at London, saying; "Master Wyatt and we of Kent do much dislike the marriage with Spain, and the coming of the Spaniards for diverse respects: howbeit, if other countries dislike them as Kent does, they shall be but hardly welcome", and so they parted. Shortly after Throckmorton met with Vaughan in Paul's, to whom Throckmorton declared with sundry circumstances, that the Western men were in a readiness to come forwards, and that sir Peter Carew had sent to him even now, and that he had in order a good band of horsemen, and another of footmen.

Then Vaughan demanded what the Earl of Devonshire would do?

Throckmorton answered "he will marvel, for he will not go hence, and yet Sir Peter Carew would meet him with a band, both of horsemen and footmen, by the way at Andover for his safeguard, and also he should have been well accompanied from hence with other gentlemen, yet all this will not move him to depart hence. Moreover, the said earl has (as is said) discovered all the whole matter to the chancellor, or else it is come out by his tailor, about the trimming of a shirt on mail, and the making of a cloak". At another time, Vaughan said, Throck-morton showed him that he had sent a post to Sir Peter Carew, to come forward with as much speed as might be, and to bring his force with him. And also Throckmorton advised Vaughan to will Master Wyatt to come forward with his power: for now was the time, in as much as the Londoners would take his part if the matter were presented to them. Vaughan said also, that Throckmorton and Warner should have ridden with the said earl westward. Moreover the said Vaughan deposed that Throckmorton showed him in talk of the Earl of Pembroke, that the said earl would not fight against them, though he would not take their parts. Also Vaughan said, that Throckmorton showed him that he would ride down into Berkshire to Sir Francis Englefield's, house, there to meet his eldest brother, to move him to take his part. And this was the sum of Cuthbert Vaughan's confession.

Stanford. Now say you? Does not here appear evident matter to prove you a principal, who not only gave order to Sir Peter Carew and his adherents, for their rebellious acts in the west country, but also procured Wyatt to make his rebellion, appointing him and the others also, when they should attempt their enterprise, and how they should order their doings from time to time. Besides all this evident matter, you were specially appointed to go away with the Earl of Devon as one that would direct all things, and give order to all men. And there-fore Throckmorton with this matter is so manifest, and the evidence so apparent, I would advise you to confess you fault and submit yourself to the queen's mercy.

Bromley. How say you, will you confess the matter, and it will be best for you?

Throckmorton. No, I will never accuse myself unjustly, but in as much as I am come hither to be tried, I pray ye let me have the law favorably.

Attorney. It is apparent that you lay at London as a factor, to give intel-ligence as well to them in the west, as to Wyatt in Kent.

Throckmorton. How prove you that, or who does accuse me but this condemned man?

Attorney. Why will you deny this matter? You shall have Vaughan justify his whole confession here before your face.

Throckmorton. It shall not need, I know his unshamefastness, he has avowed some of the untrue talk before this time to my face, and it is not otherwise like, considering the price, but he will do the same again.

Attorney. My lord and masters, you shall have Vaughan to justify this here before you all, and confirm it with a book oath.

Throckmorton. He that has said and lied, will not being in this case strike to swear and lie.

Then was Cuthbert Vaughan brought into the open court.

Sendall. How say you Cuthbert Vaughan, is this your own confession, and will you abide by all that is here written?

Vaughan. Let me see it and I will tell you.

Then his confession was showed him.

Attorney. Because you of the jury the better may credit him, I pray you my lords let Vaughan be sworn.

Then was Vaughn sworn on a book to say nothing but the truth.

Vaughan. It may please you my lords and masters, I could have been will content to have chose seven years imprisonment, though I had been a free man in the law, rather than I would this day have given evidence against Sir Nicholas Throckmorton; against whom I bear no displeasure: but with I must needs confess my knowledge, I must confess all that is there written is true. How say you master Throckmorton, was there any displeasure between you and me, to move me to say aught against you?

Throckmorton. None that I know, how say you Vaughn, what acquaintance was there between you and me, and what letters of credit or token did you bring me from Wyatt, or any other, to move me to trust you?

Vaughan. As for acquaintance, I knew you as I did other gentlemen: and as for letters, I brought you none other but commendations from Master Wyatt, as I did to diverse other of his acquaintance at London.

Throckmorton. You might as well forge the commendations as the rest: but if you have done with Vaughan my lords, I pray you give me leave to answer.

Bromley. Speak and be short.

Throckmorton. I speak generally to all that be here present, but specially to you of my jury, touching the credit of Vaughn's depositions against me, a condemned man, and after to matter: and note I pray you the circumstance, as somewhat material to induce the better. First I pray you remember the small similarity between Vaughan and me, as he has avowed before you, and moreover, to procure credit at my hand, brought neither letter nor token from Wyatt, nor from any other to me, which he also has confessed here: and I will suppose Vaughan to be in as good condition as any other man here, that is to say, an uncondemned man; yet I refer it to your good judgment, whether it were like that I knowing only Vaughan's person from another man, and having none other acquaintance with him, would so frankly discover my mind to him in so dangerous a matter. How like (I say) is this, when diverse of these gentlemen now in captivity, being my very familiars, could not depose any such matter against me, and nevertheless upon their examinations have said what they could and though I be no wise man, I am not so rash as to utter to an unknown man (for so I may call him in comparison) a matter so dangerous for me to speak, and him to hear.

But because my truth and his falsehood shall the better appear to you, I will declare his inconstancy in uttering this his evidence. And for my better credit, it may please you Master Southwell, I take you to witness, when Vaughan first insinuated this his unjust accusation against me before the Lord Paget, the Lord Chamberlain, you Master Southwell, and other, he referred the confirmation of this his surmised matter, to a letter sent from him to Sir Thomas Wyatt, which letter does neither appear, not any testimony of the said Master Wyatt against me touching the matter; for I doubt not Sir Thomas Wyatt has been examined of me, and has said what he could directly or indirectly. Also Vaughan said that young Edward Wyatt could confirm this matter, as one that knew this pretended discourse betwixt Vaughan and me, and there upon I made suit that Edward Wyatt might either be brought face to face to me, or otherwise be examined.

Southwell. Master Throckmorton you mistake your matter, for Vaughan said, that Edward Wyatt did know some part of the matter, and also was privy of the letter that Vaughan sent Sir Thomas Wyatt.

Throckmorton. Yea sir, that was Vaughan last shift, when I charged him before the master of the horse and you with his former allegations touching his witness, whom when he espied would not do so lewdly as he though, then he appears neither his first nor his last tale to be true. For you know Master Bridges, and so does my lord your brother, that I desired twice or thrice Edward Wyatt should be examined and I am sure, and most assured he has been willed to say what he could, and here is nothing deposed by him against me, either touching any letter of other conference. Or where is Vaughan's letter sent by Sir Thomas Wyatt concerning my talk?

But now I will speak of Vaughan's present estate in that he is a condemned man, whose testimony is nothing worth by any law. And because false witness is mentioned in the gospel, treating of accusation, hear I pray you what St. Jerome said, expounding that place. It is demanded while Croft's accusers be called false witness, which did report Christ's words not as he spoke them. "They be false witness" said St. Jerome, "which do add, alter, wrest, double, or do speak for hope to avoid death, or for malice easily gather he cannot speak truly of me, or in the case of another man's life, where he has hope of his own by accusation". Thus much speak St. Jerome of false witness. By the evil law there be many exceptions to taken against such testimonies: but because we be not governed by that law, neither have I my trial by it, it shall be superfluous to trouble you there with, and therefore you shall hear what your own law does say. There was a statue made in my late sovereign lord and master his time, touching accusation, and there be the words.

Be it enacted that no person nor persons shall be indicted, arraigned, condemned, or convicted for any offense of treason, petit treason, misprision of treason, for which the same offender shall suffer any pains of death, imprisonment, loss or forfeiture of his goods, lands, and unless the same offender be accused by two sufficient and lawful witnesses of shall willingly without violence confess the same. And also in the sixth year of his reign, it is thus ratified as ensued.

That no person nor persons shall be indicted, arraigned, condemned, convicted or attainted of the treasons or offenses aforesaid, or for any other treasons that now be, or hereafter shall be; unless the same offender or offenders be thereof accused (if they be then living) shall be brought in person before the said party accused, and avow and maintain that they have to say against the said party, to prove him guilty of the treason or offense contained in the bill of indictment laid against the party arraigned, unless the said party arraigned shall be willing without violence to confess the same. Here note (I pray you) that our law does require two lawful and sufficient accusers to be bought face to face, and Vaughan is but one, and the same most unlawful and insufficient. For who can be more unlawful and insufficient, than a condemned man, and such one as knows to accuse me is the mean to save his own life? Remember (I pray you) how long and how many times Vaughn's execution has been respited, and how often he has been conjured to accuse (which by Gods grace he withstood until the last hour) what time perceiving there was no way to live, but to speak against me or some other (his former grace being taken away) did redeem his life most unjustly and shamefully, as you see.

Hare. Why should he accuse you more than any other, seeing there was no displeasure between you, if the matter had not been true?

Throckmorton. Because he must either speak of some man, or suffer death, and then he did rather choose to hurt him whom he least knew and so loved least, than any other well known to him, whom he loved most. But to you of jury I speak specially, and therefore I pray you not what I say. In a matter of less weight than trial of life and land, a man may by the law take exceptions to such as he impaneled, to try the controversies between the parties: as for example. A man may challenge that the sheriff is his enemy, and therefore has made a partial return; or because one of the jury is the sheriff my adversaries servant: and also in case my adversaries villain or bondman be impaneled, I may lawfully challenge him, because the adversarial part has the use of his body for servile office: much more I may of right take exception to Vaughan's testimony, my life and all that I have depending thereupon, and the same Vaughan beings more bound to the queen's highness my adversary (that woe is me therefore) but so the law does here so term her majesty, than any villain is to his lord: for her highness has not only power over his body, lands and goods, but over his life also.

Stanford. Yea, the exception are to be taken against the jury in that case, but not against the witness or accuser and therefore your argument serves little for you.

Throckmorton. That is not so, for the use of the jury, and the witness and the effect of their doings does serve me to my purpose, as the law shall discuss. And thus I make my comparison. By the civil law the judge does give sentence upon the depositions of the witness and by your law the judge does give judgment upon the verdict of the jury; so as the effect is both one to finish the matter, trial in law, as well by the depositions of the witness, as by the jury's verdict, though they vary in form and circumstance: and so Vaughan's testimony being credited, may be the material cause on my condemnation, as the jury to be induced by his depositions to speak their verdict, and so finally there upon the judge to give sentence. Therefore I may use the same expectations against the jury, or any of them, as the principal mean that shall occasion my condemnation.

Bromley. Why do you deny that every part of Vaughan's tale is untrue?

Attorney. You may see he will deny all, and say there was no such communication between them.

Throckmorton. I confess some part of Vaughan confession to be true, as the name, the places, the time, and some part of the matter.

Attorney. So you of the jury may perceive the prisoner does confess something to be true.

Throckmorton. As touching my sending to Sir Peter Carew, of his sending to me, or concerning my advice to master Wyatt to stir or to repair hither, or touching the Earl of Devonshire parting hence, and my going with him, and also concerning the matter of the Earl of Pembroke, I do avow and say that Vaughan has said untruly.

Southwell. As for my lord of Pembroke, you need not excuse the matter, for he has showed himself clear in these matters like a noble man, and that we all know.

Hare. Why what was the talk betwixt Vaughan and you so long in Paul's, if these were not so, and what meant you oft meetings?

Throckmorton. As for our meetings, they were of no act purpose, but by chance, and yet no oftener than twice. But since you would know what communication passed between us in Paul's church, I will declare. We talked of the incommodities of the marriage of the queen with the prince of Spain, and how grievous the Spaniards would be to us here. Vaughan said, "that it should be very dangerous for any man, that truly professed the gospel to live here, such was the Spaniards cruelty, and especially against Christian men". Whereto I answered "it was the plague of God justly come upon us, and now almighty God dealt with us as he did with the Israelites, taking from them for their unthankfulness their godly kings, and did send tyrants to reign over them. Even so he handled us Englishmen, which had a most godly and virtuous prince to reign over us, my late sovereign lord and master King Edward, under whom we might both falsely and lawfully profess Gods word, which with our lewd doings, demeanor, and living, we handled so irreverently, that to whip us for our faults he would send so stranger, yea such very tyrants to exercise great tyranny over us, and did take away the virtuous and faithful king from amongst us: for every man of every estate did color his naughty affections with a pretense of religion, and made the gospel a stalking horse to bring their evil desires to effect". This was the sum of our talk in Paul's somewhat more dilated.

Stanford. That it may appear yet more evidently how Throckmorton was a principal doer and counselor in this matter, you shall hear his own confession of his own handwriting.

The clerk began to read, Throckmorton desired Master Stanford to read it, and the jury well to mark it. Then Master Stanford did read the prisoners own confession to this effect: that Throckmorton had conference with Wyatt, Carew, Crofts, Rogers, and Warner, as well of the queen's marriage with the prince of Spain, as also of religion, and did particularly confer with every the forenamed, of the matters aforesaid. Moreover, with Sir Thomas Wyatt the prisoner talked of the brute that the Western men should much dislike the coming of the Spaniards into the realm, being reported also that they intended to interrupt their arrival here. And also that it was said, that they were in consolation about the same at Exeter. Wyatt also did say, that Sir Peter Carew could not bring the same matter to good effect, not that there was any man so need to bring it to good effect, as the Earl of Devonshire, and specially in the west parts, insomuch as they drew not all by one line.

Then Throckmorton asked how the Kentish men were affected to Spaniards?

Wyatt said; "The people like them evil enough, and that appeared now at the coming of the count of Egmount, for they were ready to stir against him and his train, supposing it had been the prince." "But" said Wyatt, "Sir Robert Southwell, Master Baker and Master Noile, and their affinity, which be in good credit in some places of the shire, will for other malicious respects hinder the liberty of their country". Then Throckmorton should say; "Though I know there has been an unkindness between Master Southwell and you for a money matter, wherein I traveled to make you friends, I doubt not, but in so honest a matter as there is, he will for the safeguard of his country join with you, and so you may be sure of the lord Abergavenny and his force." Then Wyatt said, "It is for another matter than for money that we disagree, wherein he has handled me and others very doubly and unneighborly, howbeit, he can do no other, neither to me, nor to any other man and therefore I forgive him.

Item, with Sir Peter Carew, Throckmorton had conference touching the impeachment of the landing of the said prince, and touching provision of amour and munitions as ensued, that is to say, that Sir Peter Carew told Throckmorton that he trusted his countrymen would be true Englishmen, and would not agree to let the Spaniards to govern them.

Item, the said Sir Peter Carew said, the matter importing the French king, as it did, he thought the French king would work to hinder the Spaniards coming hither, with whom the said Sir Peter did think good to practice for amour, munitions, and money.

Then Throckmorton did advise him to beware that he brought any Frenchmen into the realm forcibly, inasmuch as he could as evil abide the Frenchmen after that sort as the Spaniards. And also Throckmorton thought the French king unable to give aid to us, by means of the great consumption in their own wars. Master Carew said; as touching the bringing in of the Frenchmen, he meant it not, for he loved neither party, but to serve his own country, and to help his country from bondage: declaring further to Throckmorton, that he had a small bark of his own to work his practice by and so he said, that shortly he intended to depart to his own country, to understand the devotion of his countrymen.

Item, Throckmorton did say, he would for his part hinder the coming in of the Spaniards as much as he could by persuasion.

Item, to Sir Edward Warner, he had and did become his own estate, and the tyranny of the time extended upon diverse honest persons for religion, and wished it were lawful for all of each religion to live safely according to their conscience; for the law will be intolerable and the clergies discipline now may rather be resembled to the Turks tyranny, than to the teaching of Christian religion.

This was the sum of the matter which was read in the foresaid confession, as maters most grievous against the prisoner.

Then Throckmorton said, since Master Sergeant you have read and gathered the place (as you think) that makes most against me, I pray you take the pains, and read further, that hereafter whatsoever become of me, my words be not perverted and abused to the hurt of some others, and especially against the great personages, of whom I have been sundry times (as appears by my answers) examined, for I perceive the net was not cast only for little fishes, but for the great ones.

Stanford. It shall be but loss of time, and we have other things to charge you withal, and this that you desire does make nothing for you.

Dyer. And for the better confirmation of all the treasons objected against the prisoner, and therein to prove him guilty, you for the jury shall hear the duke of Suffolk's depositions against him, who was a prisoner, amounting to this effect, that the lord Thomas Grey did inform the said duke, that Sir Nicholas Throckmorton was privy to the whole devises against the Spaniards, and was one that should go into the west country with the Earl of Devonshire.

Throckmorton. But what does the principal author of this matter say against me, I mean the lord Thomas Grey who is yet living? Why be not his depositions brought against me, for so it ought to be, if he can say anything? Will you know the truth? Neither the lord Thomas Grey has said, can say, or will say anything against me, notwithstanding the duke his brothers confession and accusation, who has affirmed many other things besides the truth. I speak not without certain knowledge: for the lord Thomas Grey being my prison-fellow for a small time, informed me, that the duke his brother had misreported him in many things, amongst others in matters touching me, which he had declared to you Master Southwell, and other the examiners not long ago. I am sure if the lord Thomas could, or would have said anything, it should have been here now. And as to the duke's confession, it is not material: for he does refer to the matter to the lord Thomas report who has made my purgation.

The attorney. And it please you my lords, and you my masters of the jury, besides these matters touching Wyatt's rebellion, Sir Peter Carew's treasons and confederating with the duke of Suffolk, and besides the prisoners conspiracy with the Earl of Devonshire, with Crofts, Rogers, Warner and sundry others in sundry places, it shall manifestly appear to you, that Throckmorton did conspire the queen's majesties death, with William Thomas, Sir Nicholas Arnold, and other traitors intending the same, which is the greatest matter of all others, and most to be abhorred. And for proof hereof, you shall hear what Arnold said.

Then was Sir Nicholas Arnold's confession read, saying that Throckmorton showed to him, riding between Hinam and Crossland in Gloucestershire, that John Fitzwilliams was very much displease with William Thomas.

Attorney. William Thomas devised, that John Fitzwilliams should kill the queen, and Throckmorton knew of it, as appears by Arnold's confession.

Throckmorton. First I deny that I said any such thing to Master Arnold, and though he be an honest man, he may either forget himself, or devise means how to unburden himself of so weighty a matter as this is; for he is charged with the matter as principal. Which I did perceive when he charged me with his tale, and therefore I do blame him the less, that he seeks how to discharge himself, using me as a witness, if he could so transfer the devise to William Thomas. But truly I never spoke any such words to him. And for my better declaration, I did see John Fitzwilliams here even now, who can testify, that he never showed me of any displeasure between them, and as I know nothing of the displeasure between them, so I know nothing of the cause: I pray you my lords let him be called to depose in this matter what he can.

Then John Fitzwilliams drew to the bar, and presented himself to depose his knowledge in the matter in open court.

The Attorney. I pray you my lords suffer him not to be sworn, neither to speak, we have nothing to do with him.

Throckmorton. Why should he not be suffered to tell the truth? And why be ye not so well contented to hear truth for me as untruth against me?

Hare. Who called you hither Fitzwilliams, or commanded you to speak? You are a very busy officer.

Throckmorton. I called him, and do humbly desire that he may speak, and be heard as will as Vaughan; or else I am not indifferently used, especially seeing master attorney does so press this matter against me.

Southwell. Go your ways Fitzwilliams, the court has nothing to do with you: peradventure you would not be so ready in a good cause.

Then John Fitzwilliams departed the court, and was not suffered to speak.

Throckmorton. Since this gentleman's declaration may not be admitted, I trust you of the jury can perceive, it was not for anything he had to say against me, but contrariwise that it was feared he would speak for me. And now to Master Arnold's depositions against me, I say I did not tell him any such words, so as if it were material, there is but his yea and my nay. But because the words be not sore strained against me, I pray you Master Attorney why might not I have told Master Arnold, that John Fitzwilliams was angry with William Thomas, and yet know no cause of the anger? It might be understood, to disagree oftentimes. Who does confess that I know anything of William Thomas's devise touching the queen's death? I will answer, No man for Master Arnold does mention no word of that matter, but of the displeasures between them. And to speak that, does neither prove treason. Is here all the evidence against me that you have to bring me within the compassed of the indictment?

Stanford. Me think the matters confessed by others against you, together with your own confession, will weigh shrewdly. But how say you to the rising in Kent, and Wyatt's attempt against the queen's royal person at her palace.

Bromley. Why do you not read Wyatt's accusation to him, which does make him partner to his treasons?

Southwell. Wyatt has grievously accused you, and in many things that others have confirmed.

Throckmorton. Whatsoever Wyatt has said of me in hope of his life, he unsaid it at his death. For since I came into this hall, I heard one say (but I know him not) that Wyatt upon the scaffold did not only purge my lady Elizabeth her grace, and the Earl of Devonshire, but also all the gentlemen in the tower, saying they were all ignorant of the stir and commotion. In which number I take myself.

Hare. Notwithstanding he said, all that he had written and confessed to the council, was true.

Throckmorton. Nay sir, by your patience, Master Wyatt said not so, that was master doctors addition.

Southwell. It appears you have had good intelligence.

Throckmorton. Almighty God provided that revelation for me this day since I came hither: for I have been in close prison these eight and fifty days, where I heard nothing but what the birds told me, which did fly over my head. And now to you of my jury I speak specially, whom I desire to mark attentively what shall be said. I have been indicted, as it appears, and now am arraigned of compassing the queen majesties death, of levying was against the queen, of taking the Tower of London, of deposing and depriving the queen of her royal estate, and finally to destroy her, and of adherence to the queen's enemies. Of all which treasons, to prove me guilty, the queen's learned counsel has given in evidence these points material; that is to say: for the compassing or imagining the queen's death; and the destruction of her royal person,

Sir Nicholas Arnold's depositions, which is, that I should say to the said Sir Nicholas in Gloucestershire, that Master John Fitzwilliams was angry with William Thomas.

Whereto I have answered, as you have heard, both denying the matter: and for the proof on my side, do take exceptions prove nothing concerning the queen's death. For levying of war against the queen, there is alleged my conference with Sir Thomas Wyatt, Sir James Crofts, Sir Edward Rogers, Sir Edward Warner. Against the marriage with Spain, and the coming of the Spaniards hither, which talk I do not deny in sort as I spoke it, and meant it: and notwithstanding the malicious gathering this day of my conference, proves yet no levying of war. There is also alleged for proof of the same article, Sir James Croft's confession, which (as you remember) implied no such thing, but general talk against the marriage with Spain. And of my departing westward with the Earl of Devon, which the said James does not avow, and therefore I pray you consider it as not spoken. There is also for proof of the said article, the duke of Suffolk's confession, with whom I never had conference; and therefore he avouched the tale of his brothers mouth, who has made my purgation in those matters; and yet if the matter were proved, they be not greatly material in law.

There is also alleged for the further proof of the same article, and for deposing and depriving the queen of her royal estate, and for my adhering to the queens enemies, Cuthbert Vaughan's confession, whose testimony I have sufficiently disproved by sundry authorities and circumstances, and principally by your own law, which does require two lawful and sufficient witnesses to be brought face to face. Also for the taking of the Tower of London, there is alleged Winter's depositions, which uttered my disliking, when he uttered to me Sir Thomas Wyatt's resolution and devise for attempting of the said peace. And last of all, to enforce these matters, mine own confession is ingreeved against me, wherein there does appear neither treason, neither concealment of treason, neither whispering of treason, nor procurement of treason.

And forasmuch as I am come hither to be tried by the law, though my innocence of all these points material objected, be apparent to acquit me, where to I do principally clean: yet I will for your better credit and satisfactions, show you evidently, that if you would believe all the depositions laid against me, which I trust you will not do, I ought not to be attainted of the treason comprised within my indictment, considering the statute of repeals the last parliament, of all treasons, other than such as be declared in the five and twentieth year of King

Edward the Third, both which statutes, I pray you my lords, may be read here to the inquest.

Bromley. No sir, there shall be no books brought at your desire, we do all know the law sufficiently without book.

Throckmorton. Do you bring me hither to try me by the law, and will not show me the law? What is your knowledge of the law to these men's satisfactions, which have my trial in hand? I pray you my lords, and my lords all let the statutes be read, as will for the queen as for me.

Stanford. My Lord Chief Justice can show the law, and will, if the jury do doubt of any point.

Throckmorton. You know it were indifferent that I should know and hear the law whereby I am adjudged, and for as much as the stature is in English, men of meaner learning than the justices can understand it, or else how should we know when he offend?

Hare. You know not what belongs to your case, and therefore we must teach you: it appertained not to us to provide books for you, neither sit we here to be taught of you, you should have taken better heed to the law before you had come hither.

Throckmorton. Because I am ignorant, I would learn, and therefore I have more need to see the law, and partly as well for the instructions of the jury, as for my own satisfaction, which me think were for the honor of this presence. And now if it please you my Lord Chief Justice, I do direct my speech specially to you. What time it please the queen's majesty, to call you to this honorable office, I did learn of a great personage of her highness privy council, that amongst other good instructions, her majesty charged and enjoined you to minister the law and justice indifferently without respect of persons.

And notwithstanding the old error amongst you, which did not admit any witness to speak, or any other matter to be heard in the favor of the adversary, her majesty being party; her highnesses pleasure was, that whatsoever could be brought in favor of the subject, should be admitted to be heard. And moreover that you specially and likewise all other justices, should not persuade themselves to sit in judgment otherwise for her highness, than for her subject. Therefore this manner of indifferent proceeding being principally enjoined by Gods commandment, which I had thought partly to have remembered you and others here in commission, in the beginning, if I might have had leave; and the same also being commanded you by the queens own mouth: me think you ought of right to suffer me to have the statutes read openly, and also to reject nothing that could be spoken in my defense; and in thus doing, you shall show your selves worthy ministers, and fit for so worthy a mistress.

Bromley. You mistake the matter; the queen spoke those words to Master Morgan chief justice of the common pleas: but you have no cause to complain, for you have been suffered to talk at your pleasure.

Hare. What would you do with the statute book? The jury does not require it, they have heard the evidence, and they must upon their conscience try whether you be guilty or no, so as the book needs not; if they will not credit the evidence so apparent, then they know what they have to do.

Cholmley. You ought not to have any books read here at your appointment, for where does arise any doubt in the law, the judges sit here to inform the court, and now you do but spend time.

The attorney. I pray you my Lord Chief Justice repeat the evidence for the queen, and give the jury their charge, for the prisoner will keep you here all day.

Bromley. How say you? Have you any more to say for yourself?

Throckmorton. You seem to give and offer me the law, but in very deed I have only the form and image of the law, nevertheless, with I cannot be suffered to have the statutes read openly in the book, I will by your patience guess at them as I may, and I pray you to help me if I mistake, for it is long since I did see them. The statute of repeal made the last parliament, has these words: be it enacted by the queen, that from henceforth none act, deed, of offense, being by act of parliament or statute made treason, petit treason, of misprision of treason, by words, writing, printing, ciphering, deeds, or otherwise whatsoever, shall be taken, had deemed, or adjudged treason, petit treason: but only such as be declared of expressed to be treason, in or by an act of parliament made in the five and twentieth year of Edward the third, touching and concerning treasons, and the declaration of treason, and none other.

Here may you see, this statute does refer all the offenses aforesaid, to the statute of the five and twentieth year of Edward the third, which statute has these words touching and concerning the treasons that I am indicted and arraigned of, that is to say: Whosoever does compass of imagine the death of the king, or levy war against the king in his realm, or being adherent to the kings enemies within this realm, or elsewhere, and be therefore probably attainted by open deed by people of their condition; shall be judged a traitor. Now I pray you of my jury which have my life in trial, note well what things at this day be treasons, and how these treasons must be tried and discerned; that is to say, by open deed, which the laws does at some time term. And now I ask notwithstanding my indictment, which is but matter alleged, where dooly appear the open deed of any compassing of imagining the queen's death? Or where does appear any open deed of being adherent to the queen's enemies, giving to them aid and comfort? Or where does appear any open deed of taking the Tower of London?

Bromley. Why do not you of the queen's learned counsel answer him? Me think, Throckmorton, you need not have the statutes, for you have them meetly perfectly.

Stanford. You are deceived to conclude all treasons in the statute of the five and twentieth year of Edward the third, for that statute is but a declaration of certain treasons, which were treason before at the common law. Even so there did remain divers other treasons at this day at the common law, which be expressed by that statue, as the judges can declare. Nevertheless, there is matter so lucent alleged and proved against you, to bring you within the compass of the same statute.

Throckmorton. I pray you express those matters that bring me within the compass of the statute of Edward the third. For the words be these: and be thereof attainted by open deed: by people of like condition.

Bromley. Throckmorton you deceive yourself, and mistake these words; by people of their condition. For thereby the law does understand the discovering of your treasons. As for example, Wyatt and the other rebels, attainted for their great treasons, already declare you to be his and their adherent, in as mind as diverse and sundry times you had conference with him and them about the treason, so as Wyatt is now one of your condition, who (as all the words knows) has committed an open traitorous fact.

Throckmorton. By your leave my lord, this is a very strange and singular understanding. For I suppose the meaning of the law-makers did understand these words: but people of their condition; for the state and condition of those persons which should be on the inquest to try the party arraigned, guilty or not guilty, and nothing to the betraying of the offense by another man's act, as you say. For what have I to do with Wyatt's acts, that was not nigh him by one hundred miles?

The Attorney. Will you take upon you to still better of the law than the judges? I doubt not but you of the jury will credit as it becomes you.

Cholmley. Concerning the true understanding of these words: By people of their condition, my Lord Chief Justice here has declared the truth, for Wyatt was one of your condition, that is to say, of your conspiracy.

Hare. You do not deny, Throckmorton, that there has been conference and sending between Wyatt and you: and he and Winter does confess the same, with others, so as it is plain; Wyatt may be called one of your condition.

Throckmorton. Well, seeing you my judges rule the understanding of their words in the statute, by people of your condition, thus strangely against me: I will not stand longer upon them. But where does appear in me an open deed whereto the treason is specially referred?

Bromley. If three of four do talk, devise, and conspire together of a traitorous act to be done, and afterwards one of them does commit treason, as Wyatt did, then the law does repute them, and every of them as their acts, so as Wyatt's acts do imply and argue of your open deed, and so the law does term it and take it.

Throckmorton. These be marvelous expositions and wonderful implications, that another man's act whereof I was not privy, should be accounted mine: for Wyatt did purge me that I knew nothing of his stir.

Hare. Yea sir, but you were a principal procurer and contriver of Wyatt's rebellion, though you were not with him when he made the stir. And as my lord Hare has said, the law always does procure treason, or any other man to commit treason, of a traitorous act, as you did Wyatt and others: for so the overt act of those which did it by your procurement, shall in this case be accounted your open deed. We have a common case in the law, if one by procurement should diseize you of your land, the law holds us both wrong doers and gives remedy as well against the one as the other.

Throckmorton. For God's sake apply not such constructions against me, and though my present estate does not move you, yet it were well you should consider your office, and think what measure you give to others, you your selves I say shall assuredly receive the same again. The state of mortal life is such, that men know full little what hangs over them. I put on within these XIJ months such a mind, that I most woeful right was as unlike to stand here, as some of you that sit there. As to your case last recited, whereby you would conclude; I have remembered and learned of you Master Hare, and you Master Stanford in the parliament house, where you did sit to make laws, to expound and explain the ambiguities and doubts of law sincerely, and that without affections.

There I say I learned of you, and others my master of the law, this difference between such cases as you remembered one even now, and the statute whereby I am to be tried. There is a maxim of principle in the law, which ought not to be violated, that no penal statute may, ought, or should be conferred, expounded, extended, of wrested, other-wise than the simple words and nude letter of the same statute does warrant and signify. And amongst diverse good and notable reasons by you there in the parliament house debated (Master Sergeant Stanford) I noted this one, while the said maxim ought so be inviolable. You said, considering the private affections many times both of princes and ministers within this realm, for that they were men, and would and could err, it should be no security, but very dangerous to the subject, to refer the construction and extending of penal statutes to any judges equity (as you termed it) which might either by fear of the higher powers be seduced, or by ignorance and folly abused: and that is an answer by procurement.

Bromley. Notwithstanding the principal (as you allege it) and the preciseness of your sticking to the bare words of the statute, it does appear and remain of record in our learning, that diverse cases have been adjudged treason, without the express words of the statute, as the queen's learned counsel there can declare.

The Attorney. It does appear the prisoner did not only entice or procure Wyatt, Carew, Rogers, and others, to commit their traitorous act, and there does his open facts appear, which Vaughan's confession does witness, but also he did mind shortly after to affect at himself with those traitors: for he minded to have departed with the Earl of Devonshire westward.

Throckmorton. My innocence concerning these matters I trust sufficiently appears by my former answers, notwithstanding the condemned mans unjust accusation. But because the true under-standing of the statute is in question, I say procurement, and specially by words only, is without the compass of it, and that I do learn and prove by the principle which I learned of Master Stanford.

Stanford. Master Throckmorton, you and I may not agree this day in the understanding of the law, for I am for the queen, and you are for yourself: the judges must determine the matter.

Bromley. He that does procure another man to commit a felony or a murder, I am sure you know well enough the law does adjudge the procurer there a felon or a murderer; and in case of treason it has been always so taken and reputed.

Throckmorton. I do and must clean to my innocence, for procured no man to commit treason: but yet for my learning I desire to hear some case so ruled when the law was as it is now. I do confess it, that at such time there were statutes provided for the procurer, counselor, aide, abettor, and such like, as there were in King Henry the eights time; you might lawfully make this cruel construction, and bring the procurer within the compass of the law. But these statutes being repealed, you ought not now so to do: and as to the principal procurer in felony and murder, it is not like as in treason; for the principal and accessories in felony and murder be triable and punishable by the common law: and so in those cases the judges may use their equity, extending the determination of the fault as they think good: but in treason it is otherwise, the same being limited by statute, which I say and avow is restrained from any judges construction, by the maxim that I recited.

Stanford. Your lordships do know a case in Richard the thirds time, where the procurer, to counterfeit false money, was judged a traitor, and the law was as it is now.

Hare. Master Sergeant does remember you Throckmorton of an experience before our time, that the law has been so taken: and yet the procurer was not expressed in the statute, but the law has been always so taken.

Throckmorton. I never studied the law, whereof I do much repent me: yet I remember, while penal statutes were talked of in the parliament house, you the learned men of the house remembered some cases contrary to this last spoken of. And if I misreport them, I pray you help me. In the like case you speak of concerning the procurer to counterfeit false money at one time the procurer was judged a felon, and at another time neither felon nor traitor: so as some of your predecessors adjudged the procurer no traitor in the same case, but leaned to their principal, though some other extend their constructions too large. And here is two cases with me, for one against me.

Bromley. Because you reply upon the principal, I will remember where one taking the great seal of England from one writing, and putting it to another, was adjudged a traitor in Henry the fourths time, and yet his act was not within the express words of the statute of Edward to third. There be diverse other such like cases that may be alleged and need were.

Throckmorton. I pray you my Lord Chief Justice call to your good remembrance, that in the self same case of the seal, Justice Spellman, a grave and well learned man, since that time, would not condemn the offender, but did reprove that former judgment by you last remembered, as erroneous.

Stanford. If I had thought you had been so well furnished in book cases, I would have been better provided for you.

Throckmorton. I have nothing but I learned of you specially Master Sergeant, and of others my masters of the law in the parliament house and therefore I may say with the prophet (salutem ex inimicis nostris).

Southwell. You have a very good memory.

The Attorney. If the prisoner may avoid his treasons after this manner, the queen's surety shall be in great jeopardy. For Jack Cade and the blacksmith, and diverse other traitors, sometime alleging the law for them, sometime they meant no harm to the king, but against his counsel, as Wyatt, the Duke of Suffolk and these did against the Spaniards, when there was no Spaniards within the realm. The duke and his brethren did mistake the law, as you do, yet at length did confess their ignorance, and submitted themselves: and so were you best to do.

Throckmorton. As to Cade and the blacksmith, I am no so well acquainted with their treasons as you be: but I have read in the chronicle, they were in the field with a force against the prince, whereby a manifest act did appear. As to the Duke of Suffolk's doings, they appertain not to me. And though you would compare my speech and talk against the Spaniards to the dukes acts, who assembled a force in armies, it is evident they differ much. I am sorry to in grieve any other mans doings, but it serves me for a peace of my defense, and therefore I wish that no man should gather evil of it: God forbid that words and acts be thus confounded.

The Attorney. Sir William Stanley used this shift that the prisoner uses now; he said he did not levy war against King Henry the seventh, but said to the Duke of Buckingham, that is a good quarrel he would aid him with five hundred men; and nevertheless Stanley was for those words attained, who (as all the world knows) had before that time served the king very faithfully and truly.

Throckmorton. I pay you Master Attorney do not conclude against me by blind contraries. Whether you allege Stanley's case truly or no. I know not. But admit it be as you say, what does there prove against me? I promised no aid to Master Wyatt nor to any other. The Duke of Buckingham levied war against the king, with whom Stanley was confederate so to do as you say.

The Attorney. I pray you my lords that be the queens commissioners, suffer not the prisoner to use the queen's learned counsel thus, I was never interrupted thus in my life, nor I never knew any thus suffered to talk, as this prisoner is suffered; some of us will come no more at the bar and we be thus handled.

Bromley. Throckmorton you must suffer the queen's learned counsel to speak, or else we must take order with you, you have had keeve to talk at your pleasure.

Hare. It is proved that you did talk with Wyatt, against the coming of the Spaniards, and devised to interrupt their arrival: and you promised to do what you could against them: where upon Wyatt being incorporated by you, did levy a force, and attempted war against the queen's royal person.

Throckmorton. It was no treason nor procurement of treason, to talk against the coming hither of the Spaniards, neither was it treason for me to say I would hinder their coming hither as much as I could (understanding me rightly as I mean it) yea though you would extend it to the worst, it was but words, it was not treason at this day as the law stands. And as for Wyatt's doing, they touch me nothing; for at his death when, it was not time to report untruly, he purged me.

Bromley. By sundry cases remembered here by the queen's learned counsel (as you have heard) that procurement which did appear none otherwise but by words and those you would make nothing, has been of long time, and by sundry will learned men in the laws adjudged treason. And therefore, your procurement being so evident as it is, we may lawfully say it was treason, because Wyatt performed a traitorous act.

Throckmorton. As to the said alleged fore precedents against me, I have recited as many for me, and I would you my Lord Chief Justice should incline your misjudgments rather after the example of your honorable predecessors, justice Markham, and others, which did ensure corrupt judgments, judging directly and sincerely, after the law and the principles in the same, than after such men as swerving from the truth, the maxim, and the law, did judge corruptly, maliciously, and affectionately.

Bromley. Justice Markham had reason to warrant his doings: for it did appear, a merchant of London was arraigned and slanderously accused of treason for compassing and imagining the kings death, he did say he would make his son heir of the crown, and the merchant meant it of a house in Cheapside at the sign of the crown, but your case is not so.

Throckmorton. My case does differ I grant, but specially because I have not such a judge: yet there is another cause to restrain these your strange and extraordinary constructions: that is to say, a provide in the latter end of the statute of Edward the third, having these words: Provided always, if any other case of supposed treason shall chance hereafter to come in supposed treason shall chance hereafter to come in question of trial before any justice, other than is in the said statute expressed, that then the justice shall forbear to adjudge the said case, until it be showed to the parliament to try whether it should be treason or felony. Here you are restrained by express words to adjudge any case, that is not manifest mentioned before, and until it be showed to the parliament.

Postman. That provision is understood of cases that may come in trail which has been in use, but the law has always taken the procurer to be a principal offender.

Sanders. The law always in cases of treason does account all principals and no accessories as in other offenses, and therefore a man offending in treason, either by covert act of procurement, whereupon an open deed has insured, as in this case, is adjudged by the law a principal traitor.

Throckmorton. You adjudge (me think) procurement very hardly, besides the principal, and besides the good proviso, and besides the good example of you best and most godly learned predecessors, the judges of the realm, as I have partly declares, and notwithstanding this grievous racking and extending of this word procurement, I am not in the danger of it, for it does appear by no disposition that I procured neither one or other to attempt any act.

Stanford. The jury have to try whether it be so or not, let it weigh as it will.

Hare. I know no mean so apparent to try procurement as by words and that mean is probable enough against you, as well by your own confession, as by other men's depositions.

Throckmorton. To talk of the queen's marriage with the prince of Spain, and also the coming hither of the Spaniards, is not to procure treason to be done: for then the whole parliament house, I mean the common house did procure treason. But with you will make no difference between words and acts, I pray you remember a statute made in my late sovereign lord and masters time, King Edward the first, which apparently expressed the difference. These be the words: Whosoever does compass of imagine to depose the king of his royal estate by poem preaching, express words or sayings, shall for the first offense loose and forfeit to the king all his and their goods and cattle, and also shall suffer imprisonment of their bodies at the kings will and pleasure.

Whosoever and for the second offence shall loose and forfeit to the king the whole issues and profits of all his or their lands, tenements and other hereditariness, benefices, prebends, and other spiritual promotions. Whosoever and for the third offense, shall for term of life or lives of such offender or offenders, and shall also forfeit to the kings majesty, all his or their goods and cattle, and suffer during his or their lives perpetual imprisonment of his or their bodies. But whosoever and by writing, ciphering, or act and shall for the first offense be adjudged a traitor, and suffer the pains of death. Here you may perceive how the whole realm and all your judgments has before this understood words and acts diversely and apparently. And therefore the judgments of the parliament did assign diversity of punishments, because they would not confound the true understanding of words and deeds, appointed for compassing and imagining by word, imprisonments: and for compassing and imagining by open deed, pains of death.

Bromley. It is agreed by the whole bench, that the procurer and the adherent be deemed always traitors, when as a traitorous act was committed by any one of the same conspiracy: and there is apparent proof of your adhering to Wyatt, both by your own confession and other ways.

Throckmorton. Adhering and procuring be not all one, for the statute of Edward the third does speak of adhering, but not of procuring; and yet adhering ought not to be further extended, than to the queen's enemies within her realm, for so the statute does limit the understanding. And

Wyatt was not the queen's enemy, for he was not so reputed when I talked with him last, and our speech implied no enemy, neither tended to any treason, or procuring of treason: and therefore I pray you of the jury note, though I argue the law, I allege my innocence, as the best part of my defense.

Hare. Your adhering to the queen's enemy within the realm, is evidently proved: for Wyatt was the queen's enemy within the realm, as the whole realm knows it, and he has confessed it both at his arraignment and at his death.

Throckmorton. By your leave, neither Wyatt at his arraignment nor at this death, did confess that he was the queen's enemy when I talked last with him; neither was he reputed not taken in fourteen days after, until he assembled a force in arms, what time I was at your house master Englefield, where I learned the first intelligence of Wyatt's stir. And I ask you who does depose that there passed any manner of advertisement between Wyatt and me, after he had discovered his doings, and showed himself an enemy? I had been so disposed, who did let me that I did not repair to Wyatt, or to send to him, or to the Duke of Suffolk either, who was in my own country, and thither I might have gone and conveyed myself with him, unsuspected for my departing homewards.

Englefield. It is true that you were there at my house, accompanied with others your brethren, and to my knowledge, ignorant of these matters.

Bromley. Throckmorton, you confessed you talked with Wyatt and others against the coming of the Spaniards, and of the taking of the Tower of London, whereupon Wyatt levied a force of men against the Spaniards he said, and so you say all: but in deed it was against the queen, which he confessed at length: therefore Wyatt's acts do prove you counselor, and procurer, howsoever you would avoid the matter.

Throckmorton. Me think you would conclude against me with a misshapen argument in logic, and you will give me leave, I will make another.

Stanford. The judges sit not here to make disputations, but to declare the law, which has been sufficiently done, if you would consider it.

Hare. You have heard reason and the law, if you ill conceive it.

Throckmorton. Oh merciful God, oh eternal father, which sees all things, what manner of proceedings are these? To what purpose serves the statute of repeal the last parliament, where I heard some of you here present, and diverse other of the queen's learned counsel, grievously inveigh against the cruel and bloody laws of King Henry the eight, and against some laws made in my late sovereign lord and master's time, King Edward the first. Some termed them Dracos laws, which were written in blood: some said they were more intolerable than any laws that Dionysius or any other tyrant made. In conclusion, as many men, so many bitter terms and names those laws had.

And moreover, the preface of the same statute does recite, that for words only, many great personages, and others of good behavior, have been most cruelly cast away by these former sanguinolent thirsty laws, with many other suggestions for the repeal of the same. And now let us put on indifferent eyes, and thoroughly consider with ourselves, as you the judges handle the constructions of the statute of Edward the third, with your equity and extensions, whether we be not in much worse case now than we were when those cruel laws yoked us. These laws albeit they were grievous and captious, yet they had the very property of a law after Saint Paul's description. For these laws did admonish us, and discover our sins plainly to us, and when a man is warned, he is half armed.

These laws, as they be handled, be very baits to catch us and only prepared for the same, and no laws: for at the first sight they ascertain us we be delivered from our old bondage, and by the late repeal the last parliament, we live in more security. But when it pleases the higher powers to call any mans life and sayings in question, then there be constructions, interpretations, and extensions reserved to the justices and judges equate, that the party triable, as I am now, shall find himself in much worse case than before when those cruel laws stood in force. Thus our amendment is from God's blessing into the warm sun. But I require you honest men which are to try my life, consider there opinions of my life, judges be rather agreeable so the time, than to the truth: for their judgments be repugnant to their own principle, repugnant to their godly and best learned predecessors opinions, repugnant I say to the proviso in the statute of repeal made in the last parliament.

The attorney. Master Throckmorton quiet yourself, and it shall be the better for you.

Throckmorton. Master attorney, I am not so unquiet as you be, and yet our cases are not alike: but because I am so tedious to you, and have long troubled this presence, it may please my Lord Chief Justice to repeat the evidence wherewith I am charged, and my answers to all the objections, if there be no other matter to lay against me.

Then the chief justice remembered particularly all the depositions and evidences given against the prisoner, and either for want of good memory, or good will, the prisoners answers were in part not recited: whereupon the prisoner craved indifference, and did help the judges old memory with his own recital.

Sendall. My masters of the jury, you have to inquire whether Sir Nicholas Throckmorton knight, here prisoner at the bar, be guilty of these treasons, or any of them, whereof he has been indicted and this day arraigned, yea or no. And if you find him guilty, you shall inquire what lands, tenements, goods, and cattle he had at the day of his treasons committed, of any time since: and whether he fled for the treasons or no, if you find him not guilty.

Throckmorton. Have you said what is to be said?

Sendall. Yea for this time.

Throckmorton. Then I pray you give me leave to speak a few words to the jury. The weight and gravity of my cause has greatly occasioned me to trouble you here long, with any prolix oration: you perceive not withstanding this day great contention between the judges and queen's learned counsel on the one party, and me the poor and woeful prisoner on the other party. The trial of our whole controversy, the trial of my innocence, the trial of my life, lands, and goods, and the destruction of my posterity forever, does rest in your good judgments. And albeit many this day have greatly inveighed against me, the final determination thereof is transferred only to you. How grievous and horrible the shedding of innocent's blood is in the fight of almighty God, I trust you do remember. Therefore take heed (I say) for Christ's sake, do not defile your consciences with such heinous and notable crimes. They by grievously and terribly punished, as in this world and vale of misery upon the children's children to the third and forth gener-ation, and in the world to come with everlasting fire and damnation. Lift up your minds to God, and care not too much for the world, look not back to the fleshpots of Egypt, which will allure you from heavenly respects, to worldly security, and can thereof neither make you any surety. Believe I pray you, the queen and her magistrates be more delighted with favorable equity, than with rash cruelty. And in that you be all citizens, I will take my leave of you with St. Paul's farewell to the Ephesians, citizens also you be, whom he took to record that he was pure from shedding any blood, a special token and doctrine left for your instruction, that every of you may wash his hands of innocents bloodshed, when you shall take your leave of this wretched world. The Holy Ghost be among you.

Sendall. Come hither sergeant, take the jury with you, and suffer no man to come at them, but to be ordered as the law appoints, until they be agreed upon their verdict.

Throckmorton. It may please you my lords and masters which be commissioners, to give order that no person have access or conference with the jury, neither that any of the queen's learned counsel be suffered to repair them, or to talk with any of them, until they present themselves here in open court, to publish their verdict.

Upon the prisoners suit on this behalf, the bench gave order that two sergeants were sworn to suffer no man to repair to the jury, until they were agreed according to order. Whereupon then the prisoner was by commandment of the bench withdrawn from the bar, and the court adjourned until three of the clock at afternoon, at which hour the commissioners returned to the Guildhall, and there did tarry until the jury were agreed upon the verdict. And about five of the clock, their agreement being advertised to the commissioners, the said prisoner, Sir Nicholas Throckmorton was again brought to the bar, where also the jury did repair; and being demanded whether they were agreed upon their verdict, answered universally with one voice, Yea. Then it was asked who should speak for them: they answered, Whetston the foreman.

Sendall. Nicholas Throckmorton knight, hold up thy hand.

Throckmorton. Then the prisoner did so upon the summons.

Sendall. You that be of the jury, look upon the prisoner.

Jury. The jury did as they were enjoined.

Sendall. How say you, is Master Throckmorton knight there prisoner at the bar, guilty of the treasons whereof be has been indicted and arraigned in manner and form, yea or no?

Whetston. No.

Sendall. How say you, did he flee upon them?

Whetston. No, we find no such thing.

Throckmorton. I had forgotten to answer that question before, but you have found according to truth: and for the better warranty of your doings, understand that I came to London, and so to the queen's counsel unbrought, when I understood they demanded for me: and yet I was almost an hundred miles hence, where if I had not presumed upon my truth, I could have withdrawn myself from catching.

Bromley. How say you the rest of you, is Whetston's verdict all your verdicts?

Jury. The whole inquest answered Yea.

Bromley. Remember your selves better, have you considered substantially the whole evidence in sort as it was declared and recited; the matter does touch the queen's highness, and yourselves also, take good heed what you do.

Whetston. My lord, we have thoroughly considered the evidence laid against the prisoner, and his answers to all these matters, and accordingly we have found him not guilty agreeable to all our consciences.

Bromley. If you have done well, it is the better for you.

Throckmorton. It is better to be tried, than to live suspected. Blessed be the Lord God of Israel, for he has visited and redeemed his people, and has raised up a mighty salvation for us in the house of his servant David. And it may please you my Lord Chief Justice, forasmuch as I have been indicted and arraigned of sundry treasons, and have according to law put my trial to God and my country, that is to say, to these honest men which have found me not guilty, I humbly beseech you to give me such benefit, acquittal and judgment, as the law in this case does appoint,

When the prisoner had said these words the commissioners consulted together.

Throckmorton. May it please you my Lord Chief Justice to pronounce sentence for my discharge?

Bromley. Whereas you do ask the benefit that the law in such case does appoint, I will give it you; to wit, that where you have been here this day before the queen's commissioners and justices arraigned of the said treasons, whereto you have pleaded not guilty, and have for trial therein put yourself on God and your country, and they have found you not guilty, the court does award that you be clearly discharged paying your fees. Notwithstanding Master Lieutenant take him with you again, for there are other matters to charge him withal.

Throckmorton. It may please you my lords and masters of the queen's highness privy council, to be on my behalf humble suitors to her majesty, that like as the law this day (God be praised) has purged me of the treasons wherewith I was most dangerously charged: so it might please her excellent majesty to purge me in her private judgment, and both forgive and forget my over rash boldness, that I used in talk of her highness's marriage with the prince of Spain, matter too far above my capacity, and I very unable to consider the gravity thereof, a matter impertinent for me a private person to talk of, which did appertain to her highness privy council to have in deliberation. And if it shall please her highness of her bountiful liberality, to remit my former oversights, I shall think myself happy for trial of the danger that I have this day escaped, and may thereby admonish me to eschew things above my reach, and also to instruct me to deal with matters agreeable to my vocation. And God save the queens majesty, and grant the same long to reign over us. And the same Lord be praised for you the magistrates, before whom I have had my trial this day indifferently by the law, and you have proceeded with me accordingly and the grace of God be amongst you now and ever.

There was no answer made by any of the bench to the prisoner's suit, but the attorney did speak these words.

The attorney. And it please you my lords, forasmuch as it seems these men of the jury which have strangely acquitted the prisoner of his treasons whereof he was indicted, will forthwith depart the court. I pray you for the queen, that they, and every of them may be bound in recognizance of five hundred pounds apiece, to answer to such matters as they shall be charged with in the queen's behalf, whosoever they shall be charged or called.

Whetston. I pray you my lords be good to us and let us not be molested for discharging our consciences truly. We be poor merchantmen, and have great charge upon our hands, and our livings do depend upon our travels, therefore it may please you to appoint us a certain day for our appearance, for perhaps some of us may be in foreign parts about our business.

Thus much for Sir Nicholas Throckmorton arraignment, wherein is to be considered, that the repealing of certain statute in the last parliament, was the chief matter he had to allege for his advantage: whereas the repealing of the same statutes was meant notwithstanding for another purpose (as before you have partly heard) which statutes, of the effect of the chief branched of them have been since that time again revived, as by the books of the statutes it may better appear, to the which I refer the reader.

Holinshed, The First and Second volumes of Chronicles, pg. 1104-1117.

There is no genuine parallel between Sir Nicholas's trial and those of today. From the beginning to the conclusion of the trial, the court and council employed tactics that would not be seen in a modern court, such as literally baiting Sir Nicholas with questions and accusations to induce him to confess his culpability. Sir Nicholas's dexterity is evidence of his intellect and talent, and his audacity afforded him extraordinary advantages in his disputes with the justices and council. A man of lesser abilities would not have been able to defend himself, which is why this trial is so well documented in history because he was completely acquitted of the charge of high treason, which was unheard of during that period of turbulent Tudor history, especially in light of the hundreds of executions that followed Wyatt's rebellion.

Sir Nicholas was unquestionably in contact with the insurgents. Unknown is whether he actually pledged to accompany Edward Courtenay into the west. I am confident that Nicholas had numerous conversations with Thomas Wyatt, but the nature of these conversations can only be conjectured.

An early historian suggested that the jury's conscience had less trouble with the evidence against Sir Nicholas than with the guilt affixed to those facts. The verdict may have been a rebuke for the mass executions carried out by the crown; ambassador Simon Renard reported to the emperor that the verdict was an affront to the crown and that Mary was ailing for three days as a result. Renard notes that a throng welcomed Sir Nicholas following the trial by throwing their caps in the air and shouting. The queen ordered that the jurors be punished; consequently, they were apprehended and incarcerated for nearly eight months.

Despite having avoided execution, Nicholas remained in the Tower of London following his trial. Dr. Wotton wrote in a letter to Sir William Petre (a member of the council) on 14 July 1554 that he had not yet heard what the queen intended to do with Sir Nicholas and that Nicholas had not yet been granted mercy by her. In addition, Sir Nicholas was in such dire need of money that he requested to serve her Majesty in 'these conflicts' and promised not to join the insurgents but to work for the Gascons (those who resided in southwest France).

Dr. Wotton to Sir William Petre. Has not yet received her Majesty's pleasure concerning Throckmorton, who, he is informed, continues his suit still to be received to mercy, and is now driven to such extremity that he must needs serve in these wars, having no other means whereby to live. But he will not, he understands, serve with the rebels, and labors to be employed with the Gascons. Would be glad to learn what answer to make concerning him. Yesterday Cardinal Tournon told one of the Ambassadors that it is understood the Prince of Spain has returned from the sea-coast, because of the mortality among the soldiers that should come with him : wherefore it is thought he will not be in England so soon as expected. The siege of Sienna is said to be raised ; save that the Florentines have left 5,000 men in the forts near the town, and that Pietro Strozzi is joined with the French aid of Italians and others who were at Mirandola, so that he now seems to be strong enough to resist the Duke of Florence. The latter is said, however, to expect great succor shortly from Milan and Naples. The French have embarked in their own navy a number of troops for Sienna; and they say that the navy of Algiers joins that of France to conduct it safely, but it is thought Prince Doria is ready to meet them by the way, as strong, or stronger than they are. [One page. The first portion, relating to Throckmorton, in cipher, deciphered.]

Calendar of State Papers, Foreign Series, Mary 1553–1558. #223, pg. 96-97.

Sir Nicholas Throckmorton was freed from the Tower of London on 18 January 1555 after paying a fine, according to a pair of records. Several other people were released from the Tower of London on the same day, and Henry Machyn notes in his diary, 'and then there was a great firing of guns.' In addition, it was around this time that Sir Nicholas's jury was ultimately released upon payment of a 2,000-pound fine.

Chapter 3: Transition

Upon his release from confinement, Nicholas found England to be in a very turbulent state, primarily due to the change in religion, and the situation was deteriorating. A letter from a 'reverend and distinguished bishop' provides a clear summary of this, but the author's name has not been recorded, possibly out of dread of punishment for speaking out.

> 'The proceedings of that parliament, wherein all her father's doings in religion were condemned, seemed to confirm what Martin [in his book against priests' marriage] said, that all the heresies in King Edward's days proceeded from the queen's father. And if so, he was to be condemned with the rest of the Protestants. Wherefore, it was to be though, seeing Almighty God had suffered some of them to suffer martyrdom by fire, by bloody persecution, and the tyranny of the Pope's laws, and torments for professing the truth of God's word, that now the body of that noble prince the queen's father, because he was the beginner of all this, and the continuer of it twenty-five years, as the proceeding of the parliament seemed to pronounce, should be taken up at Windsor, and burnt as Wickliff's was.'

Strype. *Memorials Ecclesiastical Relating Chiefly to Religion.* Volume 3:1, pg. 251-252

By the time the majority of those involved in Wyatt's rebellion had been persecuted and executed, many fled England in terror for their lives due to the religious persecutions. Nicholas chose to depart for France in the early months of 1556, possibly arriving there in late February or early March.

In March 1556, the council received official intelligence of a new conspiracy that would later be dubbed 'the Dudley Conspiracy' after its chief instigator, Henry Dudley, a relative of the late John Dudley, Duke of Northumberland. It was a scheme to remove Mary from the throne and possibly send her to Spain with her new spouse, then to position Elizabeth on the throne and marry her to Edward Courtenay. The rebellion would be financed with exchequer funds that would be secreted into France to employ ships and mercenaries.

Nicholas Throckmorton's inclusion with Henry Dudley, William and Edward Courtenay, and John Throckmorton as one of the primary instigators is rather peculiar. However, Nicholas was in France at the time, and no evidence was found in early archives to support this. In addition, it should not be forgotten that he escaped execution on account of his intelligence and intellect and was just released from prison. If Queen Mary had even the slightest evidence that Sir Nicholas was implicated in another plot against her, she would stop at nothing to have him promptly tried and executed. Nicholas was an intelligent man, and the repercussions of his involvement in another insurrection would have outweighed the possibility that he would have eventually learned of the conspiracy through his extensive network of contacts in France. It is plausible that the omission of the first name in conjunction with the mention of a Throckmorton's involvement misled some historians.

Nicholas arrived in Saint Malo, France, on 27 June 1556. Even though he suffered only minor injuries when his horse collapsed on him en route to Paris in early July, it made further travel extremely uncomfortable, and he could only ride for brief distances. He notified Dr. Wotton via letter that he was unable to complete the journey to Paris (417 kilometers, or about 259 miles). Nicholas reaffirmed in his letter to Wotton that he had not spoken to another Englishman while in France and had no plans to do so except with Wotton. He also expressed a need for money. Nicholas was again cautioned by Dr. Wotton not to contact the dissidents, as doing so would be detrimental to his business. Nicholas stated that he would never support Henry Dudley's activities or the rebellion.

By 4 August, both Wotton and Nicholas were in Paris, and Wotton wrote to the queen to confirm that Nicholas had not spoken to any Englishmen while in Paris and that Nicholas had requested a meeting in a secret location out of fear of danger; however, no additional information is provided regarding the nature of the danger or the information to be discussed. Perhaps he desired to share information he heard while at the French court.

Nicholas sent an emissary to Dr. Wotton to inquire about a number of Englishmen, why they were in Paris, and whether they were there for him.

Wotton responded in the negative. Nicholas remarked to his emissary that it was odd that not only was his presence in Paris known, but also that one of Wotton's men had spotted him in the street while traveling to the palace.

Perhaps it is just a coincidence, but the editor of the manuscript collection has marked as absent a number of letters to and from Nicholas during the period he was in France. In all the letters that I have reviewed to this point, I have discovered minuscule spaces where letters should have been. I conclude this based on how often Nicholas communicated. The compilers of the numerous Calendars of papers that I have reviewed undoubtedly undertook a monumental task in assembling thousands of documents into numerous reference volumes, so it is unknown when these particular letters disappeared. It appears that the original correspondence referenced in the Calendars made reference to the missing letters from that time period. The first time I encountered absent letters from the same time period was while gathering information for A Shadow of the White Rose about Edward Courtenay. Permit me to recall those early discoveries, as they have relevance to both the same time period and related individuals.

Edward Courtenay perished on 18 September 1556 in Padua, Italy, under the suspicion that he was poisoned. During the last few months of his life, there is very little correspondence to and from Courtenay, but prior to that, he wrote many letters, sometimes six per week. Upon his demise, the Council of Ten in Venice discovered a large cache of his correspondence, and a number of these letters were withdrawn from the box, never to be read by anyone.

The short trail began on 17 November 1556, when the Council of Ten in Venice instructed the bailiff of Padua to wrap the casket (box) containing Courtenay's correspondence in a wrapping that would conceal its contents for transportation and to perform this task attentively and in secret without informing or discussing it with anyone. Three days later, the Council of Ten unanimously approved a motion to hire a carpenter with specific qualifications and to require him to remain silent. They would open the sealed casket (box) and read all the letters contained within, after which the carpenter would return the casket to its original state. By 26 November, all of the letters contained in the casket had been reviewed, and the Council of Ten had marked each letter with a small cross. Some were returned to their bundles, while others were returned to their linen coverings, sewn shut, and placed back in the casket to make it appear as though they had not been disturbed. The coffin was then sealed in the presence of Courtenay's entourage and sealed with his official seal.

Rawdon Brown, editor of the *Calendar of State Papers and Manuscripts, Relating to English Affairs Existing in the Archives and Collections of Venice*, indicated that the thirty-two manuscripts of letters to and from Courtenay that he reviewed, dating from 8 May 1555 to 22 February 1556 and preserved in the Venetian archives at the time, did not contain a cross. On the basis of this evidence, it is reasonable to assume that the letters were either of personal or political significance, perhaps correspondence to or from the French king expressing his desire to position Courtenay and Elizabeth on the English throne.

The absent Nicholas Throckmorton letters are from June to July of the same year. Perhaps the Council of Ten confiscated Courtenay's correspondence at the request of the French ambassador to Venice, the Bishop of Lodeve. There appears to be no reason for the Republic of Venice to perpetrate an act of state larceny by opening a sealed container, as they had no reason to be inquisitive about the letters, whereas the French would. Doctor Wotton wrote to Queen Mary on 21 June 1557, which is the last known mention of certain letters, to describe an interview with a gentleman named Lant, who had ties with the French and told a correspondent of Doctor Wotton that he possessed certain letters that had belonged to Courtenay. Later, when questioned about them, he denied ever having said such a thing or possessing letters from the deceased Courtenay.

There are no additional indications or suggestions regarding the fate of the letters, who received them, how many there actually were, or the location or disposition of the Council-marked letters. They were likely destroyed, with their contents hidden indefinitely, not only to safeguard Courtenay's name but also anyone mentioned in the letters and their plots. Perhaps some of these letters are concealed in an obscure collection of undiscovered manuscripts. Edward Courtenay's involvement in the 'Dudley Conspiracy' has been mentioned by both ancient and modern historians, and his name appears with the same frequency as that of Nicholas Throckmorton. It was relatively simple to trace Courtenay's movements in his final years, and there are records of him in Paris in 1555, but none in 1556. It is also known that Peter Carew traveled to both France and Italy around the same time. These individuals share certain characteristics that raise numerous concerns. Nicholas was familiar with Carew and Courtney.

Over the course of three months, records of arrests and interrogations of those suspected conspirators in the Dudley conspiracy reveal that torture was used to obtain valuable information that ultimately led to the indictment of thirty-six individuals and the execution of ten for their role in the conspiracy. Dudley, who was in France when the arrests commenced, remained there until 1563, when he returned to England. Several early and modern historians indicate that Nicholas and other conspirators were judged and executed on 28 April 1556. I am pleased to report that Sir Nicholas lived an additional fourteen years.

Lady Throckmorton appeared before the council on 7 October 1556 and requested permission to send her husband desperately required funds. The council granted her request a single time, and the queen authorized a maximum of forty crowns. It is conceivable that the council limited the quantity of money because they feared Nicholas would fund a rebellion or aid those who would.

By late October, tensions between England and France were evident in the increased troop movements of 8,000 to 12,000 French soldiers, according to some reports. Nicholas remained in Paris and reported frequently to Dr. Wotton, but despite his skills and diligence, he was unable to obtain credible information regarding the reason the soldiers were in transit.

On 1 December, King Philip II of Spain was relieved by the arrival of the Earl of Pembroke and wrote to his wife that he could now repel any French attacks. The French king was alarmed by the Earl of Pembroke's presence on 12 December and promptly sent a letter to Queen Mary inquiring about her intentions. By mid-January 1557, Dr. Wotton reported that there was only speculation of war while he was in Poissy, France.

Dr. Wotton was in Paris around 16 March, and it is safe to presume that Sir Nicholas was nearby, as he was able to convey information regarding the installation of English ordinance on a marshy ground near Guises, with the intention of seizing the town. Dr. Wotton relocated to La Ferte Milon by 27 April, and Nicholas reported from Paris that the French had as many ships prepared for war as they did troops. On 29 May, Queen Mary recalled Dr. Wotton, and she informed King Henry II of France of his withdrawal. On 1 June 1557, after receiving word that her army had arrived in Calais, Queen Mary sent a commission to the French King.

During the Battle of St. Quentin, the Earl of Pembroke commanded a force. Pay records and muster documents do not indicate what Sir Nicholas was doing or where he was, but it is safe to assume that he served as an ambassador and did not serve in the military. The few records that mention him only describe his correspondence, with no mention of him in battle.

The conflict of St. Quentin occurred around 8:00 a.m. on St. Lawrence's Day, 10 August 1557. Contemporary accounts of the battle differ from source to source, but the common facts seem to indicate that the constable arrived at St. Quentin with 30 ensigns of German and 18 ensigns of French troops to be assaulted by the Duke of Savoy, who broke and scattered the French troop lines. Numerous German soldiers were slain, while several thousand were captured. Several thousand French soldiers were slain, and an even greater number were captured; however, these figures differ depending on the source examined. According to the records, only a few members of Philip's army were injured, and one gentleman was slain.

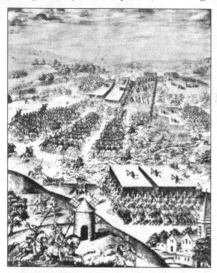

Fig. 10. Battle of St. Quentin, from the fresco by Granello. Public domain usage, photo number M0012864, Welcome Images. Public domain usage, photo number M0012864, Welcome Images.

There are very few records indicating where Nicholas was for the next ten to twelve months, and no known correspondence from or to him, including with his wife. Nicholas may have realized that he could not advance in Mary's court and began to consort more with Princess Elizabeth than he did before Mary ascended the throne, according to one early historian.

Nicholas may have returned to England immediately after the Battle of St. Quentin, based on these scant details. In addition, there is a letter from Dr. Wotton conveying Nicholas' request to expedite his relief shortly before

Fig. 11. Francis II, heir to the French throne, aged 14, married Mary, Queen of Scots, aged 15, on 24 April 1558, at Notre Dame Cathedral in Paris. Histories document a lavish event with all the pomp and circumstance of a regal wedding. Young, G. F. *The Medici, with Portraits and Illustrations*. London, 1913.

Mary Tudor fell ill during the summer of 1558, and by November it was evident that she would pass away. Her husband, Philip, advised her to recognize Elizabeth as her successor in a message. Mary died 17 November 1558, and when the news was proclaimed during a session of parliament, a moment of stillness was observed, followed by the resounding chant, "God save Queen Elizabeth, reign she most long, reign she most happily!"

QUEEN ELIZABETH. BY ZUCCHERO.

Fig. 12. Law, Ernest. The Royal Gallery of Hampton Court. London, 1898.

Elizabeth remained at her residence in Hatfield when the news of her sister's death arrived, and although she had made preparations in the event of her sister's passing, she immediately dispatched Nicholas to confirm the news. Elizabeth instructed Nicholas to 'Haste to the palace and beseech one of the ladies of the bedchamber who was in her confidence; if the queen were truly deceased, send her as a token the black enameled ring that her majesty wore at night.' Several peers of the council arrived at Hatfield to greet their new queen before Nicholas's return. It wasn't long before the streets of London were filled with shouts of delight as church bells rang, bonfires were lighted, and people ate, drank, and made general merriment in honor of the new queen's accession.

Cardinal Reginald Pole (Reginald Pole was an English cardinal of the Roman Catholic Church and the last Roman Catholic archbishop of Canterbury, serving from 1556 to 1558 during the Counter-Reformation) died at his residence in Lambeth Place on the same day as Mary, and it appears that their deaths occurred within a few hours of each other.

An early historian notes that after Nicholas delivered the ring to Elizabeth, he was advised to travel to the residence of Cardinal Pole and examine his depositories for documents and correspondence that could reveal state secrets. Upon his return from the lengthy and fruitless task, he discovered that his absence had been used to fill all the lucrative positions in the new administration to his exclusion. However, the queen granted him the position of England's senior butler and then appointed him chamberlain of the exchequer. Queen Elizabeth was also officially proclaimed queen and Sir William Cecil was appointed as her secretary of state on this day.

Nicholas confronted Elizabeth about the thirteen privy councilors she retained from Mary's tenure who practiced the old religion, according to an anecdote preserved by history. Nicholas told her in no uncertain terms how inconvenient and risky it would be to counsel such individuals "Who, if they should once get her into their counsel and confidence, would either gain her to their religion, or if they found they could not carry that point, would endeavor to take her away by violence or poison."

Elizabeth responded swiftly, "God's death, villain! I will have thy head."

Nicholas calmly replied, "You will do well to consider first, Madam, how long you will then be able to keep your own on your shoulders." Nicholas left the enraged queen. Long-standing friendship with her permitted him to address her in such a fashion.

As with all monarchs before her, France and Scotland were of the utmost importance when Queen Elizabeth began addressing the issues of the realm. Elizabeth needed to appoint a trustworthy diplomat and ambassador to France, and her longtime friend Sir Nicholas Throckmorton seemed to be the ideal candidate, as he had spent considerable time in France, spoke the language, and was familiar with the country's customs.

Nicholas was at Westminster on 3 May 1559 when he received his appointment as Ambassador Resident to the French court. The queen issued him the following directives to observe while in France:

> 1. After having accomplished the purposes for which he is associated with the Lord Howard of Effingham and Dr. Wotton, he shall continue as ambassador resident with the French King, and in this capacity is to promote the increase of amity between the two realms.

> 2. In the transmission of intelligence he shall send duplicates of all letters of importance, either by the merchants of Rouen, or Dieppe, or by way of Germany, from Geneva or Strasburg.

> 3. He shall continue to act in the matter respecting "the detention of certain Frenchmen, counterfeiters of monies, both English, French, and Spanish."

> *Calendar of State Papers, Foreign Series, Elizabeth, 1558–1559,* pg. 241.

Shortly thereafter, Nicholas returned to France, but this time in an official capacity. He was well-received at the French court, and the monarch ensured that he received several gifts, including a boar and other essentials. During the first couple of months, he complied with the queen's requests and kept her informed of the French court's activities.

King Henry II of France celebrated the wedding of his daughter Elizabeth of France (1527-1598) to King Philip II of Spain at St. Quentin on 30 June 1559. He was injured during a joust with the commander of the Scottish Guard, Comte de Montgomery, despite being warned by members of his court not to engage in jousts or any other form of combat. The monarch presumably received the warning from Michel de Nostradamus in the form of a quatrain the previous year.

> The young lion shall overcome the old one,
> In martial field by a single duel,
> In a golden cage he shall put out his eye,
> Two wounds from one, then he shall die a cruel death.

Garencieres, Ophilus. *The True Prophecies or Prognostications of Michael Nostradamus*. Century 1, XXXV, pg. 24.

The fractured lance of his opponent pierced King Henry II's right eye and temple, inflicting a fatal injury. Nicholas was a spectator at the event and sent a letter to the English council on 1 July 1559 detailing the incident.

The Duke of Savoy was not financed till the XXVII of this present, at night; which was done at Meigret, a house of the constable's near the place of the jousts, with great triumph; which evening also an entry was made for the beginning of the jousts. And forasmuch as I was neither desired to be at the same, nor at the first running at tilt, which was the XXVIII of this present; I did take occasion the XXIX of this present (the rather for that I had an inkling of some disliking towards) to speak to the constable touching Stranguish; supposing, partly by his countenance and otherwise, to decipher him. And after I had according to your Lordships instructions spoken to him, he made me answer (with a very good countenance, as me seemed) that he would forthwith cause letters to be written to all the ports in France, naming them apart to me; and that in case the said Stranguish (whom, he said, he had cause to know) did repair to any of these ports; that he should their neither receive any successor, nor be suffered to escape, if he arrived in any of the same; adding further, that he was ready to do the queen's majesty all the service that should lie in him: whereupon he willed, that Stranguish's name should be left with him in writing; which was done.

It may like your lordships further to be advertised, that the XXVIII of this present, which day the king dauphin's band began the jousts, two heralds which came before his band were Scots, fair set out with the king dauphin and queen dauphins' armies, with escutcheon of England set forth to the show; as all the world might safely perceive, the same being embroidered upon purple-velvet, and set out with armory upon their breasts, backs, and upon their sleeves.

The XXIX of this present, the bands of the prince de Condé, of the Duke de Longueville, and the Duke of Bouillon, ran against the challengers; at which triumph were the pope's Nuncio, the ambassador of Venice, and I, in a place appointed by the constable. The ambassador of Portugal was their, but not in our company; who stood in a house right over against us: which affair, as I could learn, was of his own provision.

The last of this present, the prince of Nevers, otherwise called count d' Eu, came to the tilt with his band; where I was to see them run, and none ambassador Elles. Whereat it happened, that the king, after he had run a good many courses very well and fair, meeting with young Monsieur de Lorges, captain of the Scottish guard, received at the said de Lorge his hands such a counterbluff, as, the blow first light-ning upon the king's head, and taking away the pinnate which was fastened to his headpiece with iron, he did break his staff withal; and so with the rest of the staff hitting the king upon the face gave him such a counterbluff, as he drove a splinter right over his eye on his right side: the force of which stroke was so vehement, and the pain he had withal so great, as he was much astonished, and had great ado (with reeling to and from) to keep himself on horseback; and his horse in like manner did somewhat yield. Whereupon with all expedition he was unarmed in the field, even against the place where I stood: and as I could discern, the hurt seemed not to be great; whereby I judge, he is but in little danger. Merry, I saw a splint taken out of a good bigness; and nothing else was done to him upon the field: but I noted him to be very weak, and to have the since of all his limbs almost benumbed for being carried away, as he lay along, nothing covered but his face, he moved neither hand nor foot, but lay as one amassed. Whether there were any more splints entered in, as in such cases it happened, it was not known. There was marvelous great lamentation made for him, and weeping of all sorts both men and women. Thus your lordships may see, what God sometimes does to show what he is, and to be known;

that amongst all these triumphs, and even in the very midst and pride of the same, suffered such mischance and heaviness to happen.

Forbes, Dr. Patrick. *A Full View of the Public Transactions in the Reign of Q. Elizabeth*, pg. 150-151.

Eleven days later, King Henry II of France passed away. Nicholas notified England on 13 July.

By mid-July, the queen expressed her satisfaction with Nicholas' administration of her affairs, including those between France and Scotland. Nicholas reminded Elizabeth in late August that his first three months had passed, and despite his earlier request to return home, the queen asked him to stay for an additional three months.

Queen Elizabeth sent to him on 28 August a petition from Sir Thomas Cotton, who claimed that his son had been abducted in Calais and was being held for ransom by a Madam Crezecques. The queen had pleaded with Nicholas to use his influence with the Duke of Guise to resolve the matter and the unreasonable ransom demand.

On September 10, Nicholas informed Queen Elizabeth of the rising religious tensions in France.

I am informed, that they here begin to persecute again for religion more than ever they did; and that at Paris there are three or four executed for the same, and diverse great personages threatened shortly to be called to answer for their religion. Wherein the cardinal of Lorraine having been spoken to, within these two days, has said, that it is not his fault; and that there is no man that more hates extremis, then he does: and yet it is known, that it is, notwithstanding, all together by his occasion.

Forbes, Dr. Patrick. *A Full View of the Public Transactions in the Reign of Q. Elizabeth*, pg. 226-227.

Nicholas was able to provide the Duke of Guise with additional information about Madame Crezecques and her actions on 12 September. Nicholas discovered that she abducted Mr. Cotton's son in retaliation for her son's capture and confinement by a Burundian rather than an Englishman.

Nicholas sent a request to the duke, based on a vow the duke made at the time Calais was captured that no women or children would be captured, to resolve the matter and pay for the safe return of Mr. Cotton's son. The next day, Nicholas received a response from the duke stating that Mr. Cotton's son would be released only if Madam Crezecques's son was released without ransom.

Francis II departed for Rheims on September 18 for his coronation. Nicholas accompanied the young monarch as the procession left Villiers Coste-rez and proceeded towards the magnificent cathedral.

> The XI of this present the king removed from Villiers Coste-rez to an abbey two leagues of, called Longpoint; the next day to La Fere in Tartenois, a house of the contestable; from there, the day following, to Fymes; and the XIIII of this present to an abbey three leagues from Reims: where the XV of this month he made his entry, and was first received at the gate by a maid representing the town of Reims; who (after a few words spoken of submission) delivered the keys thereof to the king, who gave the same to his lieutenant the duke of Nevers to open the gates which he found shut. There was in that place very little or no show at all saving that the arms of England, France, and Scotland quartered were very trimly set out to the show over the gate. From there he was straight conducted to the church of Nostredame, and there received by the cardinal of Lorraine and the cardinals Givry, Burbon, and Chastillon in their pontifications, accompanied with some crosses, and a number of priests in copes. When the king was once entered into the church, the cardinal of Lorraine made an oration to him: which ended, the king proceeded towards the chore, being lad on his right side with the cardinal of Givry, and on his left side by the cardinal Chastillon; by whom he was brought to the high altar: where after he had kneeled a while and made his prayers, he offered to the altar a golden image of St. Francis, and kissed the crown, and so went to his palace, without any other ceremony or show at all. The king himself and about XVI of his order who came with him were appareled only in black velvet coats; having thereupon their collars, without any other show. Soon after, the same day, the young French queen made her entry, and was received at the gate with a little oration, without any other ceremony, and so with a small train conducted to the palace.

> The sacred and coronation, which was appointed to have been the XVII of this month, for that the duke of Savoy was the same day troubled with his ague, was differed till the XVIII of the same: which day the said sacred and coronation were executed; whereat there were the six perish of the church, and the six pairs of the temporality, in their habit accustomed for the like ceremony. The perish of spirituality were placed with the bishops on the right side of the chore; and the temporal perish, viz. the king of Navarre representing the duke of Burgundy, the duke of Guise the duke of Normandy, the duke of Nevers the duke of Guyon, the duke of Monpensier the count of Flanders, the

duke d'Aumale the count of Champaign, and the constable the count of Toulouse, on the left side; on which were also the knights of the order, and the ambassadors of the pope, the king of Spain, of Portugal, of Mantua, and two gentlemen sent from the state of Siena. For the rest of the ceremonies, the same were executed in such sort as has been heretofore accustomed. The old queen, her daughters, and all the ladies of the court (except the young French queen) were all appareled in the dueill. The knights of the order, and all others, who had no robes, wore only velvet, or some other silk black, without either goldsmiths work or embroidery. The duke of Savoy was present at these ceremonies.

Forbes, Dr. Patrick. *A Full View of the Public Transactions in the Reign of Q. Elizabeth*, pg. 231-232.

Nicholas received word of his wife's illness 'vexed with ague and in more fear than danger, we trust.' On 11 October 1559, Queen Elizabeth authorized his return to England to be with her. In addition, the queen instructed Nicholas to notify the Cardinal of Lorraine and the Duke of Guise that Henry Killigrew would stand in for his absence for approximately four to five days before returning to France.

Henry Killigrew wrote to Secretary Cecil on 18 November, informing him that the cardinal and Duke of Guise believed Nicholas's return home was for a covert reason and that his wife was not truly unwell, 'for some purpose besides, which was small, pour leur advantage.'

Killigrew also reported that French Queen Mary had fallen ill and spent several days in her chamber as rumors circulated that Francis had become a leper and the children were removed from Chatelherault out of fear that the monarch would visit. Several physicians treating the king feared that he would die shortly, but he recovered and resumed hunting, his favored pastime.

The French ambassador Noailles wrote at the end of December that Nicholas's return to England was a ruse and that he was certain Nicholas was aiding the separatists in Scotland, as he had been informed that certain individuals had been seen entering his lodging. Nicholas's leave was significantly longer than four to five days, and he left Dover on 24 January 1560, and arrived in Paris on 4 February 1560. Nicholas informed England that several of his subordinates requested permission to return to Scotland due to ill treatment and that he was unable to meet with the king because he was hunting, despite the fact that there were no records in the archives indicating his presence in Scotland.

Nicholas was eventually permitted to meet with the King of France on 27 February and invited to remain for dinner. After apologizing for his absence due to his wife's illness, the conversation turned to the tensions between Scotland, England, and France after the Cardinal of Lorraine drew him aside after dinner to discuss current events. Several individuals who acted without authority regarding the Scottish Reformation were to be punished, according to the cardinal. In addition, the cardinal voiced his concern regarding rumors that the queen would side with Scotland against France.

Nicholas assured the cardinal that he was oblivious of any plans by the queen to support Scotland. Before Nicholas was to meet with the king again, he visited with the queen and the queen's mother, who wished their sister Elizabeth 'good health.'

Fig. 13. Robert Dudley, Earl of Leicester. Cust, Lionel. The National Portrait Gallery. #447, p. 51.

Since that time, historians have debated Nicholas's relationship with Robert Dudley, Earl of Leicester, but less is known about Leicester and Cecil's tense relationship. Nicholas expressed his displeasure to Secretary Cecil upon hearing rumors that the earl was considering a marriage to Queen Elizabeth.

Sir, the XXV of October, in the night, I received the queen's majesty's packet, with the letters and writings mentioned in the same, by my servant Davis; and also a letter from you, which amongst other things contained your advice to have me write to her majesty, to move the same for order to be taken in the better dispatch of her affairs, which, you say, are too much neglected. For answer whereto, I say, I know not where to begin: I looked by your last to be somewhat satisfied and resolved, touching the greatest matter of all, I mean the queen's marriage. I know not what to think, nor how to understand your letter in that point. And the bruits be so brim, and so maliciously reported here, touching the marriage of the lord Robert, and the death of his wife, as I know not where to turn me, nor what countenance to bear. Sir, I thank God I had rather perish and quail with honesty, than live and beguile a little time with shame.

 And therefore I tell you plainly, until I hear of, or on, what you think in that matter, I see no reason in the advising of her majesty. Merry, to you I say in private, that albeit I do like him for some respects well, and esteem him for many good parts and gifts of nature, that be in him, and do wish him well to do; yet the love, duty, and affection, that I bear to the queen's majesty, and to the surety of herself, and her realm, does, and shall, during my life, take more place in me, than any friendship, or any particular case. And therefore I say, if that marriage takes place, I know not to what purpose any advice or counsel should be given; for as I see into the matter, none would serve. If you think, that I have any small skill or judgment in things at home, or on this side, or can conjecture sequels, I do assure you, the matter succeeding, our state is in great danger of utter ruin and destruction. And so far I think I see into the matter, as I wish myself already dead, because I would not live in that time. I beseech you, like as I deal plainly with you, so to signify plainly to me, not only what is done in that matter, but what you think will be the end. Thereupon you shall perceive, that I will write to her majesty my poor advice, in such sort, as becomes a true and faithful servant. And if the matter be not already determined, and so far past, as advice will, not serve, I require you, as you bear a true and faithful heart to her majesty and the realm, and do desire to keep them from utter desolation, & in *visceribus Jesu Christi*, I conjure you to do all your endeavor to hinder that marriage. For, if it takes place, there is no counsel or advice that can help. Who would be either patron or mariner, when there is no remedy to keep the ship from sinking? As we begin already to be in derision and hatred, for the bruit only, and nothing taken here on this side more assured than our destruction; so if it take place, we shall be *opprobrium hominum et abjeclit plebis*. God and religion, which be the fundaments, shall be out of estimation; the queen our sovereign discredited, contemned, and neglected; our country ruined, undone, and made prey. Wherefore with tears and sighs, as one being already almost confounded, I beseech you again and again, set to your wits, and all your help to stay the commonwealth, which lies now in great hazard.

Let us remember what this noble wise man said, when he used these words: "Ego enim existimo melius agi Cum civibus privatim, u si tota respublica fortunata fit, quam si pet singulos elves felix fit, publice vero labefactetur. Nam quum evertitur patria, is cui privatim bene est, nihil tamen minus et ipse evertitur; cui autem male, is in ilia prospere agente, multo magis incolumis est." For your letters, they be as safe in my hand as in your own, and more safe in mine than in any messenger's. Think it assuredly, I am as jealous of your safety and well doing, as yourself; and so conceive of me.

If you will be pleased to write to me sooner than you shall have occasion to send a post, my cousin H. Middlemore, my steward, can, I suppose, convey your letters safely to me. I am much beguiled, if he be not an honest and faithful young man; I pray you deal with my letters as I do with yours; for all is not gold that glitters, and that you may well perceive by some men's new haunts. It may like you to show this bearer some favor for my sake, in his suit. I pray you also, let my lord of Creigh find courtesy at your hands. The man is well affected to you, for the bruit that ruin of you. Thus I humbly take my leave of you. From Paris the XXVIII of October, 1560. Yours, &c. N. Throckmorton.

Miscellaneous State Papers, Vol. I, pg. 121-124.

In the concluding paragraph of a letter to Secretary Cecil, Nicholas revisited the same subject when he was informed that such a marriage would have severe negative effects on negotiations.

And lastly and chiefly, that they take it for truth and certain, that her majesty will marry the Lord Robert Dudley; whereby they assure themselves, that all foreign alliance and aid is shook off, and do expect more discontinuation thereby amongst yourselves. Thus you see your fore; God grant it do not with rankling fester too far and too dangerously. Thus I humbly take my leave of you, from Orleans the XVII of November, 1560. Yours, &c. N. Throckmorton.

Miscellaneous State Papers, Vol. I, pg. 144-146.

Queen Elizabeth I of England and the Scottish and French representatives of King Francis II of France (husband of Mary Queen of Scots) drew up the Treaty of Edinburgh in order to formally end the siege of Leith, replace the

Auld Alliance with France with a new Anglo-Scottish accord, and maintain peace between England and France.

The treaty between France and Scotland had not been ratified by mid-November, and after numerous requests, Nicholas was granted an audience with the French King. He then sought an audience with the queen, expecting for a better outcome, as his meeting had not yielded a definitive answer. She told him, 'My subjects in Scotland do their duty in nothing, nor have they performed one point that belongs to them. I am their queen, and so they call me; but they use me not so.' Scotland was dissatisfied with the terms of the treaty.

Late in November, King Francis II of France became sick with what is commonly known as a fever and catarrh, and his physicians predicted that he would pass away within a few months. The young king recovered for a brief time, and it appeared that he could avert death, but Nicholas remained near to court to report on changes, knowing that if the young king died, changes would occur not only in France but also in Scotland.

> Sir Nicholas Throckmorton to the queen. It may like your majesty, since my letters of the XXIX of November to your majesty, wherein I advertised your highness, of the French King's state in his sickness, I understand, that he is somewhat amended, but yet very weak, and so feeble, as he was not able to keep the feast of the Golden Fleece, on St. Andrew's day, whereof he is knight; and now the physicians mistrust no danger of his life for this time.
>
> And whereas in the same letter I wrote to your highness, that the French Queen was not then minded to send your majesty her picture, nor letter, which she had promised, as I advertised your highness by my letter of the XXVIII of the last; I understand now, that she has given order, that my lord Seton shall both bring a letter from her to your majesty, and also her picture. Whether it come of her better mood, or by the said lord Seton's importune suit, to have the carrying thereof to your highness, I know not. I understand, that the French king has pressed two and thirty captains, they to be ready with their bands upon the next warning.
>
> And thus I pray God long to preserve your majesty in health, honor, and all felicity. From Orleans the 1 of December 1560. Your Majesty's, &c. N. Throckmorton.
>
> *Miscellaneous State Papers,* Vol. I, pg. 160-161.

At 11 p.m. on 5 December 1560, the sixteen-year-old French king passed away. On 8 December, he was interred in the church's crypt of Saint Croix. Mary, Queen of Scots was now the solitary sovereign of Scotland due to her descent from King Henry VIII's eldest sister, Queen Margaret.

Charles IX ascended to the French throne upon the demise of his older sibling on the same day that Catherine de Medici became his guardian. One of their initial actions was to release the Prince of Conde, but he refused to depart, stating, "Until my accusers were confined here." He quickly accepted his liberation and traveled to La Fere.

Nicholas was confident that he would be permitted to return to England after the death of the king, and he indicated as much in the majority of his correspondence at the time. Queen Elizabeth's intentions were different.

Fig. 14. The Queen Mother, Catherine Medici. Young, G. F. *The Medici, with Portraits and Illustrations.* London, 1913.

Nicholas visited Catherine Medici, mother of Francis II, after Christmas to discuss the treaty. She informed Nicholas that now, with the death of the king, the Queen of Scotland was responsible for all matters. The Queen Mother concluded their meeting by extolling Nicholas's management of the government's affairs.

In the first few weeks of January 1561, Queen Mary was still in mourning, but she sent four men to Scotland with a commission stating that she would marry where and to whom she wished. There were rumors that Mary had no intention of returning to Scotland and that she would marry a Frenchman instead.

Nicholas was instructed to refocus his efforts on preventing the Queen Mother from advancing Papism and overturning Protestantism in France. The Queen Mother indicated in a diplomatic manner that she was inclined to advance the true religion, but that she "is forced to show a good face to the adversary."

Lady Throckmorton traveled to Elizabeth's court in late February, hoping to find a sympathetic ear regarding Nicholas's request to return home. At the end of the letter Secretary Cecil wrote to Nicholas, he mentioned that Lady Throckmorton addressed it, 'To my loving husband, Sir N. Throckmorton, Knt, the queen's ambassador in France.' Nicholas learned that his wife would presumably join him in Paris by the end of March, and he notified Secretary Cecil that he hoped to return to England by the end of April. Nicholas was concerned that his son's affection for a young French lady residing near Paris and his presence in Paris had caused a scandal. Nicholas ordered two of his attendants to use any means necessary to discourage his son from pursing his passionate displays of affection. Nicholas was also concerned with the Paris epidemic.

Nicholas was informed that he would soon be relieved of his duties as he prepared for a meeting with Queen Elizabeth and Queen Mary, though the details were still being finalized. Queen Mary had finally begun her arduous voyage to Scotland when she became sick in Joinville. Nicholas met with her in early April to negotiate the treaty, but Mary would not ratify the agreement between France and Scotland without the advice of her council. Nicholas revealed to Secretary Cecil that he believed Queen Mary had fabricated her ailment in order to avoid ratifying the treaty.

Among the many matters Throckmorton was handling, the matter of Thomas Cotton's son remained unresolved. On 19 April 1561, the Duke of Guise delegated De la Haye to pursue the release of young Mr. Cotton, but his efforts were unsuccessful, and Elizabeth pressed Nicholas Throckmorton for resolution.

Queen Elizabeth granted Lady Throckmorton permission to travel to France to be with her spouse on the same day, and by 8 May, she was en route.

Nicholas eventually obtained an audience with Queen Mary in mid-June after much persistence. Obviously, the ratification of the treaty was the primary focus of the meeting. Mary maintained that she could not ratify the treaty without her council and had not altered her position. Nicholas and the Queen discussed various religious topics after he realized he was unable to advance the argument.

Queen Mary requested a passport to travel through England in the event that her ship was required to disembark anywhere on English soil and transit through to Scotland. If she ratified the treaty, Queen Elizabeth responded, she would be allowed to travel through England. Mary's request for a passport was granted by Queen Elizabeth at the beginning of August, despite the fact that this did not elicit the anticipated response.

Nicholas arrived in Abbeville, France, at the request of Queen Mary, and conferred with her. Nicholas naturally brought up the treaty. Queen Mary discussed the treaty's articles and stated that her youth and inexperience precluded her from ratifying the treaty without the advice of her council, and that she would write to Queen Elizabeth prior to her departure.

On 19 August, Queen Mary and her two uncles landed at Leith, Scotland, early in the morning with two galleys. She did not receive a warm welcome because her exact arrival date and time were unknown. In spite of this, she did receive a warm welcome after word rapidly spread of their queen's arrival.

On 3 September, a master of the household to the Queen of Scotland traveled to Paris to present Lady Throckmorton with tokens of devotion from Mary. Lady Throckmorton was given two basins, two ewers, two salts, and a standing cup, all of which were guilted and weighed a total of 398 oz. Before departing, the gentleman relayed kind words from the queen to Nicholas, who was evidently confined to his bed.

Mary, Queen of Scots, was in her homeland on 20 September 1561, when a border survey titled 'The bounds and meres of the batable land belonging to England and Scotland' was published. The results determined where the River Esk entered the sea, with the English ground measuring eight miles in length and four miles in width and the Scottish ground measuring seven miles in length and four miles in width.

Reports of a recently published obscene and libelous book rapidly reached Elizabeth's court. Gabriel De Sacconay, precentor of the church of Lyons, wrote that King Henry VIII's separation from the church of Rome was due to the influence of Ann Boleyn (mother of Queen Elizabeth), whom he compared to Solomon's pagan wives, dubbing her Jezebel, and asserting that she was appropriately punished for her wickedness. Nicholas was instructed by Queen Elizabeth to suppress the book by any means necessary, and he addressed the king and Queen Mother, who assured him they would cooperate. The king ordered Sacconay to modify the objectionable passages and the printer to cease all sales, but Queen Elizabeth pressed for a harsher punishment, possibly because the book contained information Elizabeth did not want made public. By the beginning of October, the book had been altered, all known editions of approximately 800 copies had been confiscated, and Queen Elizabeth had reviewed and approved two copies. If any copies survived the destruction, I was unable to find them.

Elizabeth's rightful claim to the throne over Mary, Queen of Scots, was revived by the book. Nicholas was visited by D'Oysel (Henri Cleutin Oysel, seigneur d'Oisel et de Villeparisis was the representative of France in Scotland from 1546 to 1560, a gentleman of the chamber of the king of France, and a diplomat in Rome from 1564 to 1566 during the French Wars of Religion) at his home in Paris, and they immediately engaged in a lengthy conversation. D'Oysel indicated that Nicholas could deduce from Sacconaye's book that not everyone shared the same opinion regarding Queen Elizabeth's title, and that she had no reason to resend the matter to Queen Mary or her council. If Queen Elizabeth perished without a progeny, Queen Mary would ascend to the throne of England.

The precise date of Thomas Cotton's son's release is unknown, but in a letter dated 4 March 1562, it is mentioned that a letter was conveyed by Sir Thomas Cotton's son. The archives contain no additional information regarding Madame Crezecque or the offspring of Sir Thomas Cotton after this point. Unknown is Nicholas's contribution to the resolution of the issue.

At this juncture in English and French history, religious differences undoubtedly sparked numerous, sometimes heated debates, but they were hardly remarkable. Though uncommon, generally minor disturbances escalated into serious conflicts, and in mid-October, Nicholas reported that between 7,000 and 8,000 Protestants had gathered approximately one mile outside of Paris to hear a minister preach. Many were injured, as the Papists had closed the city's gates, obstructing their path back inside. On both parties, there were reported casualties. Nicholas feared that the frequency and magnitude of these conflicts would increase.

Nicholas was informed by Secretary Cecil that Sir Peter Mewtas had visited Queen Mary to discuss the treaty. The queen indicated that there were provisions in the treaty that affected her late husband, King Francis, and that she believed a new review would be prudent and that Nicholas should be consulted on the matter.

The Earl of Bedford informed Nicholas on 14 November that Sir Thomas Smith had been named as his successor, but that the decision had not yet been finalized.

Christmas in Paris was anything but tranquil when Protestants gathered at Fanburg, St. Marceau, and Papists gathered at St. Medard with the intent to attack. One of the Protestants was slain by a Papist sword, and when the Protestant guards attempted to retaliate, they were battered and driven back, with many individuals being beaten and injured, by the king's lieutenant.

THE PRINCE DE CONDÉ.

HENRY OF GUISE.

Fig. 15. Yorston's *Popular History of the World, Ancient, Mediaeval and Modern.* Yorston and Co., New York, 1884. V. 5, pg. 140-141.

The Bishop of Carlisle delivered fourteen articles of religious doctrine to Secretary Cecil on 14 January 1562. No one of the new doctrines was permitted to convene among them under the threat of being burnt, and everyone was required to live according to the Roman Catholic Church or face the death penalty. This included the Duke of Guise's declaration that he would defend the venerable religion "to the last drop of my blood!"

Nicholas informed Secretary Cecil that his wife would return to England by the end of March and that he hoped to return by the end of April. He was concerned about the unrest in Paris and the epidemic. His wife actually left for England on 9 March.

By mid-March, two names appeared more frequently in reports: the Protestant-Huguenot Prince of Conde and the Catholic Duke of Guise. Each side kept a careful eye on the other as their numbers grew, and on 20 March it was rumored that there were between nine and ten thousand soldiers.

As what is commonly known as the Spanish Inquisition reached its apogee at this time, the Spanish council announced their disapproval of the Scottish queen's tolerance of Protestants. As many in the French court aligned with their allies and Queen Elizabeth requested that Nicholas encourage the Queen Mother, the Queen of Navarre, and the Prince of Conde to maintain their beliefs, Germany and Italy also spoke on the subject of religion.

In addition, a rendezvous location for Queen Elizabeth and Queen Mary was being organized. Queen Elizabeth expressed her desire "not" to visit Scotland, while Queen Mary expressed her desire to visit England. The most reasonable location would be south of the Scottish border, perhaps in York.

On 10 April, the Prince of Conde departed Paris with 1,500 soldiers en route to Orleans. The Queen Mother, the king, and the Duke of Orleans relocated to Melun, a strong town that could shield them from danger for four to five days if necessary, out of concern for the king's safety. The king issued orders for the prince to disarm, but the prince disregarded them because he did not believe they originated from the king.

The king dispatched commissionaires to Switzerland for the assistance of 6,000 soldiers and to Germany for an additional 3,000 pistoleers. All soldiers, with the exception of those belonging to the Prince of Conde, were ordered to hasten their arrival. Between 15 and 17 April, the Burgundian Papists murdered and injured two hundred people. Nicholas reported to Elizabeth that according to what he had heard, Scotland would not rise up as France had. "But contrariwise, it would be well that the Protestants there had a watchword to look to their case and surety, and to take heed that their adversaries grow not too great, nor too bold."

Late in April, Nicholas received additional reports of his son's overzealous behavior toward a young woman, prompting him to request that Secretary Cecil write to his son about the irrational display of affection with a young gentlewoman residing outside of Paris and warn him to cease. "She is a maid, and her friends will hardly bear the violating of her." Nicholas anticipated Cecil would have a greater impact on his son than he would. Nicholas was unable to transport his son to Paris because of the unrest in the city and the presence of the epidemic.

In Paris, Papists ravaged the residences of three Protestants, continuing the religious discord. This action led to the execution of the criminals. In retaliation, the Protestants defaced images, copes, and surplices in every church in Orleans. Two Protestants were publicly executed by Papists in Paris under the protection of 2,000 to 3,000 armed men.

The King of Spain offered the King of England 30,000 infantry and 6,000 cavalry to assist in the suppression of the rebellion. Nicholas advised the queen that a diplomatic solution would be preferable to the use of force. Queen Elizabeth sent Henry Sidney, the president of the council of the marches of Wales, to assist Nicholas with the unfolding events in France. On 8 May, Nicholas and Sidney jointly addressed the king, queen mother, and duke of Guise.

The prince of Conde composed 'Occurrence to the advantage/ disadvantage of the Prince of Conde' which included seventeen articles, and in one he dubbed the turmoil 'war,' during this period.

The prince responded to Nicholas' letter by stating that he was delighted with Queen Elizabeth's stance on the matter and that the situation would not have progressed as far as it has if his opponents had taken the same stance.

Queen Mary informed Queen Elizabeth that she would remain in Scotland until all religious disputes in France were resolved by the end of June. In addition, she indicated that their annual meeting would not take place. Sidney had returned to England to meet with Elizabeth, and he informed Nicholas that, despite Queen Mary's objections, Elizabeth had indicated that the meeting would take place in York or on the English side of the River Trent on Bartholomew Tide (24 August), and orders were issued to prepare for the meeting. Very soon after, a proclamation was issued stating that the monarchs had consented to meet at Nottingham Castle at the start of September.

Nicholas learned from his informants that the Prince of Conde's camp was two leagues from Orleans and four leagues from the Duke of Guise's camp. The prince had thirty-four ensigns, or approximately 7,000–8,000 poorly armed foot soldiers, and the cavalry had approximately 5,000 horse soldiers who wore long white coats of serge, kersey, or stamell with long sleeves of armor.

It was reported that the duke had 27 ensigns, or approximately 6,000 foot soldiers, and approximately 7,000 cavalry.

As tensions continued to escalate, both factions were receiving additional outside support in the form of men, weapons, powder, and provisions, but the prince had acquired the wealth of the city of Bourges and several other locations to advance his campaign.

THE CALVINISTS

DESTROYING IMAGES AND DECORATIONS OF CHURCHES AND CATHEDRALS,
From the Original, by A. De Neuville.

Fig. 16. *Yorston's Popular History of the World, Ancient, Mediaeval and Modern.* Yorston and Co., New York, 1884. V.5, pg. 142.

Nicholas was determined to accomplish Elizabeth's request that he mediate between the two forces on her behalf, as evidenced by the massive quantity of correspondence between the prince, duke, king, and queen mother over the course of several months, some of which did not go so well.

Nicholas encountered an unanticipated problem as a result of the conflicts: some of his letters were intercepted and never delivered.

On 9 June, the Queen Mother and the King of Navarre convened with the Prince of Conde to negotiate the terms of a treaty that was only partially accepted. The first conference lasted approximately two hours, during which time soldiers from both sides stood poised approximately 1,000 paces apart. The king proposed new articles, and the prince concurred with some of them. The conference lasted three days, but no definitive agreement was reached. The queen remarked that both camps were so close together that it was impossible to exit one without confronting the other, resulting in conflict.

By 12 July, hangings, burnings, the destruction of homes and religious objects, and the murder of men, women, and children were once again all too common. Nicholas's servant was robbed and shot while conveying crucial letters to Queen Elizabeth; a record of the incident indicates that Nicholas himself was fired at, although he never mentions it in his correspondence.

> A servant of Throckmorton the ambassador is forcibly taken in the open street by Francis, grand prior of France, the Duke of Guise his brother, and thrust in the gallies, pistols are discharged at the ambassador himself within the walls.
>
> Camden, William. *The History of the Most Renowned and Victorious Princess Elizabeth*, pg. 34-35.

After the treaty was signed, soldiers who had left their respective locations began to return accompanied by new soldiers and cavalry. As hostilities increased, so did the number of people slain in battles and skirmishes; furthermore, these numbers were augmented by plague fatalities. Nicholas grew extremely fearful for his own safety, and on 5 August he told Queen Elizabeth, 'The daily despites, injuries, and threats put in use towards me and my servants by the insolent raging people of this town, so assure me of my own destruction and that I am not ashamed to declare that I am afraid.'

Reports on the estimates of forces made on 2 September indicate the Duke of Deux Ponts led 2,500 foot soldiers and 1,000 pistoleers, in addition to 6,000 Swiss, and the Baron Des Adrets with 4,000; the Queen of Navarre with other lords of Gascony, joined with an additional 8,000 foot soldiers and 1,500 cavalry; and the Prince de Pourcain joined the Prince of Conde's forces with 600 cavalry and 2,000 foot soldiers.

In Beaugency, the Duke of Guise had 2,000 cavalry and was joined by twenty ensigns (approximately 4,000 men) of Germans, twenty-seven ensigns (approximately 6,000 men) of French, and approximately 3,000 Swiss, but many were lost to the epidemic rather than in battle. About 4,000 additional soldiers from other regions comprised the remainder of the duke's forces. Obviously, these statistics differ depending on the source examined, but these are the averages. Nicholas acknowledged that he had an obligation to report accurate information to Queen Elizabeth so that she could make informed decisions concerning her realm and subjects.

Nicholas announced his intention to travel from Paris to Burges on 8 August, and Marshal Brisac suggested a safer route. Nicholas began his voyage on 1 September, but it is unknown if he heeded Brisac's advice when he encountered an artillery unit with five hundred cavalry and three hundred foot soldiers. Nicholas attempted to retreat to safety as the Catholic forces simultaneously attacked him. Conde's forces annihilated the attacking forces of the Duke of Guise, losing three hundred soldiers, six cannons, and powder wagons. Nicholas was spared death due to his neutrality, but he lost everything he owned because it was confiscated, including letters from Queen Elizabeth containing special instructions and ciphers as well as a substantial amount of cash. Nicholas traveled approximately twenty-two miles with Conde's force to Orleans, where he remained at the admiral's home for an additional eight days.

On 6 September, spies informed Nicholas that the king would endeavor to recapture Newhaven and Orleans. By that time, Nicholas had recovered a number of stolen items, including letters, ciphers, and horses. He expressed a strong desire to return home and reminded the queen of his three and a half years of service in France. Elizabeth was confident that she had hired the most qualified candidate.

On 3 October, English troops arrived in Newhaven, France. No man was permitted to be with a woman other than his wife, which was one of sixteen orders issued to the soldiers, mostly concerning their conduct in France. Four days later, Queen Elizabeth instructed the Earl of Warwick to assist and aid the Prince of Conde.

Henry Smith arrived in France on 6 October, and encountered Nicholas, who requested permission to introduce his replacement to the Queen Mother and the king, but was denied permission.

By mid-October, Nicholas eventually received permission from Queen Elizabeth to return to England; Henry Smith had assumed his responsibilities as ambassador, but the Queen Mother refused to issue Nicholas a passport to leave France or return to court. The king was advised to deny Nicholas's request and instead use Smith. In addition, Marshal Brisac, the lieutenant general of Normandy, is cited regarding Nicholas on 15 October 1562:

"That whatever it cost they must get him into their hands, and without delay must cut off his head, he being the most dangerous instrument of his nation for them; and that they will find articles enough to make his process."

Calendar of State Papers-Foreign, Elizabeth-V-5 (1562). Letter 848-#3, pg. 368.

On 8 November, the Prince of Conde captured Pluvieres from the Duke of Guise with approximately 6,000 foot soldiers and 2,000 mounted troops. As an act of vengeance, Conde's forces executed anyone who displayed arms or attempted a show of force against them. This retaliation was in response to the duke's massacre of Conde's soldiers at Rhone.

In the following letter to Queen Elizabeth, Nicholas vividly describes the rising religious tensions in France.

To the queen's majesty. It may please your majesty, I sent you a dispatch from Orleans of the XXX of October, for answer to your last letters of the XVII of September, which came to my hands the XXV of October; and also did by the same dispatch advertise your majesty of such matters and occurrences, as I thought was convenient for your majesty's knowledge at that time. I sent the same dispatch by one of my own servants to Dieppe, and gave him in charge to pass therewith into England. He approached near to Dieppe the same day the town was rendered to the Marshall Montmorency; so as he could by no means, neither pass himself, nor send the dispatch safely into England. And thereupon my said servant returned to me with the said dispatch addressed to your majesty: which I have thought need to send once again to your majesty by the way of Sir Thomas Smith; for that the same does contain in part matters need for your knowledge and confederation, albeit the loss of Rone and Dieppe may alter a great part of the determination and resolution convenient for that time and state. And to the intent your majesty may the better advice and give order for your own affairs; I have thought convenient to advertise you of the proceedings of the Prince of Conde since my said last dispatch, and of such other occurrences as be come to my knowledge.

The Prince of Conde and the admiral with their force, that is to say, of footmen six thousand armed so, and of horsemen near about two thousand of all sorts, marched from Orleans the VIII day of November. The IX day the said prince sent a trumpet to the town of Pluvieres to render; a town in the Beaulse, between Paris and Orleans, fortified and held by the faction of the Duke of Guise ever since the beginning of these troubles. The XI day the said prince made his approaches before the said town; and the said X day was so much of the faulxbourgs of the town, as was left unburned by them within. The XI day, about eight of the clock in the morning, the battery was made to the said town, of two cannons only: and there was also two scares employed to beat the flanks and defenses. The battery profited so well and the sap together, that the town was rendered to the prince about twelve of the clock the same day; upon no other capitulation, but the whole town and all the people therein to stand to the prince's mercy. The prince gave pardon to all the inhabitants of the town which bare no arms: the captains, soldiers, and such as bare arms, were all executed; except the governor only, who is yet held alive as prisoner, and is named Monsieur de la Masiere. There was four ensigns of footmen within the town. The said XI day Monsieur d' Andelot made the Almain force, brought by him under the conduct of the Marshall of Hesse, to join with the said prince's force. There is three thousand and five hundred righters, very well armed and mounted: there is also four thousand footmen, as well armed, and men of as good show as ever I saw. The Marshal of Hesse is the most moderate and advised Almain that I have seen; but the people under his charge be very Almain soldiers, which do spoil all things where they go.

The said XI day Monsieur de Gonorre, knight of the order and brother to the Marshall Brisac, arrived at the prince's camp, immediately after the winning of the town of Pluvieres; who proposed to the prince and to the admiral, in general terms, a plausible accord and composition: saying to them, they should have what they would desire, so as they would find the means to rid the realm of France of the Englishmen which were entered, and the Almain also; but especially the Englishmen, for that they did possess the principal port of this realm. The said Monsieur Gonorre remained in the prince's camp all night, and lodged in the admiral's lodging; and made many long and sundry discourses to them, with overtures of fair show; always concluding upon the conditions before spoken of.

The next morning the prince and the admiral made me privy to all this conference; and asked my opinion, what answer they should make. I told them, that Monsieur de Gonorre's fair words and other such like had heretofore much abused them, and done them much harm; having diverted them from their advantage taking upon their enemies: and I thought, his coming and legation at this time tended to no other end; for now their enemy's forces was not comparable to theirs, and therefore they had no other means to serve their turns but fair words. I put them in remembrance to consider, what surety they might have to have promise kept of anything promised them by their enemies; putting them also in remembrance of their performance in times past, both of the king's edicts, the ordinance of the estates, and their own promise.

Then the Prince of Conde and the admiral said to me: We do consider this that you do say to be true; but in case things be reduced to such points as we may be assured of a good end, what shall we say of the queen your mistress determination? I answered: You see the queen my mistress determination by her protestation; and you know, she is a princess of her word, and will keep promise both with you and with herself. But, quote I, I see by no possibility how you can be well assured, if the queen my mistress's force were further of this realm: for at this present if English men and Almain were not here; you know, your own force to be so small of your own nation, as your enemies would not be assured of them, nor offer you so largely as they do; whereof you have had good proof this four months past, in which time neither Englishmen nor Almain for you were in this realm. In the end they said: monsieur l' ambassador, assure you, and we pray you to assure the queen your mistress, that we will no end but such as shall stand with her pleasure: and yet we pray you, let us know by as good speed as you can her opinion in these matters. We will answer Monsieur de Gonorre, and by him the Queen Mother and the king's council, that we can see no surety for ourselves, nor repose for this realm, unless the queen of England and the princes of Almain do make the end. And thereupon the prince and the admiral dispatched Monsieur de Gonorre the XII day in the morning, in such sort as they told me before mentioned.

The severity used at Pluvieres by the Prince of Conde against the captains and soldiers proceeded chiefly in revenge of the great cruelty exercised by the Duke of Guise and his party at Rone against the soldiers there, but especially against your majesty's subjects: and in recompense of the cruel putting to death of the presidents Maunderville, Marlorat, Cotton, and others, the Prince of Conde caused to be executed at Orleans, before his departure, a counselor of the parliament of Paris named Sappin, and an Abbot appertaining to the Cardinal of Lorraine. The said XII day, in the afternoon, the prince caused his whole camp to march from Pluvieres towards Etampes.

The XIII day eleven ensigns of footmen of the papist's camp, being left in Etampes to guard the town, and perceiving the prince's forces approaching, did abandon the town; which they sacked before their departing. The XIIII day in the morning, the inhabitants of the town of Etampes, perceiving the Prince of Conde to be encamped but three miles from their town, sent the key of their said town, with their submission to the prince; offering to him to aid him of victual's and all other things that they were able to furnish. The prince accepted their offer in good part, and would not suffer his camp to enter into the town: so as the XV day his camp marched towards Paris, leaving the town of Etampes on the left hand, taking the way towards Corbeil: which town was kept by the enemy, the passage being there by bridge over the river of Seyne, and but eight leagues from Paris.

The XV day the prince approached with his camp within three leagues of Corbeil aforesaid; and was constrained there to sojourn some time, by means of a great straight which his army had to pass at a town named Ferte-Allan: nevertheless his light horse occupied both them of Melun, Corbeil, and Paris with alarums, the time of his sojourning. The same day there arrived a messenger from my Lord of Warwick in the prince's camp, who brought a letter from my said lord to the Prince of Conde. The said messenger also declared to the prince in my hearing, that your majesty had sent over one hundred thousand crowns and above, to aid the said prince; and that the same was there ready for him, whenever he should send for it. Whereupon, I suppose, the prince will send commission to monsieur de Bricquemort, or Monsieur de Beauvois, or both, to repair to your majesty very shortly. The prince's desire is, that some good number of your force, under the leading of my Lord of Warwick, should join with his force: which cannot be safely done, unless the prince should send a good band of his horsemen to guard them. The said messenger did also declare to the Prince of Conde, and the same was confirmed by letters from Monsieur de Bricquemore and Monsieur de Beauvois, that the Count of Rhingrave desired my Lord of Warwick to make fair and neighborly war, and so doing he should find the like at his hands: which be but baits to insinuate the said count into my Lord of Warwick's good opinion, that thereby he might the easier abuse him.

I do think, your majesty is by the advertisement of Sir Thomas Smith now well advertised, in what evil terms I stand here with the Queen Mother and the council about her: whose color and malice was so great, as she could not but discover the same vehemently to your said ambassador at his last audience; whereof partly he has of late advertised me, advising me to beware, how I fall into her or their hands. So as, whatever information has been given your majesty of my preciseness and scrupulosity, or that I have formed myself a fear without cause, your majesty may now perceive by more indifferent testimony than my own, that I had reason to eschew to committee myself either to the Queen Mother's or the king's councilors courteously, without a sufficient safe conduct for my safety: which to obtain for me, the Prince of Conde and the admiral have of late required Monsieur de Gonorre to solicit the Queen Mother that I may retire myself further of this country, according to your majesty's commandment. And besides this your ambassador's confirmation of my hard case with the said Queen Mother, and the king's council; I am very well able to assure your majesty by very good means, as you shall know at my access to you, that she and they did mean, having me in their hands, being untied by safe conduct promise, to dispatch me forth of the world.

It may please your majesty, it is taken here for a matter concluded, that Maximilian the King of Bohemia either is or shall be chosen King of Romains: whose election not being already solemnized in my simple opinion, it shall be very convenient for your majesty's purpose to recommend the said King of Bohemia favorably to your friends the Princes of Almain: which your majesty's friendly recommendation cannot but be thankfully taken of the emperor, the King of Bohemia, and his brethren, together with the said Princes of Almain.

Of late here have been sundry rumors spread of your majesty's late sickness, and of the manor of it; your friends and well-wishers in this country fearing, that the same has proceeded of some malicious violence of your enemies: but now, thanks be to God, your said friends be now all well comforted, in that your majesty has escaped the danger thereof. About this your majesty's sickness, your estate, and the state of your realm, here has been very strange discourses: and it is here believed for certain, that very lately the grand prior, disguised in very secrete ways, repaired into your realm, there to practice things upon all events whose practices, it is said here, were accompanied with some peril to your own person. I will not assure your majesty, that this is true; for that I am not so well ascertained thereof as I could wish: but it may please you, that this advertisement, as it is, may thus far forth serve, as to move you to be vigilant of your own safety, as well in your feeding as otherwise, and to have an eye to the practices within your realm.

I am very loathe to call things in question which be past, and past recovery; but it seems very strange to the Prince of Conde, to the admiral, and to me your majesty's minister here, that the town, castle, and new fortifications of Dieppe was by your men and by the French captains there so abandoned as it was: for, howsoever your majesty has been given to understand, the town was much more guardable than Rone was, considering the force which was in it; and the enemy was not in case, both for lack of powder and other things necessary, either to assail it or force it, but (as they say) with bonne mine: for they had no means to make their artillery to march, and to be employed; and who would give over such a town without any cannon shot? Moreover please it your majesty, suppose the case at the worst, that they had been vehemently assailed, and could be by no means, either by the Prince of Conde or otherwise, succored: yet in all extremities they might have retired themselves, as they did, by sea.

The loss of that piece was of great importance, and came very ill to pass, not only for your majesty's own affairs but also for your friends and favorers in this country: who can by no means give you intelligence from time to time of their doings; Newhaven being situate as it is, and being as it were besieged; Harflute, Humflute, Cauldebeck, Rone, Feckam, and Dieppe being held by the enemies; and the count Rhingrave, with force of horsemen Almain, and French footmen, being in these parties, as it were to make a violent siege to Newhaven. And moreover, besides Newhaven, there is no port now in this country at your and your friend's devotion: the navigation is much more freer and stronger for the enemy, by the loss of Dieppe, then it was. This I can assure your majesty, the French captains that were in Deep shall never be well looked on that gave advice to abandon the same in sort as it was, neither by the Prince of Conde, nor by the Admiral.

Your majesty can consider, it is a dangerous matter to give your enemy scope, and to tie yourself to one straight and place. The matter had need now to be so handled, as Newhaven and your ships may impeach the navigation and trade of the river of Seyne, and also impeach the herring fishing amongst that cost; for there is no one thing will more grieve these men, nor be more intolerable to them, than that. The said count does practice, that two of his ensigns, under color of revolting from him for religion's sake, should enter into Newhaven to serve under my Lord of Warwick: which bait is but to betray the peace; for assure your majesty, there is no good meaning in the count Rhingrave, nor in none other under his charge. It may therefore please your majesty to admonish my Lord of Warwick, to beware of these cunning dealings, like as I have already something written to him in this matter, if my letter may safely come to his hands.

It may please your majesty, it is taken here for an assured truth, that the King of Navarre is either dead, or will be dead within few days; and that the Prince of Conde, having this great force together, shall be able to enjoy the place and authority that the king his brother did enjoy within this realm. And for that I do perceive, there is already practices in hand set on by the Queen Mother, secretly so to accord with the Prince of Conde, as that the Cardinal of Ferrare, the house of Guise, the constable, and the Marshall St. Andre may still remain in their estates in court and council about the king; which tends but to exclude the admiral, his brethren, and such as favor the religion and be no good Spaniards; which being brought to pass, the Queen Mother does think herself well fortified to do her will, and also to be in case to lead the Prince of Conde to all intents and purposes, through his easy nature and facility, as me did the king his brother: these matters thus coming to pass will frame toward and unprofitably for your majesty's affairs. Therefore it may please you, as it were by way of advise and for good amities' sake, to advise the Prince of Conde by letter in general terms, and by speech in particular to Monsieur de la Haye and to Monsieur de Briquemore to admonish the Prince of Conde, that the proceedings of the king his brother, abandoning the advancement of religion, his faithful friends and servants, as he did, may be to him a glass and teaching, to see the danger that may ensue to him, if he do the like: and that he has good cause to value and esteem the admiral, his house, and all such noblemen and gentlemen as have taken his part in this quarrel, rather than such as have sought his ruin and destruction; as the persons afore named have done, with divers other, many of them forgetting, that they were his kinsmen. I do see some apparent cause to write thus much to your majesty and therefore it may please you to consider graciously of it, and to give order for the same in time.

I do also perceive great presumption, that, amongst other accords for the troubles in this realm, the matter of religion is like to be compounded by means of an interim, (after the same manner as it was in Germany in the time of the Emperor Charles, or according to the present state there) until by some council there may be some universal reformation ordained for the church. What will ensue hereof, I will not take upon me to say; but I suppose, in a kingdom it will not work most quietness. And therefore it may please your majesty so to provide for the quietness of your own state, as no practice, mourner, nor dangerous instrument win not that credit at your majesty's hands, nor be not suffered so to work within your realm, go as that an interim may be introduced to take place in your realm, after the example of France and Germany: for, your majesty not offended, whosoever will open that gate, to introit such a change within your realm, does not mean the repose and conservation of your estate; and therefore such overtures would be cut of, without any manner of toleration.

Presently the Prince of Conde does write to your majesty and to the Earl of Warwick, and by his means to convey his letters to your majesty by the hands of Monsieur de Bricquemore. Monsieur de la Haye has somewhat complained, or at the lest the Prince of Conde is given to understand, that the said De la Haye is not most grateful to your majesty. It should better succeed for your service, as the case stands, that your majesty would by your gracious usage to him move him to change that opinion. For, as the case stands presently, the good usage of the Prince of Conde's minister shall more advance your service, and turn more to your commodity, then the good usage of Monsieur de Foix: for he is taken to be the Queen Mother's and the papists minister, and the other is the minister of your majesty's good friends and well willers; to whom open good treatment may be no we as well avowed to be used and moved by your majesty and your ministers, as to the other.

The Prince of Conde, the admiral, and other your majesty's good friends in this country, be somewhat jealous, that Sir Thomas Smith, your majesty's ambassador has such intelligence, and does make such court to the Cardinal of Ferrare: and albeit I know nothing thereof, yet I have done the best I can to satisfy them; assuring them, his actions does tend nothing to their prejudice. I have given Sir Thomas Smith a watchword in this matter, to eschew those haunts and intelligences with the cardinal, especially at this time, unless your majesty have given him instructions so to do.

It may please your majesty, the prince and his force have been driven to consume the XVII, XVIII, and XIX of this month, before he could make his approaches to Corbeil; partly for the repose of the Almain after their long travail, and also for mustering of them; and partly for that the passage was very straight, as aforesaid, to pass so much carriage as is in this army, wherein there is to fight six thousand horsemen of all sorts and nations and ten thousand footmen. The cause why the prince and his force do amuse themselves before the said town of Corbeil is, as well for that the same town, standing as it does, may impeach and cut of their victuals coming to them from Orleans, Pluvieres, and the Beaulse; as also for that the enemy, enjoying the same, shall have the river of Seyne on that side at commandment to succor the town of Paris of victuals and other things necessary from time to time. For these respects aforesaid the prince does assay to recover the said town to his devotion, if it be possible; although there will be somewhat ado there about, for that there is within the said town, as it is said, of the enemies four thousand footmen and two thousand horse, and the Duke of Nevers and the Marshall St. Andre be within the said town. At the dispatch hereof the artillery to batter the town of Corbell was in planting: whereabouts there has been lost both good captains and some number of good soldiers, and namely the lieutenant to Monsieur de Grandmont, named Chanterat; which Monsieur de Grandmont is colonel of all the Gascoigne footmen. It may please your majesty, the XVIII day of this month the King of Navarre departed this life between Roan and Paris, being brought up by water. It may please your majesty, if you be disposed to aid the Prince of Conde with money, to stay a while the payment thereof, until you may see how the Queen Mother and he will agree. N. Throckmorton. 20 November 1562.

Forbes, *A Full View of the Public Transactions*, Vol. II, pg. 195-203.

BATTLE OF DREUX, DECEMBER 19, 1562
(Bib. Nat., Estampes, *Histoire de France*, Q. b)

Fig. 17. Caldwell-Marsh, Anne. *The Protestant Reformation in France*, pg. 392.

Nicholas was in the prince's camp at the beginning of December and reported to Queen Elizabeth that she should continue to provide the prince with men and funds to ensure a safe and uncontested occupation of Newhaven. Nicholas reported that artillery and supplies continued to increase on both sides. It culminated on 19 December, at Dreux, when both sides collided and a significant battle ensued. Sir Nicholas Throckmorton's account is perhaps the most vivid of the few surviving accounts of the battle of Dreux; I will leave his words to speak for themselves.

Both the armies were minded, as it seemed by their proceedings and issue, to give the battle; the Prince of Conde being resolved to pass the river of Dure at Dreux, the constable and Duke of Guise being likewise resolved to impeach that passage at that place. Thus each party persisting in their opinions, the battle began about XII of the clock at noon, and continued till the night did separate them. The vanguard of the Prince of Conde's side being conducted by the admiral and his brother, accompanied with the Marshal of Hesse and five cornets of reighters, did defeat the battle of his enemies led by the constable: at which defeat the constable was taken, being hurt with a pistol shot on his neither lip, but not dangerously; who was forthwith with great speed led to Orleans. And the said vanguard, having thus defeated the constable's battle, followed the chase of their enemies so broken. The vanguard led by the Duke of Guise stood firm in a place of advantage. The Prince of Conde with some disadvantage charged the same: whereat he was defeated; and the prince taken by Monsieur d'Ampville. Four cornets' of freighters accompanying the said prince's battle were so estranged with two or three shots of great artillery, that they would never come to the fight.

The footmen on the Duke of Guise's side did their devoir very well, but especially the Swiss's. The footmen of the Prince of Conde's side, as well Frenchmen as Almains, (and the same both in the vanguard and the battle) did behave themselves very ill; and such as had the leading of them behaved themselves much worse. The constable and the Duke of Guise having XXII pieces of artillery, that is to say, XIII in the vanguard, and VIII in the battle, did shoot four volleys against their enemies. But the prince's artillery was so ill conducted, having four field pieces, two cannons and a culverin that they never shot a shot, nor stood him instead. The Duke d'Aumale was overthrown, and in great danger of taking; but very well rescued by the succors of his brother the Duke of Guise, who came in season for that purpose.

That day the said duke stood himself, his friends, and his case in great stead: for surely he behaved himself like a great and valiant captain: and such victory as remained to him and his party that day was to be ascribed to him, in manner, only. Such victory, and it please your majesty, I may say; because, if all be well considered, it is very doubtful; and the damage is rather greater to them which challenge the victory, than to the other side which is said to be defeated. Indeed, as having regard to the ceremonies of the war, the Duke of Guise may challenge to himself that day's victory: for his footmen remained lords of the field, and kept their place: he won four pieces of the prince's artillery, and kept them: he encamped over the dead bodies: albeit, the admiral with his force went not far from there that night. The said duke caused the view to be made of the dead bodies, and his army had the spoil of them; and caused divers of them to be buried. His army won and bares away the ensigns of the prince's footmen; which were offered up with procession and great solemnity upon Christmas day at Dreux. For these respects your Majesty may perceive, as I said, the Duke of Guise was victor.

But when it is remembered, that as well the constable, being chief of the one army, is taken, as the prince, being chief of the other; the Marshal St Andre slain, who is said to have had the principal leading of the vanguard, and the Duke of Guise the leading of the horsemen; the Duke of Nevers so hurt, as he is never like to escape (although the same happened by casualty, and not by fight;) Messieurs de la Brosse and Givry, knights of the order, slain; Monsieur de Montbron, the constable's son, and many other gentlemen of good behavior slain and sore hurt; and six or seven score gentlemen of credit and quality being prisoners; in counterpace whereof only, of men of quality to speak of, Monsieur d'Arpation was slain on the prince's side, Monsieur de Muy and Monsieur de la Curee taken prisoners; the prince not having lost above seven score of his horsemen, as the admiral has sent me word since the battle; the adversaries having lost, as it is said, at the least three hundred gentlemen: the circumstances, as I said before, being well weighed and considered; I think, and it please your majesty, the victory may be called doubtful, and not greatly advantageous to the Prince of Conde's adversaries; but, I am sure, I may boldly say, nothing to the advantage of the French King and his country.

The Almain footmen on the prince's side did never strike a stroke; and therefore they were wholly defeated, in running away. Nevertheless the Duke of Guise took to mercy 2,000 of them: whereof he had sent without weapon, having white robes in their hands, 1,500 into Almain; which have made other never to bear arms against this king, nor him the said duke. The other five hundred, being very well armed, as I hear, have taken other to serve the king against your majesty, and so are sent with Bassanpiero, the Rhingrave lieutenant, (who has also led with him the ten ensigns of Almains which were under his leading to the count Rhingrave, his chief) into Normandy, there to be employed against your majesty's force: whether also is sent, to be lieutenant for the king, Monsieur de Vielleville, now Marshal of France, having the state of the Marshal St Andre.

Forbes. *A Full View of the Public Transactions in the Reign of Q. Elizabeth.* V. 2, pg. 251-253.

Nicholas is frequently depicted in recent accounts as having been captured and sometimes tortured during the conflict, but he describes the experience somewhat differently. When Nicholas witnessed the apprehension of the Prince of Conde, he and three of his servants fled to Nogent le Roy, a town approximately two leagues from the battlefield, to seek refuge at the castle of the Duchess of Bouillon.

Fig. 18. Bouchot, Henri. *Les Portraits aux Crayons. Front piece.*

The duchess promptly informed the duke about Nicholas, and soldiers were dispatched to observe him. Nicholas spent five days with the widow duchess at the castle, where he dined and was treated well, according to a rare account of the time period. There is a single, very early rumor that the two had an affair, but I was unable to find evidence to substantiate this claim. I will defer to the creative conceptions of fiction writers on this matter.

On Christmas Eve, Nicholas was transferred to the duke's camp, where they dined, and the duke questioned him at length about his role in the battle to ascertain whether or not Nicholas was armed and mounted on horse. Nicholas assured the Duke of Guise that he was not armed, nor mounted on a horse. The duke expressed his opinion regarding Queen Elizabeth's role in the affair, stating, "Her proceedings against us may be a means to move others to do unto her as she does unto us." As a minister to Queen Elizabeth in France, the duke informed Nicholas that he was suspected and accused of causing all of their problems. Nicholas was escorted to St. Germains, where he was informed that he, "Should be constituted a prisoner in the castle," where he stayed for four days before being transferred to St. Denis on 3 January 1563.

The Queen Mother instructed M. De Sevre once more to work exclusively with Smith. According to an uncorroborated source, this was done to discredit Nicholas's remarks. Nicholas was informed that a member of the privy council had stated that he "He should be taken and executed;" this was an entirely different person than Marshal Brisac.

So, what occurred? I was only able to locate information from a memoir written by Michael de Castelnau, who served in numerous military capacities during the time period. I will defer to his assessment.

> Upon this, their majesties made me a great many fine promises, and ordered me immediately (before my men were disbanded) towards Rouen, to meet the two English ambassadors who were upon their way to court; the king being not resolved to receive or see them. Mr. Smith the ordinary resident was one of them, and Throgmorton his predecessor the other; both which were ordered by the queen, their mistress to wait upon their majesties at Haure; but happened to come too late, though Throgmorton let the other go before to try what reception or success they were likely to meet with. But because de Foix the French resident was narrowly watched and treated like a prisoner in England, the king was therefore advised to use Smith in the same manner, and not to receive Throgmorton upon any account, but have him confined as the chief author of the rupture contrary to the treaty which was concluded with his mistress at Cambray; and since he had presumed to come into France without his majesty's leave or passport, that he could not do less than make a prisoner of him. All which, the king commanded me to acquaint him with and moreover, that he was so hated by the army (both Protestants as well as Catholics) and all the people of France, that there was no way of preserving his person from danger, but by putting him in a place of safety."

> Castelnau, Michael. *Memoirs of the Reigns of Francis II and Charles IX*, pg. 262-263.

Castelnau is quoted in a letter as saying that when he disclosed this information to Nicholas, Nicholas, "he being a passionate, fiery person, began to justify himself and bluster a good deal about his mistress's power." This resulted in the summoning of a garrison to accompany Nicholas to the castle of St. Germains. Castelnau then met with Smith, knowing that he would be treated similarly to Nicholas for the same reasons, and Smith was sent to the castle of Melun for a brief time before returning to his lodgings in Paris. Smith told Castelnau that if Nicholas had not opposed Queen Elizabeth's desires, the two realms would have remained allies. Castelnau observed that Nicholas and Smith were not close companions based on the way they spoke to one another.

After satisfying the duke's concerns, Nicholas was released to begin the New Year, not as a prisoner but as a man under close observation. While at St. Denis on 3 January 1563, he sent his account of the battle to Queen Elizabeth at the earliest opportunity. Three days later, he moved to Chartres to report that the duke and admiral's legions had crossed the Loyre River (the original line of demarcation between the two forces at Derux) and that the prince was still being held captive but would be transferred to Chartres under guard. In addition, Nicholas received reports that new companies of men had arrived and that surrounding communities had taken on new leadership as fighting continued.

Nicholas returned to Portsmouth on 18 January to receive approximately fourteen thousand Pounds, after which he returned to France to distribute the funds, primarily as remuneration for the admiral's forces. Nicholas was extremely cautious when transporting such a large sum of money, which he referred to as 'treasure.' In order to avoid attracting attention, he would leave on one ship while the money followed on another. On his voyage from Portsmouth to Newhaven, the ship he was on was attacked by three small French vessels. They readily repelled the assault and captured one of the attackers. He arrived at Boulogne on 26 January, to return to Dover without incident. Nicholas departed Newhaven with a ship full of artillery and ammunition, as requested by the Earl of Warwick for the admiral to capture the Caen castle. Nicholas explained that the castle was more effectively protected by nature than by design.

Nicholas shared a vivid account of the death of the Duke of Guise on 24 February.

> The Duke of Guise died of his hurt the XXIV of February, which he received the XVIII, of the same, being given him after a strange manner: for a gentleman, named Merey, of no great appearance, nor show of any great manliness, belonging to Monsieur de Subize, governor at Lyons for the Prince of Conde, did shoot a pistol at the said Duke, who was accompanied with three or four gentlemen, returning from Portreau of Orleans to a place named St. Mesme where he lodged. The said de Merey, which did this act, was alone, appareled like a reightre,

mounted on a genet: who after he had discharged his pistol, and struck the duke in the shoulder, (which at the first appeared to be no mortal wound) retired himself, and traveled all that night. In which time he might have had time enough to have retired himself into some place of surety: but God, who govern all men's doings to one end or other, suffered the man to be so confused, as he could not retire himself far off from the place where he was apprehended, which was within two miles of the Duke of Guise's camp. And since his apprehension and examination, as I understand, he confessed very assuredly, that it was he that shot the pistol at monsieur de Guise, with resolute intent to kill him; moved and solicit thereto only, as he said, by his own zeal to revenge the tyranny which the Duke of Guise had committed against the Christians, and was like to exercise, if he might have any long life: and this was, said he, the end that God provided for all insolent and tyrannical princes.

Forbes. *A Full View of the Public Transactions in the Reign of Q. Elizabeth.* V. 2, pg. 343.

At some point between the middle and end of March, Nicholas returned to England, which must have been a welcome respite from the pressures in France. Nicholas must have relished his sabbatical because nothing is heard from, to, or about him until the end of July, when the peace treaty between France and England has been drafted. The king and the queen mother agreed to the terms, and Queen Elizabeth deemed them sincere enough to dispatch Nicholas back to France. On 25 July, Nicholas arrived in Rouen and stayed with the governor.

Nicholas hoped that hostility toward him had subsided, but when he returned to France, he immediately discovered that it still existed; he was detained and again held captive, unable to leave. He was informed that he was not a prisoner but rather under security for his safety. It would appear that Queen Elizabeth and the Queen Mother misunderstood who should preside over the proposed treaty, and Nicholas found himself at the center of a controversy. The Queen Mother expressed her apprehension that 'He would again stir some sedition in the realm.' His confinement was partially a result of the English's confinement of the French ambassador. Although the Queen Mother tried to reassure Queen Elizabeth that Nicholas was not a prisoner, it is fair to say that he was both.

In addition, Smith and Nicholas' animosity only exacerbated the situation. Nicholas wrote in a letter to Secretary Cecil: 'Now sir (Secretary

Cecil) you will see that this man's malice to me will neither suffer him to do his duty to the queen nor to behave to me, his colleague, as an honest man,'

Nicholas received the improved treatment, and he informed Smith in late August that he resided in the castle of St. Germain. Eventually, tensions between Smith and Nicholas subsided, albeit marginally. He described the nearly comfortable chambers in which he and his servants resided, as well as the fact that they were permitted to take brief walks in the corridors and garden, but that he was locked in his room each evening at approximately 6:00 p.m. Nicholas was unaware at the time that Smith was also being confined as a prisoner in the castle of Melum and receiving the same treatment. Nonetheless, Smith was released around 13 October, and on the same day, Nicholas told Cecil that he regretted accepting the assignment in France.

Negotiations continued for Nicholas's release and to employ the commission he was granted in the ratification of the Cambresis Treaty, but not all parties involved permitted it. Regardless of Nicholas's feelings toward Smith, it appeared that Smith was his foremost advocate for his liberation.

On 26 October, Cecil issued an ultimatum to the French, demanding that Nicholas be released to use his commission and return to England, while another ambassador with a similar commission be sent in his place. Queen Elizabeth dispatched a commission to Nicholas on the same day, indifferent to the French response. In addition, if the French declined to approve the commission, the treaty would not be ratified. Obviously, Elizabeth desired Nicholas's presence.

As a result of a speculation that he would attempt to escape, Nicholas began the month of November complaining about his increased confinement with additional guards who monitored and rigorously controlled his activities. Nicholas assured everyone that he had no plans to do so, but his circumstances did not improve. On 5 November, King Charles IX informed Smith that he would release Nicholas if he promised not to leave France without his permission, and a few days later, Nicholas confirmed this in writing. However, this did not improve his chances of freedom.

Nicholas was escorted by twenty members of the king's guard from St. Germain to Lignerolles on 7 November and from there to Meaux on 8 November to meet with Smith and other French court members who could not concur on Nicholas's release. Nicholas became ill and requested to see a doctor in Paris for a variety of potential causes. Nicholas was sent back to the château de Saint-Germain after the Queen Mother denied his request. But on 22 December, the Queen Mother sent her physician to see Nicholas, and although no life-threatening illness was discovered, Nicholas urged for accommodation in Paris, but he resolved to spend Christmas at the castle of St. Germain.

On 14 January 1564, the Queen Mother met Nicholas for approximately two hours in the garden of Bonnes Hommes in Paris. She told him that all issues would be resolved if the four individuals held in England were released. Nicholas was incapable of concluding such an agreement without consulting Queen Elizabeth, so he was sent back to St. Germain the next day.

Smith's displeasure at not being informed of Nicholas's encounter with the Queen Mother exacerbated the animosity between the two ambassadors. Smith sent a letter to Cecil on 24 January.

> His of the 11th shows him to be a loving and faithful friend to stick unto him against all his despisers and backbiters. He cannot learn what was the cause why Sir Nicholas should thus fall out with him. Sir Nicholas had the same allowance as he has. The writer has four or six men at the most, and never a horse. He (Nicholas) has sixteen of seventeen horses, a wagon, a cart, and twenty-four or twenty-five men. Has not had more than one lean coney at his table, which cost him fifteen sous (twenty-two pence), and a woodcock or partridge as much. The carcass of a small sheep is a mark, or 15s. The hire of his house costs him an angel a day at the least, for he pays his men a crown in gold, and furnishes them a mess of meat, bread, and wine; besides that, the host himself sits at his table.

> *Calendar of State Papers, Foreign Series, Elizabeth.* V.7. Letter 99, pg. 32-33.

CHAPTER 4: AMBASSADOR

Nicholas, ever persistent, was not deterred by the results of his first encounter with the Queen Mother. On 17 February 1564, he drafted three proposals and submitted them to the Queen Mother. The final 'Articles of Peace' were published on 16 March.

> 1. The hostages to be released from their present strict confinement, and within the space of three months from this treaty to be liberated altogether.
>
> 2. Before the departure of the said hostages from England, the king of France shall pay [blank],000 crowns of the sum to the queen, and shall provide sufficient security for the payment of a further sum of [blank],000 crowns within a year. The queen to bind herself to restore the said money in case the hostages are not set at liberty.
>
> 3. As soon at the treaty is concluded Throckmorton shall be allowed to quit France.
>
> *Calendar of State Papers, Foreign*, V7. Letter 253, pg. 82.

Despite the fact that the amount to be paid was left blank in the original document, they consented to pay 400,000 crowns. Nicholas's initial three proposals differ slightly from those of 16 March, but the Queen Mother rejected them on 5 April, and negotiations proceeded for another six days. Nicholas stayed in Troyes, where he complained that each night he was returned to the Black Friars, 'Where all the windows were purposely barred and grilled with iron, and no man suffered to have access.' On 12 April, Charles IX of France ratified the Treaty of Troyes, which included the exchange of money and Nicholas's release. On 24 June, the king consented to abide by the articles.

The next day, Smith approached Nicholas to discuss their approach to the treaty negotiations. Smith inquired as to whether he would approach the king prior to his departure, and he responded that he would not. Smith suggested that either Nicholas or Ambassador Somers should, prompting Nicholas to respond that Somers lacked the authority to do so. Smith's response that Somers had sufficient cause infuriated Nicholas, who then initiated a dispute with Smith over one of his accounts. He informed Smith that he had informed the Queen Mother, but Smith denied it. Nicholas referred to him as a deceiver and 'a horseon traitor,' to which Smith responded by affirming his loyalty to the queen. Nicholas drew his dagger and 'poured out such terms as his malicious stomach and furious rage had in store.' Nicholas referred to Smith as a 'errant knave, a beggarly knave, and a traitor,' prompting Smith to draw his dagger when Somers intervened. Nicholas took several strides towards Smith while shouting at him, while another gentleman raced into the room to assist.

Later, Smith revealed to Cecil in a letter that he contemplated thrusting his dagger at Nicholas, but retreated to allow tempers to cool. After several fraught minutes, the two men re-sheathed their daggers and parted ways. Smith informed Cecil of the incident, but Nicholas never did.

On 23 April 1564, peace was restored in France, and the calm Parisian evenings glowed with festive fires, dancing, and music. Nicholas was given a gold chain estimated to be worth more than 1,400 crowns and weighing 164 ounces. Queen Elizabeth received the treaty on 2 May, signed and sealed it, and sent it to France immediately. Six days later, half of the payment was sent, and Nicholas made arrangements to be in Boulogne on 16 or 17 May, to receive the treasure. Two French warships escorted the treasure to Calais, where it arrived without incident.

Nicholas fled France as soon as a ship became available and arrived in England at the end of April or the beginning of May, depending on channel conditions. Almost an entire year passes before he reappears, and the extant correspondence from those with whom he typically interacted expresses their concern over his whereabouts. He undoubtedly spent time with his anxious wife and children.

Nicholas was dispatched on another diplomatic mission, this time to the north, after he had rested and, presumably, recovered from his mission in France. On 11 May 1565, he arrived in Berwick, England, on a mission to dissuade Mary, Queen of Scots, from marrying Lord Darnley. The following day, he intended to depart for Edinburgh. Lord Darnley was knighted on 15 May, and subsequently elevated to the rank of baron and earl of Ross. Immediately following these ceremonies, Lord Darnley created fourteen knights at Stirling Castle in front of the queen. The next day, Darnley became the Duke of Albany.

On 15 May, Nicholas arrived at Stirling Castle to discover the gates closed and secured. He was instructed to stay at his lodging in the city. The next day, Nicholas was escorted (not as a prisoner) to a meeting with Queen Mary, during which he conveyed Queen Elizabeth's disapproval of her marriage to Darnley. Queen Mary pointed out the numerous marriage proposals made to Queen Elizabeth by European kings and stated that she would marry whomever she chose. Nicholas later informed Queen Elizabeth that Queen Mary was so adamant about the marriage that violence would be required to prevent it.

The following letter from the abundance of Nicholas's surviving correspondence reviewed for this biography is included for several reasons. Primarily, it demonstrates Nicholas's proficiency as an ambassador, which he honed over the course of many years, displaying sufficient discretion and diplomacy to gain Mary Queen of Scots's respect and enable him to offer her advice in a manner that others would not dare. Histories indicate that Mary followed his advice. In addition, and of equal importance, the letter was not included in the monumental Calendar of State Papers series or other English or Scottish public archival record collections. It remained obscure in Sir James Melvil's manuscript collection, which was published in 1683 by his descendant George Scott. Mr. Melvil spent the majority of his life in Edinburgh during the English Tudor period and chronicled the events of that time. This collection was intriguing to evaluate. Robert Trail, minister of the Gray-Fryars church and prisoner in Edinburgh, discovered the collection of manuscripts and gave them to Mr. Scott, grandson of Mr. Melvil. The contents of those manuscripts have made a substantial contribution to this Sir Nicholas Throckmorton biography.

> Your majesty hath in England many friends of all degrees, who favor your title, but for diver's respects. Some for very conscience sake, being persuaded, that in law your right is best; some for the good opinion they have conceived, by honorable report they have heard of your virtues and liberality, the consideration whereof engages them to esteem your majesty most worthy to govern; some for factions, who favor your religion; some for the ill will they bear to your competitor, seeing their own danger if Lady Katherine should come in that place.

Of these, some are Papists, some Protestants, and yet however they differ among themselves, in religion or other particulars, they are both of one mind for the advancement of your title. Your majesty hath also diverse enemies for various respects, not unlike to the other, whose study hath always been, and will be, unless they be made friends, to hinder anything that may tend to your advantage. In one point all concur, both friends and enemies, yea the whole people, that they are most desirous to have the succession of the crown declared and assured, that they may be at a certainly only the queen herself is of a contrary opinion, and would be glad the matter should always be in suspense. Your un-friends have done what they could, to take the advantage of the time, to your prejudice; and for that end, pressed the holding of the parliament, which was before continued till October last. Knowing assuredly, that if the parliament held, the succession of the crown would be called in question. And they thought the time served well for their purpose, when there was division and trouble in your own realm, and no good understanding between you and the queen of England. And her subjects your friends, for eschewing that inconvenience and winning of time to give your majesty place to work, and remove all impediments, so far as wisdom may have found the means to drive it oft till the next spring. Now their advice is, that in the meantime your majesty endeavor by wisdom to assure yourself of the whole votes, or at least of the best and most considerable of the parliament, whenever the matter shall be brought in question. Which may be done, by retaining the bearers of those you have gained already, recovering of those who are brambled, winning of the neutrals, and so many of your adversaries as may be gained for it is not to be supposed that all can be won who are already, do far addicted to the contrary faction, but when the cause of their aversion is removed the effect will cease.

Generally your majesty will do well to forebear any act that will offend the whole people, and use such means as will render you most acceptable to them. Strangers are universally suspected to the whole people, against which your majesty has in your marriage wisely provided by abstaining to match with a foreign prince. So do they advise your majesty to abstain from any league of confederacy with any foreign prince that may offend England, till you have first essayed what you can purchase by the benevolence of the born subjects thereof. Not that they would desire your majesty to forfeit your friendship with France and Spain, but rather that you should wisely entertain them both to remain at you devotion, in case afterward you have need of their favor. Nevertheless it is their wish that the same may rather remain in general terms as heretofore, then that you proceed to any special act which may offend England, which you cannot with honor bring back again when you would. As many of our adversaries as are addicted to the contrary faction for hatred of your religion, may be gained when they see your majesty continue in the religion, may be gained when they see your majesty continue in the temperance and moderation you have hitherto wised, within your own realm in matters of religion, without innovation or alternation. As many as by misreports have been carried to the contrary faction, may by true report be brought back again, when they shall hear of your clemency used towards your own subjects, which virtue in princes, of all others, most allures the hearts of people to favor, even their common enemies. As many as can deal warily and discreetly with your friends of both the religions and are only addicted for conscience sake to my Lady Katherine, being persuaded of the preference of your title in law, may be gained to your majesty by contrary persuasions, and by adducing of such reasons and arguments, as may be alleged for proof of your good cause, whereof there are abundance to be had.

Some your majesty will find in England, who will hazard as far as they dare, to serve your turn in this behalf. But because it is so dangerous to men to deal in, and may endanger lives and lands, if they be seen earnest meddlers, traveling in the point so as would be necessary, it will require such instruments of your own when time comes, who may boldly speak without danger, and with whom the subjects of England dare freely communicate their minds, and enter into conference. If any be afraid of your majesty, thinking that you have an ill opinion of them, the assurance by a trusty minister of your good will, whom they may credit, will quickly put them out of doubt and make them favorable enough. They who are constantly yours, are easily retained at your devotion: those who heretofore have born any favor, and by the late occurrences are any way brangled, will be brought home again, when they shall see your majesty, now when it is fallen in your hands to use rigor of mercy as you please, rather incline to the most plausible part, in showing you magnanimity, when you have brought your subjects to submission and gentleness, as the good pastor to reduce his sheep that were gone astray home again to the fold. Those who are yet neutrals, by the same means, and true information of your interest by law, may all be won to your side. This done, when the matter comes in question, your friends will earnestly press your interest at this parliament, and you will without controversy bear it away.

This device, in so far as concerns your reconciliation with your subjects, is not a fetch for their favor, by is though expedient for your service by many who have no favor for them, and are different from them in religion. For it will bring the Queen of England greatly to favor you, when she shall see such a union in your own kingdom, of the head and whole members together. She will not know how to disturb your majesty's estate, especially when the reconciliation takes effect in the hearts of the subjects in England. Who will think themselves in a happy condition, if they should come under the government of so benign a princess who can so readily forgive great offenses? For albeit it must be acknowledged that my Lord of Moray, has by his inconsiderate carriage, given your majesty great ground of offense, yet it is hard to persuade the Protestants that your quarrel against them has any other foundation, than that he dodders from you in religion. Upon this ground, they find themselves engaged to espouse his quarrel. If then they perceived your majesty fractiously inclined to take him again unto favor, and forgive what is by past, the Protestants in England would doubtless declare themselves more affectionate to your interest, when they shall see more of their own religion so clemently handled. And that your majesty may have experience, that it is your advancement your friends would by this means procure, and not the advantage of those with whom your majesty is offended, a middle way may be followed, as is frequently used in such like cases, where not only the multitude is spared, but the chief authors are preserved. It may please your majesty to cause a letter to be penned in good terms and form, and publish the same by proclamation, declaring the just cause of your anger against all of them; and that yet for declaring your own nature about their deserving, you are content to remit the whole, except such principles as you please to reserve and except by name from the general pardon. And that with whom you will not take such severe order as you might in law, till you have further trial and experience of the penitence. The persons so to be nominated and excepted shall depart out of England, to what country pleases your majesty, there to remain during your pleasure. In this mean time, if your majesty find that this design usage of yours, shall produce such fruit as is here spoken, your majesty may further extend your favor, as you find convenient and profitable for yourself. For your majesty has still the crimes lying about their heads. In the meantime all who favor them in England, will pleased in their cause with your majesty.

They will in no ways, if they can eschew it, be again in the Queen of England's debt, neither by obtaining of any favor at your hand by her intervention, not yet for support in the time of their banishment. But rather it may please your majesty, that their charge be allowed them of their own lands. By following this advice, which in no ways can be prejudicial to your majesty, but will much conduce for your interest, you may recover the greatest part of the bishops of England, many of the greatest nobility and gentlemen, who are yet neutral.

Scott, George. *The Memoires of Sir James Melvil of Hal-Hill.* 1683 edition, pg. 60-63.

Nicholas informed Secretary Cecil of Thomas Randolph's arrival in Edinburgh and informed Queen Elizabeth of his 'qualities' on 21 May. 'I find by 'the man' that fair promises heretofore have drawn him to spend largely and execute his charge carefully.' This remark made by Nicholas did not pertain to monetary expenditures, but rather to conversational language. This was the final piece of correspondence from Nicholas at the time, and based on a previous comment he made to Cecil, he felt he could do nothing else in Scotland, so he returned to London, possibly to resolve personal matters, in late May or early June.

Randolph wrote to Leicester on 3 June about David Rizzo, who rapidly rose through the ranks at the court of Mary, Queen of Scots, was appointed chief secretary, and served as 'sole governor to Lord Darnley.' In addition, Randolph mentions the court's divided opinions of Darnley.

The bruits (rumors) here are wonderful, men's talk very strange, the hatred towards him and his house marvelous great, his pride intolerable, his words not to be born, but were no man dare speak against. God must send him a short end, or themselves a miserable life under such a government as this is like to be.

Calendar of State Papers Relating to Scotland. V. 2. 1563-1569. Letter 191, pg. 171.

On 3 June, the Earl of Leicester participated in a conference of the English Privy Council to discuss the advantages and disadvantages of Mary's marriage to Darnley, with the disadvantages outweighing the advantages. Mary sent correspondence and couriers to Elizabeth in an attempt to persuade her to change her mind about the marriage, but Elizabeth remained steadfast in her position, and Nicholas was caught in the middle.

Elizabeth maintained a defensive stance at the boundary between England and Scotland and in Berwick. A manifest from 8 June summarizes her forces there.

Garrison (soldiers, officers, etc.) 1,202
Workmen, artificers, and laborers. 845
Freemen and their servants. 228
Stallengers and their servants. 203
Women servants and widows. 275
Children under 14. 251
Men's wives of all sorts. 507
Total. 3, 511

Calendar of State Papers, Foreign. V.7. Letter 1231, pg. 390.

Queen Elizabeth dispatched directives for behavior designated 'Ancient Statutes of the Town and Castle of Berwick,' with the complete text included in Appendix 1.

Smith, who is currently residing in France, reported on 3 July that the French ambassador, who had just returned from Scotland, informed him that Nicholas had confided in him that he would support a marriage between Mary, Queen of Scots, and the Duke of Guise. In addition, the ambassador indicated that the Scottish nobility provided Nicholas with access to the information while Nicholas was in Scotland.

The following letter demonstrates that 'misinformation' is not a recent phenomenon. This is the only account from that time period that I reviewed in any publications.

Randolph to the Queen.

Upon Monday last, the 9th, (July) this Queen was married secretly in her palace to Lord Darnley; not above seven persons were present; and went that day to bed to Lord Seton's house. This he knows by one of the priests that was present at the Mass. If this be true the Queen sees how her promise is kept, and may measure the rest of her doings. Believes unfeignedly that the Queen shall find more fair words than good meaning. Edinburgh. 16 July. 1565.

Calendar of State Papers, Foreign. V. 7. Letter 1297, pg. 407.

James Hamilton penned a letter to Nicholas on 18 July from Stirling Castle, requesting his advice and counsel, because Nicholas regarded him with great friendliness and anticipated the messenger would provide him with guidance.

Francis Bedford (Governor of Berwick) informed Secretary Cecil on 23 July that Mary, Queen of Scots, possessed an estimated 6,000 to 7,000 armed men, with more arriving daily at the frontier. The English forces in Berwick not only complained about a lack of funds, but also inadequate munitions, and other supplies. As cattle were moved further away from the borders and cornfields preventing soldiers from stealing food, hunger became a major concern. Bedford feared he would be unprepared in the event of a conflict.

Six days later, Randolph reported that Lord Darnley was proclaimed king around 9 p.m., 'by common consent of all the lords present in this town.' (Edinburgh).

John Thomworth arrived in Edinburgh not as a replacement ambassador but as a supporter of Randolph. Just before 10 August, John Thomworth arrived in Edinburgh. Eleven days later, he requested to be recalled because tensions were high in Edinburgh and along the borders. Elizabeth informed him on 28 August that she would add 600 foot soldiers and 100 cavalry to Berwick's forces. By the beginning of September, the forces in Berwick had resorted to plundering food and other supplies from homes, stables, and fields.

Thomworth left Edinburgh on 9 September following a life-threatening encounter with armed individuals over an unidentified matter. Nicholas may have remained for a brief period longer, but he escaped as tensions grew too high to guarantee his safety. By 13 October, he had fled Edinburgh and passed the 600 additional Englishmen Elizabeth had sent to the north. By mid-October, Mary, Queen of Scots had reduced her army to between 300 and 400 soldiers in an effort to avoid conflict with England.

Elizabeth notified Mary on 24 October of her desire to begin drafting articles that would eliminate all grievances between the two countries, including Mary's marriage to Lord Darnley. In addition, Elizabeth informed Mary that she would shortly dispatch an ambassador and requested that he be granted safe passage, unlike Nicholas. Four days later, Elizabeth sent Thomas Randolph in Edinburgh instructions to discuss the Edinburgh Treaty.

At the end of October, rumors were sent from England claiming that Mary was pregnant. On 9 November, the borders were once again tranquil and well-supplied, and English forces have been reduced to 600 foot soldiers and 100 cavalry. Randolph reported on 19 November that Mary was not pregnant but had 'fallen sick of her old disease that commonly takes her at this time of year in her side.' On 4 December, however, the rumors of Mary's pregnancy resumed with greater fervor.

Through Christmas, there were no reports of any activity between the two countries.

On 20 February 1566, Mary complained to Elizabeth that Randolph had provided a large sum of money to her dissidents, and Elizabeth ordered him to leave Scotland or face severe punishment; he complied and left for Berwick. Nicholas was also in Berwick at the time, and he received correspondence from a French ambassador containing less urgent information.

David Rizzio was assassinated while having supper with Mary and a small group in a closet (small dining room) adjacent to her bedroom in the tower of Holyrood House Palace on 9 March 1566. The assassination was and continues to be one of the most dramatic events in Scottish history.

Numerous well-written accounts of the incident in Scottish history have been published, but I have encountered wildly divergent early accounts of the event. Basically, Darnley entered the room and sits down next to Mary, ostensibly to calm or distract her. A group of conspirators broke into the chamber, and one of the conspirators pointed a pistol at Mary, while another drew a dagger from Darnley's waistband and stabbed Rizzio. They then dragged the wailing Rizzio from the closet into the bedroom and repeatedly stabbed him. Darnley reportedly ordered Rizzio's corpse to be thrown down the main staircase, stripped off his clothing, and buried the body as soon as possible. Documents from the time period indicate that Darnley was aware of the plot, but it did not manifest as intended and requires further explanation beyond the scope of this work. If the reader wishes to learn more about the assassination, there are a number of recently published, high-quality books available.

Mary and Darnley escaped through a subterranean conduit to Dunbar Castle prior to the brutal murder.

Following is an account that Sir James Melvil of Hal-Hill recorded from that period.

> The king was yet very young, and not well acquainted with the nature of this nation. It was supposed also, that the Earl of Lennox knew of the said design. For he had his chamber within the palace, and so had the Earl of Athol, Bothwell, and Huntley, who escaped, by leaping over a window toward the little garden where the Lyons where lodged. This vile act was done upon a Saturday at six o-clock at night, when the queen was at supper in her closet. A number of armed men entered within the court, before the closing of the gates, and took the keys from the porter. One part of them, went up through the king's chamber, conducted by the Lord Ruthuen and George Douglas; the rest remained without, with drawn swords in their hands, crying 'A Douglas, A Douglas'. The king was before gone up to the queen, and

was leaning upon her chair, when the Lord Ruthuen entered with his helmet upon his head, and George Douglas, and divers others with them, so rudely and irreverently, that the table, candles, meat and dishes were overthrown. Rixio (Rizzio) took the queen about the waist, crying for mercy, but George Douglas plucked out the king's dagger and stroke Rixio first with it, leaving it sticking in him. He making great shrieks and cry's, was rudely snatched from the queen, who could not prevail either with threats or entreaties to save him. But he was forcibly drawn forth of the closet and slain in the outer hall, and her majesty was kept as a captive.

Scott, George. *The Memoires of Sir James Melvil of Hal-Hill*, pg. 66-67.

Despite widespread concern that the trauma she endured following the murder may have caused her to miscarry, Mary gave birth to James, a healthy son of Henry Stewart, Lord Darnley, on 19 June 1566 in Edinburgh Castle, .

Early in June, it was reported that Mary and her husband continued to engage in verbal arguments and disagreements, which only served to reaffirm the opinions of many regarding Darnley.

Mary expressed a desire for the Earl of Leicester to attend the baptism and added that if he were unable to do so, the Earl of Bedford and Nicholas would be most welcome in his place.

Nicholas, who was still in England on 1 September, contemplated the purchase of Ashridge property, which included a home. On 6 September 1566, five days later, while in London, he received an honorary degree from Oxford in recognition of his numerous accomplishments.

Throckmorton, Sir Nicholas; created MA 6 September 1566, a wise and stout man lately leiger ambassador in France, 'as he had been in Scotland', chief butler of England and chamberlain of the exchequer (fourth son of Sir George, of Coughton, county Warwick); knighted by Edward VI; MP Malden 1545-7, Devizes, 1547-52, Northants March, 1553, Old Sarum Oct-Dec 1553, Lyme Regis 1559, and Tavistock 1563-7; died in London 12 February 1570-1; father of Arthur 1571.

Joseph Foster. *Alumni Oronienses: The Members of the University of Oxford*, 1500-1714 V.4.

According to A. Clark's *Register of the University of Oxford*, Vol. II, 1571-1622, the phrase 'created MA' was used to indicate that the degree was awarded to the individual in question without the completion of a university course or examinations (p. 234). Clark continues by stating it 'was the usual accompaniment of a royal visit.' Throckmorton's degree appears to have been awarded during Queen Elizabeth's visit, when 'on 6 September 1566, convocation ordered that as many earls, lords, and distinguished persons as the chancellor and the committee of convocation should determine who were to be created MA if they accepted the offer.'

Nicholas must have been traveling in early November, as Francis Earl of Bedford informed the caretaker of his residence in Melchbourn that he would provide any comfort Nicholas might require if he were to visit. Melchbourn was a small village in Bedford Borough, Bedfordshire, England.

Nicholas made up for lost time with his family and friends in London when he was not between two countries that were close to war or where attempts were made to assassinate, murder, or imprison him.

The tensions between Mary and Lord Darnley intensified. Mary wrote to her aunt, the Duchess of Guise, lamenting the loss of a jovial disposition in the past. In late autumn, her formerly vivacious demeanor appeared to be replaced by absolute despondency. Several times, she wrote, "I could wish to be dead."

Fortunately, Mary found some pleasure in her otherwise dreary existence by organizing her son's baptism. She had instructed everyone to wear certain colors and had given the closest to her: Moray a green suit, Argyll a red suit, and Bothwell a blue suit.

It is strange that almost as many distinct dates of the ceremony are mentioned at various periods in the written history of more than 450 years as the number of writers who passed on the information. In one early historical account, two distinct dates are provided, while others indicate the event occurred in 1567 or 1568.

> This was solemnized on the 17th December 1566 with great splendor in the chapel of Stirling Castle. On this occasion Queen Elizabeth had been invited to become godmother, but excused herself on the ground that however willing she was to be present, she was unable to come to Scotland, and as she should not well send an English lady so far in winter, so she caused herself to be represented by Mary's favorite half-sister, the Countess of Argyll, and likewise sent the Earl of Bedford as bared of a baptismal font of gold to be used in the baptism of the prince. The ceremony of baptism was performed according to the ritual of the Romish Church by the Archbishop of St. Andrews, Lord John Hamilton, a half-brother of the Duke of Chatelherault, assisted by three other bishops. The sovereigns of France and Savoy were also represented on this festal occasion, and after the religious part of rite was over the queen gave a splendid banquet to the foreigners and the Scottish lords, many of whom, including Bothwell himself, had refused to be present in the chapel during the ceremony so obnoxious to the

reformers. But, Darnley, who was present in the castle, did not make his appearance at all during the festive season.

Schiern, Frederik. *Life of James Hepburn, Earl of Bothwell*, pg. 90-91.

On 10 February 1567, at approximately 2:00 a.m., an explosion devastated the residence of Henry Stewart, Lord Darnley, in Kirk-o'-Field. The detonation was audible in Edinburgh. Lord Darnley was recuperating at Kirk-o-Field while his wife and son James were at Holyrood House, a short distance away. The body of Darnley was discovered in a nearby garden, half-naked, next to his attendant, with a dagger between them. An early historian wrote at the crime site that Darnley's body displayed symptoms of strangulation. The painting received by Secretary Cecil depicted the half-naked corpses of Darnley and his servant in the upper right corner, with a dagger, cloak, and chair nearby. On the left is a destroyed home marked as the murder site. James, Darnley's infant son, is depicted in the upper left corner saying, 'Judge and revenge my cause, O'lord.' The lower section depicts the removal of Darnley's corpse and the funeral of his servant.

In January 1567, the Earl of Leicester suggested Nicholas for the position of governor of the incorporated society that was to administer the possessions and revenues of the Warwickshire preachers.

Mr. Melvil's account is significant, and he adds the following:

> But many suspected that the Earl of Bothwell had some enterprise against him (Darnley) few durst advertise him because he told all again to some of his own servants, who were not all honest. Yet Lord Robert Earl of Orkny told him that if he retired not hastily out that place (Kirk-o-Field), it would cost him his life, which he told again to the queen; and my Lord Robert denied that ever he spoke it. This advertisement moved the Earl of Bothwell, to hast forward his enterprise; he had before laid a train of powder under the house where the king did lodge, and in the night did blow up the said house with the powder; but it was spoken that the king was taken forth, and brought down to a stable, where a napkin was stopped in his mouth, and therewith suffocated.

Scott, George. *The Memoires of Sir James Melvil of Hal-Hill*, pg. 78.

Nicholas was unquestionably implicated in the assassination due to his close relationship with Mary, Queen of Scots, due to the prevalence of the accusations. The murder remains an active source of investigation, as new techniques aim to uncover previously unseen evidence that will help solve the mystery. If new scientific developments permit a discovery that proves

Nicholas's involvement, I hope to include it in a revised edition. The murder of Darnley remains at the top of the list of unresolved crimes in Scotland. Equally captivating are the 'casket inscriptions.' Mary's allegedly penned letters to Bothwell implicate her in the assassination of Lord Darnley alongside Bothwell. Nicholas most likely referred to these letters as evidence in a letter he sent to Elizabeth from Edinburgh.

> Thirdly, they mean to charge her with the murder of her husband, whereof (they say) they have as apparent proof against her as may be, as well by the testimony of her own handwriting, which they have recovered, as also by sufficient witnesses.

Schiern, Frederik. *Life of James Hepburn, Earl of Bothwell*, pg. 108.

As with Darnley's assassination, the letters' veracity has been and continues to be a matter of debate, and they will continue to fascinate historians for centuries to come.

The trial of James Earl Bothwell for the murder of Henry Lord Darnley, the spouse of Mary, Queen of Scots, began on 12 April 1567 at the Senate House in Edinburgh. Even though the Earl of Bothwell was exonerated of all charges, he was aware that the world still considered him culpable.

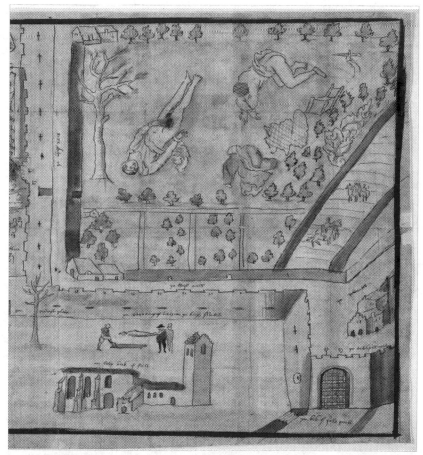

Fig. 19. [2-page span] Lord Darnley's Residence. Public domain usage. British Library Collections-Shelfmark: MPF1/366.

Following is a description of Bothwell's efforts to sway public opinion.

Further set up a paper in the market-place bearing that albeit he had been acquitted by law, yet to make his innocence the more manifest, he was ready to try the same by single combat with any man of honorable birth and reputation who would accuse him of the king's murder.

To which answer was made by another placard, set up immediately after in the same place, that forasmuch as the said Earl of Bothwell had caused a placard to be set up, signed with his own hand, whereby he challenged any man of quality and of a fair reputation who would and dared to say that he was guilty of the death of the king, adding that he who said it, or went about to import that charge, should be forced to eat his words: a gentleman of honor and good renown accepted his offer, and said he would prove by the law of arms that he was the principal author of that horrid murder, of which the judges had rashly acquitted him for fear of death after so much inquiry had been made into it. And whereas the King of France and the Queen of England required by their ambassadors that the said murder might be punished, he also entreats their majesties to insist with the queen, his sovereign lady, that by her consent a time and place may be appointed in their countries to combat the earl, according to the law of arms, in their presence, or in that of their deputies; at which time and place he promises and swears on the word of a gentleman, to be present and do his duty provided their majesties will by proclamation, grant safe conduct to him and his company to pass and re-pass through their dominions without any molestation. He refers it to the judgment of the readers and hearers what just cause he has to desire this of the King of France and the Queen of England, and by this he advertises the rest of the murderers to prepare themselves; for he will give each of them the like challenge and publish their names in writing, that they may be known to everybody.

Emlyn, Sollom. *A Complete Collection of State Trials*-V-6, pg. 81-82.

Mary visited her son James in Stirling, and upon her return to Edinburgh on 24 April 1567, Bothwell 'intercepted' her and took her to Dunbar. Too many recent accounts, including a prominent informational website, indicate that Bothwell assaulted and violated her. Perhaps this helps to sell more books, but it is disconcerting that so many people believe this distorted account of history, given that contemporary accounts depict the event differently. Sir James Melville, who was present at the time, stated, "It was with the quenis (queen's) awen (own) consent." I found no evidence that Mary was violated or assaulted in any of the accounts I examined.

In spite of the rather ostentatious accounts, it was evident that Mary and Bothwell would wed. Before the marriage could take place, Bothwell had to surmount a significant obstacle: he was still married. Lady Bothwell filed for a divorce on the basis of his adultery with one of her servants in the commissioner's court on 27 April, and it was granted the following day. There are differing accounts of her motivation for taking such action, including pressure or threats to her life, but no evidence is known to support these claims.

Bothwell was elevated to Duke of Orkney on 14 May 1567, and the following day, they were married 'in the palace of Holyrood within the old chapel by Adam, Bishop of Orkney, not with Mass, but with preaching, ten hours before noon.'

Mary's decision to marry the primary suspect in the assassination of her spouse so shortly after his death greatly diminished her popularity, and on 17 June she fled to Lochleven, which became her prison.

On 1 July, Nicholas was immediately briefed and sent to Scotland. Nicholas was dispatched to Scotland with a 'very villainous design' according to a number of accounts. However as can be seen in his correspondence, he maintained his integrity, and Queen Elizabeth's instructions would not permit him to act in such a manner.

Instructions by the Queen of England given to Sir Nicholas Throckmorton, sent into Scotland to the Queen (of Scotland), 30 June 1567.

> You shall in the beginning declare to her how much we have been of long time troubled and grieved in our mind to behold such evil accidents as of late from time to time have happened to her, wherein her fame and honor have been in all parts of Christendom much impaired and decayed; and especially upon the death of her husband, being so apparently and horribly murdered so near to herself, yea, and within so few hours after she parted with him in the night, and nothing done by her effectual for the search of the malefactors, and due punishment thereof. Next, her favoring and maintaining the Earl of Bothwell and his associates, being men of notorious evil name, whom the world charge also most of all with this detestable murder. And thirdly, with the maintenance of the same earl being so charged to procure such a strange divorce from his wife, a good lady, as never was heard that a man guilty should for his offenses put away his innocent wife, and that to be colored by form of law; but that which followed, say they, hath added to the same an immortal reproof to her, that is, suddenly, hastily, and rashly to take such a defamed person to her husband. All which things, truly you may say, have pierced our very heart with daily thoughts for many respects, as by sundry our letters to her we have friendly and plainly declared. In all which we have felt

our sorrows mixed also with offense and displeasure to her, in such sort as we thought never more to have dealt with her by way of advice, taking her by her acts a person desperate to recover her honor, and so do we know other princes, her friends and near kinsfolk, to be of the like judgment: Yet, nevertheless, now at the last, this mischief that hath followed in the end, after all these, hath stirred up in us a new alteration and passion of our mind, and hath so increased and doubled our former sorrow and grief of mind. Behold suddenly the raising an intestine trouble, in manner of war, betwixt her and her nobility and subjects, wherein finding her to have light into such hard terms, that she is restrained by her nobility and subjects, as we hear, from her liberty; our stomach so provoked, we have changed our former intention of silence and forbearing to deal in her causes.

First, to an inward commiseration of her, our sister, for this last calamity; and next, to a determination to aid and relieve her by all possible means for the recovering of her to her liberty, and not to suffer her, being by God's ordinance the prince and sovereign, to be in subjection to them that by nature and law are subjected to her. For which very purpose you shall say, we have sent you at this time to understand truly her estate, and the whole manner how the same has happened; and to confer with her what may be thought meet for us, as her sister and next neighbor, to do for her, be it by counsel, force, or otherwise; and therefore you shall require her to impart to you that which indeed she can require of us in honor to be done for her, to bring her to liberty, and her realm to concord and inward peace; and so doing you shall assure her we will do as much for her (the circumstances of her case considered) as she were our very natural sister or only daughter. And at the hearing of her declaration you shall require her to bear with you, if according to our direction you do declare also unto her wherewith her nobility and subjects charge her; and so you shall orderly make full declaration thereof, adding therewith that your meaning is not to increase her calamities, but to the end, upon the truth known, her subjects may be duly reprehended and corrected for things unduly laid to her charge: and in other things wherein her fault and oversight cannot be avoided, or well covered, the dealing therein and order thereof may be with wisdom and policy so used and tempered, as her honor may be stayed from utter ruin, and her state recovered with some better accord to follow betwixt her and her subjects. And after she shall have fully declared to you her answer, or request, or her other defenses, if she shall require our aid by force to recover her liberty, and be revenged, you shall say, that you have commission directly to charge and reprove her subjects with this their restraining of her their sovereign lady, and to procure her liberty; or otherwise to assure them plainly, that she shall not lack our aid to compel them thereto; whereunto if they shall not yield, you may tell her you will speedily advertise us, who, you doubt not, will perform our promise.

In the dealing herein also it shall behoove you to know beforehand the disposition in the nobility, whom you shall assure we neither can nor will endure, for any respect, to have her, being a queen and their sovereign, to be by them, being subjects, imprisoned, or deprived of her state, or put in any peril of her person.

And you shall also do your best in reasoning with the queen, to move her by all good persuasions to use wisdom and not passion in this her adversity, as the time required, whereunto, you shall add, that all the world seen her own defaults and oversights to have brought her; although, on the other side, we confess that her subjects ought not to be allowed to take from her and to themselves any sword or juris-diction to punish or reform her faults, but ought to seek the amend-ment of any of her faults by counsel and humble requests. And finally, not finding that they would desire to remit themselves to Almighty God, in whose hands only princes' hearts remain, you shall add, that to bring the calamity to some speedy and quiet end, you shall move her to remit and pardon such things as by rigor of law she, as their sovereign, may extend against them; and to yield also to such requests which shall be made to her, and shall tend for advancement of justice, and especially for the punishment of the murder of her husband, upon any subject whosoever the same be, being found guilty. And further also, to yield to her nobility and people such other reasonable requests as may seem convenient and necessary for the security of their lives and lands, living hereafter obediently. In which last matter you shall say, if any such thing shall be by them demanded as she cannot nor ought not to like of, nor can be induced to, if she will commit the judgment thereof to us, being a queen as she is, we will frankly deal therein, as far as possibly we can with our honor, most to her satisfaction; and in things unmeet to be granted by her, we will assist her in the plain denial thereof. And to bring this manner of end the better to pass, you may labor to persuade her, that seeing things done and past, as well of her part as on theirs, cannot now be undone, it is altogether vain to contend much hereupon; but wisdom must be used in these, and such extremities as these be, to abolish the memory of both, and yet to have principal regard of her being the prince and head.

In your discourse with her you must remember to her, that we have determined and resolved to rest upon these three heads. The first is, to recover her to her liberty with good accord of her subjects, either by persuasion, or treaty, or by force. Next, to procure a due punishment of the murder of her husband; whereunto also we have by nature good title to be a party pursuant, considering the party murdered was both our subject born and nearest kinsman of the blood royal both of England and Scotland. The third, which also nature moves unto, is to have the royal prince preserved from all such danger as manifestly he seems to be in, if the murderers of his father be justified. And concerning the first of these, which is her liberty, your coming is at this time specially; and therein we have principally charged you to labor and travel to the uttermost. For the second, which is the prosecution of the murderer, you may plainly say, though we cannot affirm any ordinary power in her subjects by force to compel her thereto, yet we would be very sorry to find her unwilling to consent thereto; for then we must needs hold her so condemned, as we would not think her free from such other compulsion as one prince and neighbor may use towards another, for punishment of such horrible and abominable facts. Neither may she think it strange, though therein we do show ourselves a party against the murderers, as a thing more properly pertaining to us for many respects, than to any other prince of Christ   endom. For the last, you may use some good reasons to her to accord that the young prince her son may be brought out of danger there, and kept and nourished in our realm, whereof, beside the good surety of his person, many other good things may ensue to him of no small moment, hereafter to be by her well allowed; and for the more surety of his person, whereof per case some busy heads may make argument, he may be so well provided for by hostages or pledges, as no doubt can be made: Which matter we would have you, according to your wisdom, warily and also earnestly prosecute, wherein we mean truly and well to the child. And of all other things by you to be compassed, we shall most esteem thereof.

You shall also do well to learn of her what the French have therein dealt with her or any other; and because in such times and matters as these are changes of proceedings may daily alter the judgment of proceeding, we remit to your discretion to order, as you shall see cause, this charge, which we commit to you in any other form of proceeding, so as always it may appear that we do not allow of her imprisonment, and yet do allow of the justifying of any her subjects for the murder. And secondly, we do not dislike to have her so delivered, as the security of them be provided which have sincerely herein dealt to punish the murder. And the last, which we also most regard, that the prince might be brought in to our realm, to be in the custody of his person with his grandmother, and that with all security that can be devised. Of which things, if you have regard to direct your negotiation, we shall very well allow you.

Keith, Robert. *History of the Affairs of Church and State in Scotland*, pg. 667-671.

During his trip to Scotland, he left an interesting trail of correspondence detailing the times and locations of his previously undocumented rest stops. On 1 July, he left London and arrived in Ware, England the following day. On 6 July, he arrived in Ferrybridge, England, followed by Newcastle the next day. In 14 days, he traveled approximately 400 miles, or 640 kilometers, arriving in Berwick 9 July, then Fastcastle, Scotland, on 12 July, and Edinburgh on the same day.

Sir Nicholas arrived in Edinburgh on 16 July 1567, according to a contemporary source; a letter he wrote to Elizabeth from Edinburgh on 14 July is a more accurate source.

Nicholas was greeted at Coldinghame by Secretary William Lethington-Laird of Maitland, who escorted him to Fascastle as soon as he entered Scotland. Upon his arrival, he discovered Sir James Melvil, Alexander Hume, and Lethington in conference. Nicholas realized that he was now dealing with cunning, prudent, and intelligent diplomats who assured him that Mary was never to be released. After the brief conference, Nicholas departed for Edinburgh accompanied by four hundred horse soldiers and Alexander Hume to Edinburgh Castle.

Nicholas was denied access to Mary, but he was informed that she was in excellent health and well protected. Mary was permitted to be served by five or six ladies, four or five gentlemen, and two chamberers. Nicholas also discovered, which was not unexpected, that the majority of the common people disapproved of Mary for a variety of reasons, most notably her choice of Bothwell so shortly after her husband's assassination. According to an early account, 'the body was not yet cold,' and the preponderance of those affected were women. Mary made it plain to everyone who inquired that she would not abandon Bothwell. Nicholas discovered the grounds for Mary's imprisonment and promptly dispatched them to England:

> And as far as I can perceive, the principle cause of her detention is, for that at these lords do see the queen being of so fervent affection towards the Earl of Bothwell as she is, and being put at, as they should be compelled to be in continual arms, and to have occasion of many battles, he being with manifest evidence notoriously detected to be the principle murderer, and the lords meaning prosecution of justice against him according to his merits.

> Robertson, William. *The History of Scotland*, pg. 449.

It is a public speech amongst all the people, and amongst all estates (saving of the counselors) that their queen hath no more liberty nor privilege to commit murder nor adultery, than any other private person, neither by God's law, nor by the laws of the realm.

Robertson, William. *The History of Scotland*, pg. 455.

Proposals delivered to Sir Nicholas Throckmorton at his going into Scotland in July 1567.

The queen to be at liberty, with these prisoners following.

The truth of Bothwell's fact to be duly proved before her; and that she may, for her satisfaction herein, be induced to believe the same by all probable means.

That thereupon a divorce be effectually made.

That she give commission to certain noblemen to proceed against Bothwell and his accomplices.

That a parliament be assembled with speed.

That a general peace be proclaimed through the realm.

That the castles of Dunbar and Dunbarton be in custody of such of the nobility, as be not partakers with Bothwell, as the queen shall name; they giving pledges to the lords which keep the prince that neither Bothwell nor any foreigners shall be therein maintained.

Proposals delivered to Sir Nicholas Throckmorton at his going into Scotland in July 1567.

The queen to be at liberty, with these prisoners following.

The truth of Bothwell's fact to be duly proved before her; and that she may, for her satisfaction herein, be induced to believe the same by all probable means.

That thereupon a divorce be effectually made.

That she give commission to certain noblemen to proceed against Bothwell and his accomplices.

That a parliament be assembled with speed.

That a general peace be proclaimed through the realm.

That the castles of Dunbar and Dunbarton be in custody of such of the nobility, as be not partakers with Bothwell, as the queen shall name; they giving pledges to the lords which keep the prince that neither Bothwell nor any foreigners shall be therein maintained.

That for the government of the realm and the prince, the queen, with the advice of the parliament, do constitute certain Wardens of the Marches, and of Edinburgh, Stirling, Dunbar, Dunbarton, Inchkeith, &c.

That all offices of wardens, chastelans, provostings, judicatures, and the principal officers of the realm, and all ecclesiastical promotions, be given by the queen, by the advice and consent of the more part of the great council.

That upon the death of any of the great council the queen name others with the consent of the rest.

That the establishing of the succession of the crown be renovated and confirmed according to the last act of parliament.

That the cause of religion be established, excepting none but the queen's person and some competent number for her attendance, not exceeding that a general pardon be granted by parliament.

That all Bothwell's lands be annexed to the crown, and be employed upon the education of the prince.

That the grand council consist upon such a number, as always there may be attending monthly at the least five or six. And;

That orders be accorded upon for their sitting in councils, and soliciting of causes to the queen.

That no strangers born bear any office in the queen's household.

That all the articles above said, and all other thereupon depending, be established by parliament; and that it be made for the first time punishable by loss of goods and imprisonment; the second time treason, whoever shall contrary it; and that it shall be lawful to all manner of persons to pursue him that shall break the same as a traitor.

That the Queen of England may be moved to become a maintainer of the same Parliament.

Keith, Robert. *History of the Affairs of Church and State in Scotland*, pg. 674-676.

Nicholas received the first of two responses from Scottish peers on 11 July 1567, and it is reasonable to assume that they had no intention of adopting the articles in their entirety. It is very difficult to honestly reach this conclusion so far removed from that time period, but the responses Nicholas received undoubtedly support his assertion.

Queen Elizabeth issued Nicholas with additional instructions to address the Scottish Council about the disorder on the borders and to quell the developing discontent there. France made it abundantly plain that they would do whatever it took to liberate Mary and bring the prince to France.

Nicholas remained aware of the situation, and he believed that Mary would be presented with an ultimatum on 23 July, when he learned that a large number of Scottish nobles had gathered for a conference. The day after, the council announced:

> 'That the lords considering her former misbehaviors as well in the government of the realm as in her own person, could not think meet that she would any more stand charged with the government and required her to give her consent that the prince might be crowned king, and a council be appointed to govern the realm in his name, and thus doing they would endeavor to save her life and honor, both which otherwise stood in great danger. And further it was resolved that is case she should not be comfortable to this motion, that her liberty should be restrained to more straightness, and the ladies and gentlemen which be about her to be sequestered from her. In case of her refusal they mind to proceed with violence and force for the coronation of the prince and her overthrow.'

Calendar of State Papers, Foreign. V.8. Letter 1509, pg. 297.

Three items were presented to Mary by the Scottish nobility. First, they asked her permission to hand over power; second, they asked for a commission to be given to the Earl of Moray while James was still a minor; and third, they listed certain nobility in case Moray did not accept the regency alone. The Earl of Moray was unable to submit his response because he was not in Edinburgh at the time. If Mary refused to give her assent, Nicholas said, the council would accuse Mary of tyranny for breach of statutes that were passed without her knowledge, including incontinence with Bothwell, and murder for killing her late husband because they had solid proof. Another indication of the increasing discontent toward Mary.

> I have also persuaded her to conform herself to renounce Bothwell for her husband, and to be contented to suffer a divorce to pass betwixt them; she hath sent me word that she will in no ways consent unto that, but rather die, grounding herself upon this reason, taking herself to be seven weeks gone with child; by renouncing Bothwell, she should acknowledge herself to be with child of a bastard, and to have forfeited her honor, which she will not do to die for it.

Schiern, Frederik. *Life of James Hepburn, Earl of Bothwell*, pg. 245.

Plans for James' coronation began on 26 July 1567, and Nicholas was invited to take part. 'That for as much as these accidents were chanced and these matters concluded contrary to his sovereign's expectation and advice, he could not assist at any such doings,' he informed the council.

On 29 July 1567, while Mr. Knox was preaching, the Bishop of Orkney, the Laird of Dun, and the Superintendent of Lothian crowned James in the parish church of Stirling. The oath was administered to the king while the prince was represented by the Earl of Morton and the Laird of Dun. The monarch vowed to uphold the truth, put an end to all false religion, rule the populace in accordance with the law, protect the privileges of the Scottish crown, put an end to all wrongdoing, and purge the world of heretics. The celebrations that followed the coronation ceremony, which featured the firing of artillery, dancing, and jubilation in the streets of Edinburgh, are described in a few early sources.

Nicholas continued to request for more time with Mary, but he continually was turned down. On 1 August, it was stated that Mary was being watched more closely because she had 'gained the favor and goodwill of those in the castle and gained intelligence,' that she might have used to flee. Mary was moved to the castle's tower.

In the meanwhile, Nicholas asked for his return from Scotland, and Elizabeth granted his request on 6 August 1567.

> Trusty and right well-beloved, we greet you well, for as much as we do consider that you have now a long time remained in those parts without expedition in the charge committed unto you, we think it not meet, seeing there hath not followed the good acceptation and fruit of our well-meaning towards that state, which good reason would have required, that you should continue there any longer, our pleasure, therefore is, that you shall immediately upon the receipt hereof, send your servant Middlemore unto the lords and estates of that realm that are assembled together, will him to declare unto them, that it cannot be seem very strange unto us, that you havening been sent from us, of such good intent, to deal with them, in matters tending so much to their own quiet, and to the benefit of the whole estate of their country, then have so far forgotten themselves, and so slightly regarded us and our good meaning, not only in delaying to hear you, and deferring your access to the queen their sovereign, but also, which is strangest of all, in not vouchsafing to make nay answer unto us. And although these dealings be such, indeed, as were not to be looked for at their hands,

yet do we find their usage and proceedings towards their sovereign and queen, overpass all the rest in so strange a degree, as we for our part, and we suppose the whole world besides, cannot but think them to have therein gone so far beyond the duty of subjects, as must needs remain to their perpetual touch forever. And therefore ye shall say, that we have thought good, without consuming any longer time in vain, to revoke you to our presence, requiring them to grant you license and passport so to do, which when you shall have obtained, we will that you make your repair hither, unto us, with as convenient speed as you may.

Robertson, William. *The History of Scotland*, pg. 458-459.

Nicholas sent a letter to Queen Elizabeth on 9 August informing her that the Earl of Bothwell, accompanied by two hundred men, had arrived in Orkney with the intent of seizing the castle and liberating his wife. The castle was protected by four ships and four hundred soldiers. There are no additional details that could improve this account.

Nicholas met the Earl of Moray en route to Edinburgh on 12 August, a few miles outside of the city, and described him as 'Very honorable, sincere, and direct, but not resolved what he will do.' The earl was welcomed upon his arrival in Edinburgh, but his request to see Mary was denied.

The next day, Nicholas informed the Bishop of St. Andrew's and the Abbot of Arbrothe that he had been recalled and wanted to know what the confederates would do to free Mary, as he suspected they would attempt such an endeavor.

Nicholas requested additional time in Scotland on 14 August, in part in the hope that the Earl of Moray would be granted access to Mary. On 19 August, Nicholas received a response from the Archbishop of St. Andrew's regarding their intentions; they stated that they all desired Mary's return to the throne, the protection of their prince, and prompt punishment for those responsible for Darnley's murder.

On 22 August 1567, James Stewart, Earl of Moray, was named regent. An oath was administered, and the earl recited the articles and pledged to abide by them before the lords. On the same day, forty summonses were issued to individuals suspected of murdering Darnley, but only three appeared in court. In addition, those who were summoned for jury duty did not appear. The case was dismissed.

JAMES STEWART, EARL OF MORAY
From the portrait belonging to the King at Holyrood Palace, Edinburgh

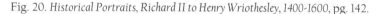

Fig. 20. *Historical Portraits, Richard II to Henry Wriothesley, 1400-1600*, pg. 142.

Moray invited Nicholas to a meeting. Nicholas arrived to discover the Earl of Moray and Secretary William Lethington conversing, and he conveyed Elizabeth's disapproval. Moray answered:

> "So far from it, Mr. Ambassador, that we wish her to be queen of all the world; but for now she is in the state of a person in the delirium of a fever, who refuses everything which may do her good, and requires everything which may do her good, and requires all that may work her harm. Be assured nothing will be more prejudicial to her interest, than for your mistress to precipitate matters. It may drive us to a strait, and compel us to measures we would gladly avoid. Hitherto have we been content to be charged with grievous and infamous titles, we have quietly suffered ourselves to be condemned as perjured rebels and unnatural traitors, rather than proceed to anything that might touch our sovereign's honor. But beware we beseech you, that your mistress, by her continual treats and defamation, by hostility, or by

soliciting other princes to attack us, do not push us beyond endurance. Think not we will lose our lives, forfeit our lands, and be challenged as rebels throughout the world, when we have the means to justify ourselves. And if there by no remedy, but your mistress will have war, sorry though we be, far rather will we take our fortune, than put our queen to liberty in her present mood, resolved as she is to retain and defend Bothwell, to hazard the life of her son, to peril the realm, and to overthrow her nobility.

For your wars, we know them well. You will burn our borders, and we shall burn yours; if you invade us, we do not dread it, and are sure of France; for your practices to nourish dissension amongst us, we have an eye upon them all. The Hamiltons will take your money, laugh you to scorn, and side with us. At this moment we have the offer of an agreement with them in our hands. The queen, your mistress, declares she wishes not only for our sovereign's liberty, and her restoration to her dignity, but is equally zealous for the preservation of the king, the punishment of the murder, and the safety of our lords. To accommo-date the first, our queen's liberty, much has been done, for the rest, absolutely nothing. Why does not her majesty fit out some ships of war, to apprehend Bothwell, and pay a thousand soldiers to reduce the forts and protect the king. When this is in hand, we shall think her sincere, but for her charge to set our sovereign forthwith at liberty, and restore her to her dignity, it is enough to reply to such strange language, that we are the subjects of another prince, and know not the queen's majesty for our sovereign."

Tytler, Fraser. *History of Scotland.* V. 7, pg. 188-190.

Nicholas expressed to Lethington his desire that every effort be made to prevent such severe measures. Nicholas addressed Lethington because he was not 'banded' with those nobles, but he realized further discussion would be futile and left.

Nicholas received the second response from the Scottish lords several days later, but their disposition was essentially the same. Nicholas accepted their invitation on 30 August, possibly in anticipation that the lords would have encouraging news.

On the 30th of August the Earl of Moray sent unto me, and required me, after the sermon, that we might go together to his lodging; whereupon the sermon being finished, I did accompany him thither, where were assembled all the lords. The L. of Lethington, in name of all the lords, made a summary repetition of all their proceedings since the beginning of this matter, yielding there these particular reasons to every their particular actions; which was in effect the same that I have heretofore in sundry of my dispatches advertised her majesty. At length he concluded, that no men in the world would be more sorry than they to have the Queen's majesty conceive otherwise than favorably of them; touching, by way of digression, the accord of religion betwixt the countries, the particular favors showed to many of them by her majesty heretofore, and the general relief that the whole country and nation received at the time of Leith; when strangers were in way to oppress them, their liberty and religion. When the L. of Lethington had finished his talk, the Earl of Moray set forth at great length what great grief it should be to him in particular to have the queen's majesty think otherwise of him than well, alleging many general reasons, and some particular touching himself, concluding there was no prince next those which he ought his chief duty unto, that the alienation of their favor might trouble him so much as the queen's majesty's.

Then the Earl of Morton said 'I will omit to speak of these things which have been touched by others, and pray you to render mine humble thanks to her majesty for the favor I received in the time of my trouble in her realm.'

Then the Earls of Moray, Athole, Morton, Mar, and Glencairn, and the L. of Lethington, led me into a little cabinet, where they had prepared a present of gilt-plate, as I esteemed it better than merits, which the Earl of Moray required me to accept by way of present, as from the king their sovereign lord. I declared that I could not accept any present from any person within that realm, but from the Queen their sovereign, of whom I would not make any difficulty to receive a present if she were in case to bestow any; but as from the King (whom I took to be the prince) I could receive none, seeing he had attained to that name by injuring the queen his mother. Whereupon the lords required me to desist from such matters, for it would but breed contention to no purpose, and so earnestly pressed me again to receive the present in the king's name, which, to be short, I refused; and so we parted, as it seemed to me they not best pleased. Then my leave being taken of them, the L. of Lethington accompanied me to my lodging, and there persisted with many persuasions to move me to change my mind from refusing the present; whereunto I did not yield, but so took my leave of him. Somewhat he required me to say unto you in his behalf, which I will declare at my return.

Keith, Robert. *History of the Affairs of Church and State in Scotland,* pg. 760-761.

On 30 August 1567, Nicholas departed Scotland disheartened and returned to England. A historical account suggests that he fled for his life, but there is no evidence to support this claim.

Moray dispatched three armed ships in quest of Bothwell, during which he apprehended five additional Confederates implicated in the assassination of Darnley. Some of the lords elected Moray to the position of regent, putting him in a problematic situation.

Bothwell was apprehended, but his ship went aground on a sandbank, allowing him to escape to Norway. The regent allegedly received a small bundle of letters and sonnets written by Mary to Bothwell, delivered by the Earl of Morton around the same time. The council and parliament examined the letters and presented them as evidence of Mary's culpability in her husband's murder. In addition, a 'bond or contract' was drafted for the assassination of the king, as stated in the same proceeding concerning Sir James Balfour. The original document was, anticipated to be, unavailable for examination. In a letter dated 28 November 1567, Drury wrote to Cecil.

> The writings, which did comprehend the names and consents of the chief for the murdering of the king, is turned into ashes, the same not unknown to the queen, and the same that concerns her part kept to be shown, which offends her.

Tytler, *History of Scotland, Volume VII*, Pg. 204.

Although there is no evidence linking the regent to the actual destruction of the 'contract,' it is reasonable to assume that he was aware of its existence.

On 15 December, the Scottish Parliament convened, and religion and Mary's incarceration were among the most vital topics discussed. The conclusion of the discussion was that Mary would remain in prison, and an act was passed to exonerate the noblemen and barons who had taken up arms to prosecute the murder.

The persistent hunt for the murderers produced positive results. John Hay of Tallo, John Hepburn of Bolton, George Dalgeish, a page or chamberlain, and William Powrie, a servant of Bothwell, were apprehended on 3 January 1568, stood trial, and in the course of their testimony implicated a number of the highest nobility in Scotland. Despite their testimony, they were arraigned, found guilty, and executed on the same day. Although Bolton proclaimed the execution of three men in connection with the murder prior to their execution, none of the men were ever arrested. One of the men that Bolton mentioned held the position of Lord Justice General. Moray, who was implicated in too many aspects, began to lose control and alienate those closest to him as people began to express sympathy for Mary's imprisonment. Nicholas Throckmorton was not among these individuals, contrary to what a few recent historians have asserted.

Mary, Queen of Scots took stock of her situation and the dependable individuals surrounding her before formulating a strategy. George Douglas, a visitor who was recently enraptured by her charisma and the attention she received, served as the inspiration for her deception. Douglas provided Mary with a disguise consisting of a garment worn by a laundress to aid in her escape. However, her attempt to flee was foiled when someone observed the 'extraordinary whiteness of her hands,' and she was returned to the castle in the same boat with which she had arrived.

Despite Douglas' banishment from the castle and Mary's increased surveillance, he maintained his determination to liberate his queen.

On 2 May 1568, Mary, Queen of Scots, did escape the castle. This report provides a vivid depiction of who was involved and how:

'Upon the second day of May a servant in Lochleven who had since his birth been nursed in the same place, and by reason thereof having credit there, stole the keys in the time of supper and thereafter passed and received the king's mother forth of her chamber and conveyed her to the boat and locked all the "yetts" [gates] upon the rest who was at supper, and spoiled the rest of the boats of their furniture, so that none was able to follow them; and when they were come to land George Douglas, brother to the Laird of Lochleven, who was in fantasy of love with her, and had provided this money of before, met her at the loch side, accompanied with the Laird of Riccarton a friend of the Lord Bothwell's and with them ten horse. They took away all the horse which pertained to the Laird of Lochleven. Within two miles Lord Seton with James Hamilton of Ormiston met her with thirty horse. In this company she passed the ferry and was met by Claud Hamilton with thirty horse, who conveyed her to Niddry, where she made some dispatches with her own hand, namely, one to John Beton to send to France, and another to the Laird of Riccarton commanding him to take the castle of Dunbar, who however failed of his enterprise. At her departing Lord Herries met her accompanied with thirty horse, and altogether conveyed her to Hamilton to the castle thereof, where she now remains, accompanied with all such as were of the motion of this conspiracy, which are not a very great number, and earnestly repents that ever they had meddling therewith. The principals of that faction are the Archbishop of St. Andrews, the Hamiltons, Herries and Seton, since they have drawn to them Eglinton and Fleming with some me gentlemen friends of Bothwell.

Calendar of State Papers, Foreign. V.8. Letter 2172, pg. 451-452.

Nicholas's years of refining his ambassadorial skills provided him with the tools necessary to inquire about Mary's fate. Without them, he would not have been the trusted and reliable ambassador on whom Queen Elizabeth relied.

Mary, Queen of Scots, eventually entered England, and as will be seen, it appears that Queen Elizabeth took great delight in preventing Mary from settling in one place for an extended period of time. Following is a brief illustration of Mary's travels between her arrival in England and her trial in October 1568; it does not encompass the entire period of time or location.

On 18 May 1568, Mary crossed the boundary from Workington (the northwest corner of England) to Cockermouth and Carlisle and wrote to Elizabeth, describing the traitorous rebels she had to endure and pleading with Elizabeth to defend her.

It is my earnest request that your majesty will send for me as soon as possible, for my condition is pitiful, not to say for a queen, but even for a simple gentlewoman. I have no other dress than that in which I escaped from the field; my first day's ride was sixty miles across the country, and I have not since dared to travel except by night.

Tytler, Patrick. *History of Scotland*, pg. 221.

The next day, Queen Elizabeth issued orders to the sheriffs of the regions instructing them to treat Mary with honor and respect, but to keep a close eye on her to prevent another escape. In addition, Elizabeth dispatched Lord Scroope and Sir Francis Knollys to prevent Mary's escape.

Mary was informed on 28 June that she was to be relocated to Bolton Castle, but the transfer was postponed as she began to assemble her belongings. Mary remained under intense security, and on 8 July, Sir George Bowes and 100 men approached the castle to free her, but she declined to leave.

On 13 July 1568, Mary left Carlisle Castle under the heavy protection of two companies of English military with twenty carriage horses and twenty-three saddled horses for her ladies and gentlemen, en route to Lowther Castle, where she would spend the night, and then Bolton Castle. Mary did indeed spend substantial time in Bolton.

Nicholas must have left Edinburgh and traveled to Dunfries, where he encountered Herries on 1 September 1568, who informed the Regent of an increase in larceny and theft reports. Nicholas was advised to appoint a virtuous and honorable man to office in order to halt this activity.

Mary was obliged to pack her belongings and depart Bolton for Tutbury under heavy guard on 26 January 1569. They arrived on 3 February 1569, after traveling through a brutally frigid winter. According to a letter she penned on 9 April, she was relocated to Wingfield Manor House around the week of Easter.

As Mary was shuffled from temporary residence to temporary residence, Moray was compelled to address the issues at hand, which caused division among the nobles surrounding him. It was rumored that he would surrender the principal fortresses, that he had consented to recognize the superiority of the English crown, that he had pursued the throne for himself, and that he was about to secure a deed of legitimatization that would position him on the throne should James die. Moray's already shaky foundation was further weakened by these reports.

In addition, while returning to England, Moray learned of a conspiracy to assassinate him and that the Duke of Norfolk and Mary were aware of the plot, which was to be carried out by the Earl of Westmoreland. This compelled Moray and Norfolk to reconcile. But Mary was not easily appeased, and she began to gather her forces. With the armies on high alert and the likelihood of bloodshed, a treaty of peace was proposed on 13 March to end all hostilities and resolve all issues. However, not all of the nobles were willing to sign, and the Duke of Chatelherault and Lord Herries were imprisoned, which infuriated many and increased hostility toward Moray.

By the beginning of July 1569, nobles such as the Earls of Arundel, Pembroke, Bedford, Northumberland, Westmoreland, Cecil, and Nicholas, who had insisted on it, were well aware of and in favor of a proposed marriage between the Duke of Norfolk and Mary. In addition, Mary had declared her willingness to divorce Bothwell. Norfolk was well-liked for numerous reasons and faced few obstacles.

Nicholas, while at Greenwich on 20 July 1569, advised Murry to contemplate and trust Lethington. The cipher translation is ambiguous regarding Nicholas, suggesting that if he (Murry) fled, his country would be in grave danger and confusion.

Moray received correspondence from Elizabeth, Mary, Sir Nicholas, and Norfolk. Elizabeth's letters contained three propositions for Mary. Mary wished to ascertain the validity of her marriage to Bothwell in her letter. Nicholas discussed Norfolk and Mary's proposed marriage.

That the time was come when he must give up all his conscientious scruple and objections. The match was now supported by a party too powerful and too numerous to be resisted. If he opposed it, his overthrow was inevitable. If he promoted it, no man's friendship would be so highly prized, no man's estimation be greater or more popular.

Of her consent (Queen Elizabeth) he need have no doubt. She was too wise a princess to risk the tranquility of her government, her own security, and the happiness of her people for the gratification of her own fancy, or the passions of any inconsiderate individual. All the wisest, noblest, and mightiest persons in England were all engaged upon their side.

Tytler, Patrick. *History of Scotland.* Vol. VI, pg. 283.

Elizabeth had not yet been apprised of the marriage proposition, despite the fact that everyone was aware of it and supported it. The English Queen was enraged when she learned of the conspiracy that had occurred behind her back, which she was unaware of. Norfolk promptly dispatched an apology to Elizabeth, clarifying that he would not have consented in full without her permission. The queen summoned Norfolk to court immediately, after which he was promptly arrested and held in the Tower of London.

Mary was given brief notice to gather her belongings and relocated from Winkfield to Tukbury. Before she packed her belongings, her residence was examined for correspondence, and she was then placed in the custody of the Earl of Huntingdon, who was frequently quite disagreeable with her. Many of her servants and attendants were dismissed and all of her incoming and outgoing correspondence was intercepted for Elizabeth to review while Nicholas monitored the information.

All of this did nothing to promote harmony in either realm, and civil unrest remained the most prevalent concern.

Nicholas found himself in a precarious situation in September 1569, when religious tensions in Northern England drew Elizabeth's attention due to rumors of the possibility of a large religious uprising, as minor revolts had already occurred. Nicholas was imprisoned in Windsor Castle on 22 September 1569, for his probable involvement in one of these revolts, specifically 'unlawful assembly in Westward Forest.'

At this juncture, many biographers, including one that I mentioned previously, indicate that Sir Nicholas Throckmorton was executed for his involvement, with some even noting the date. There are numerous additional references to 'Throckmorton's and Paget's plot' without citations or explanation that could most certainly mislead a reader or researcher. Additional investigation provided sufficient evidence for me to conclude that the involved Throckmorton was Francis Throckmorton, son of John Throckmorton and brother of our Sir Nicholas Throckmorton.

Francis Throckmorton, who was born in 1554, was a loyal envoy of Mary, Queen of Scots, who conspired with the Spanish ambassador, the French embassy, and the Duke of Guise to lead an invasion of England. Francis was executed after discovery of the scheme. Francis's marriage to Anne, a further resemblance to Nicholas's marriage to Anne Carew, inevitably misled some historians.

The intention of the November Revolt of the Northern Earls, also known as the Rising in the North, was to dethrone Elizabeth and replace her with Mary, Queen of Scots. A force commanded by Charles Neville, Earl of Westmorland, and Thomas Percy, Earl of Northumberland, occupied Durham, and a proclamation was issued in an attempt to rally all Catholics to take up arms. An estimated five to six thousand insurgents occupied Barnard Castle and the port of Hartlepool in support of the earls. Nicholas appears to have been silent at this time.

Queen Elizabeth promptly dispatched her forces, demonstrating the same skill as her father, commanded by the Earl of Sussex, to suppress the rebellion, and the earls fled to Scotland,. An early historian asserts that one of the reasons why the rebellion failed was that Nicholas perished too soon for the Catholics to gain any significant advantage from his diplomatic abilities.

Following the rebellion, Nicholas was ultimately released from Windsor Castle and returned to his London residence, possibly in late January 1570. The charges were withdrawn, and no further action was taken against him. No additional testimonies or recordings were discovered in the trials of the time.

Moray was traveling from Stirling to Edinburgh on 23 January 1570, and intended to pass through Linithgow when he was struck by a single bullet from James Hamilton of Bothwellhaugh. Accounts of the exact date differ. The bullet exited near the hip bone, killing Arthur Douglas's horse, which was riding next to him. The abrupt occurrence of the violent act caused confusion, allowing Hamilton to flee, albeit not unnoticed. He was reportedly greeted with jubilation by the Bishop of St. Andrews and a number of other nobles, who rejoiced that Scotland was once again liberated from a despot.

Moray, despite hemorrhaging, was able to walk to the palace, and initial prognoses were optimistic. However, his condition deteriorated, and he passed away shortly before midnight.

Shortly after the death of Moral, Nicholas was invited to dine with the Earl of Leicester at his home, where the fate of Moral was a topic of conversation. Following dinner, Sir Nicholas Throckmorton became gravely ill and died in Leicester House, in the parish of St. Clement Danes, without Temple Bar, London, on 12 February 1570, at the age of 57.

I found an early reference to a few letters that could have shed light on his death, but they were destroyed in the Great Fire of London in 1666. This fire, which, according to an early source, began in a baker's home in Pudding Lane and ravaged London's landscape and left an estimate of hundreds of thousands of people homeless, was the most devastating natural disaster to ever strike London. To an estimated cost of around 5 to 7 million pounds, eighty-nine parish churches, the Guildhall, and a great number of other public buildings, including marketplaces, were impacted.

The oldest report, which was published in 1641 by Leicester's own personal account, does not adequately explain the circumstances surrounding Sir Nicholas Throckmorton's death. As a result of its vivid nature, this version of the story of Nicholas's death is typically the one that is repeated the most frequently. Early contemporaneous records claim that Leicester never forgave Throckmorton for his 'vehement opposition' to the earl's intended marriage with Queen Elizabeth, and that Leicester took advantage of the chance to settle the score. I will do my best to explain why this cannot be considered reasonable in the following sentences.

Regarding the story that Leicester told, I concur with the conclusion reached in the *Dictionary of National Biography*, Volume LVI-Teach-Tollet, which states, 'No reliance need to be placed on this report.' This conclusion may be found in the brief biography of Sir Nicholas Throckmorton.

The following is a passage that was taken from Leycesters Commonwealth, Conceived, Spoken, and Published with Most Earnest Protestation... London (?), 1641.

'I was recounting unto you others made away by my Lord of Leicester with like art, and next in order I think was Sir Nicholas Throgmorton, who was a man whom my Lord of Leicester used a great while (as all the world knows) to over-thwart and cross the doings of my Lord Treasurer then Sir William Cecil, a man specially disliked always of Leicester, both in respect of his old master the Duke of Somerset, as also for that his great wisdom, zeal and singular fidelity to the realm, was like to hinder much this mans designments wherefore understanding after a certain time that these two knights were secretly made friends, and that Sir Nicholas was like to detect his doings (as he imagined) which might turn to some prejudice of his purposes: (having conceived also a secret grudge and grief against him, for that he had written to her majesty at his being ambassador in France, that he heard reported at Duke Memorances table, that the Queen of England had a meaning to marry her horse-keeper) he invited the said Sir Nicholas to a supper at his house in London and at supper time departed to the court, being called for (as he said) upon the sudden by her majesty, and so perforce would need have Sir Nicholas to sit and occupy his lordship's place, and therein to be served as he was: and soon after by a surest their taken, he died of a strange and incurable vomit. But, the day before his death, he declared to a dear friend of his, all the circumstances and cause of his disease, which he affirmed plainly to be of poison, given him in a salad at supper, inveighing in earnest against the earl's cruelty and bloody disposition, affirming him to be the wickedest, most perilous and perfidious man under heaven. But what availed this, when he had now received the bait.

Leycesters Common-wealth, pg. 42-43.

This passage was taken from the 1742 edition of Francis Peck's Legend of Sir Nicholas Throckmorton and included in *A Genealogical and Historical Account of the Throckmorton Family*.

Our author, it may be observed, mentions nothing of his uncle Sir Nicholas Throckmorton's being poisoned by Robert Dudley, Earl of Leicester. It is like he thought it might be dangerous to himself to do so: But that defect is very amply supplied by another writer (supposed to be Father Robert Parsons, the Jesuit who (in his Secret Memoirs of that Earl, 8 vo., London, 1708, p. 35) hath these words. 'I was recounting to you others made away by my Lord of Leicester with like Art, and the next in order I think was Sir Nicholas Throck-morton, a man whom my Lord of Leicester used a great while (as all the world knows) to overthwart & cross the doings of my lord treasurer, (then Sir William Cecil) a man specially always disliked of Leicester, who understanding, after a certain time, that these two knights were secretly made friends, & that Sir Nicholas Throck-morton was like to detect his doings (as he imagined) which might be some prejudice & let to his purposes; having conceived also a secret grudge & grief against him, for that he had written to her Majesty, at his being Ambassador in France, that he heard it reported at the Duke of Montmorenci's table, that the Queen of England had a meaning to marry her horse keeper (the Earl of Leicester being then her master of horse) invited the said Sir Nicholas to a supper at his house in London, & at supper time departed to the Court, being called for, as he said, on the sudden by her Majesty, & so per force would needs have Sir Nicholas to sit & occupy his lordship's place, & therein to be served as he was, & soon after by a surfet (supper) there taken, he died of a strange incurable vomit. But the day before his death he declared to a dear friend of his all the circumstances & cause of his death, which he affirmed plainly to be poison given him in a sallet (salad) at supper, inveighing most earnestly against the Earl's cruelty and bloody disposition; affirming him to be the wickedest, most perilous, & perfidious man under heaven: But what availed this when he had received the bait? After Sir Nicholas Throckmorton's death my Lord of Leicester outwardly made a great show of lamentation over him, & in a letter to Sir Francis Walsingham, the queen's Ambassador then in France, he thus expresses himself upon that occasion: 'We have lost on Monday our good friend Sir Nicholas Throckmorton, who died in my house, being there taken suddenly in great extremity on the Tuesday before his lungs were perished; but a sudden cold he had taken was the cause of his speedy death. God hath his soul, & we his friends great loss of his body.

A Genealogical and Historical Account of the Throckmorton Family, pg. 181.

Permit me to analyze briefly the relationship between Sir Nicholas Throckmorton and the Earl of Leicester through excerpts of their correspondence. Sir Nicholas Throckmorton had corresponded with the Earl of Leicester as 'patrons of puritan ministers' for many years prior to his death, as evidenced by this letter written in Edinburgh on 11 May 1565.

Sir Nicholas Throgmorton to the Earl of Leicester and Sir William Cecil.

Arrival with the Laird of Lethington at Berwick. Intended meeting of the Nobles at Stirling, concerning the marriage. Queen Mary's earnestness and vehemence about it. Her determination to send to France to declare the matter to her uncle's. Receipt of fresh instructions by the Laird of Lethington on his return to Scotland. The Queen's message contained in them, to marry whom she will, and to be fed with yea and nay no longer.

Inducements held out to William Maitland to go to France; he refuses; his great perplexity and passion. General averseness to the match. Efforts to stay himself [Throckmorton] from coming to Scotland.

Necessity of the Earl of Northumberland's being stayed. in the North. The papists are rousing themselves. Disorders in Lid desdale. Incloses,

46. 1. Thomas Randolph to Sir Nicholas Throckmorton.

Sends a paper by which he may see what haste is made to that which they would be at. Hopes that they shall both be at the marriage, though they would well be spared.

Edinburgh, May 10.

Calendar of State Papers Relating to Scotland of the Reigns of Henry VIII, Edward VI, Mary, Elizabeth-1509-1589. V. Letter #46, 46-1, Pg. 210.

The following letter from Cecil to Sir Thomas Smith, written on 16 October 1565 while Cecil was at Westminster, contains additional evidence.

To tell you truly, I think the Queen's Majesty's favor to my Lord of Leicester be not so manifest as it was, to move men to think that she will marry with him; and yet his Lordship hath favor sufficient, as I hear him say to his good satisfaction. My Lord of Sussex thinks that my Lord of Leicester might do more for him in causes of Ireland than he hath. My Lord of Norfolk loves my Lord of Sussex earnestly, and so all that stock of the Howards seem to join in friendship together, and yet in my opinion without cause to be disliked; and for the Duke, I think England hath not had in this age a nobleman more likely to prove a father and a stay to this country, and so I am glad to perceive the Queen's Majesty to have him in estimation: he is wise, just, modest, careful, et timens Deum. Sir Nicholas Throgmorton is also much noted by speech to be a director of my Lord of Leicester, but I think my Lord well able to judge what is mete or unmete, and doth use Mr. Throgmorton friendly because he doth show himself careful and devote to his Lordship.

Wright, Thomas. *Queen Elizabeth and Her Times, a Series of Original Letters.* VI, Pg. 20.

After reviewing all of the correspondence between Throckmorton and Robert Dudley, the Earl of Leicester for this biography, I was unable to discern any hostility between them that would have prompted Robert Dudley to murder Nicholas.

In a letter to the queen's ambassador in France at the time, Sir Francis Walsingham, the Earl of Leicester expressed his anguish over Nicholas' death.

We have lost on Monday our good friend Sir Nicholas Throckmorton, who died in my house, being there taken suddenly in great extremity on Tuesday before his lungs were perished; but a sudden cold he had taken was the cause of his speedy death. God hath his soul and we his friend's great loss of his body.

Digges, Dudley. *Compleat Ambassador. France*, 1655, pg. 47.

Nicholas was laid to rest on the south side of the chancel of St. Catherine Cree Church in London, beneath a 'beautiful alabaster tomb' with the following inscription:

Here lies the body of Sir Nicholas Thockmorton, Knt. The fourth son of Sir George Thockmorton, Knt. The which Sr. Nicholas was Chief Butler of England, one of the Chamberlains of the Exchequer, and Ambassador Leiger to the Queen's Majesty, Queen Elizabeth, in France, and after his return into England, he was sent ambassador again into France, and twice into Scotland. He married Anne Carew, daughter to Sir Nicholas Carew, Knt. And begat of her ten sons and three daughters. He died the 12th day of February, Anno Dom. 1570. Aged 57 years.

The English Baronetage; Containing a Genealogical and Historical Account of all the English Baronets. V.2, pg. 358.

The following passage from Francis Peck's 1740 publication The Legend of Sir Nicholas Throckmorton is relevant in this context:

Sir Nicholas Throckmorton died suddenly in Leicester house in the parish of S. Clement Danes, without Temple Bar, London on Monday the 12 Feb. 1570. Whereupon his body was carried to his own house in the parish of (S. Catherine) Cree-church near Aldgate; where resting till the 21 of the said month, it was then buried in the parish church there (*Fati Oxon*, vol. I, col. 100).

There was an early reference to someone who had observed his deteriorating health and mentioned it in a letter. According to another source, poison was added to the food during dinner. A second account of his death must not be disregarded, as it was significant enough to be included in the Throckmorton family's history.

I have been informed that, when Sir Nicholas Throckmorton was poisoned as aforesaid, and lay upon his death bad at Leicester House, he called one of his own gentlemen privately to him and charged him, "When I am dead and gone," said he, "tell that rouge Leicester that I say he hath poisoned me, but that I hope my daughter, Betty, will outlive him and (when he is also is dead gone) lift up her vardingal and piss upon his grave, and tell her for me, that I charge her, it possible to do so." But whether his said daughter (first maid of honor to Queen Elizabeth and afterwards married to the famous Sir Walter Raleigh) had ever an opportunity to comply with this odd injunction of her father I cannot tell, sure I am that the said Sir Nicholas Throckmorton having a very numerous issue and then a more numerous train of descendants, one of these latter, a gentleman of some figure (who highly honored the singular as it was, as no other than a like command to him and all the descendants of the said Sir Nicholas Throckmorton) being, a great many years after at Warwick, and seeing the above mentioned Earl of Leicester's magnificent tomb in the middle of the great church there, addressing himself to certain friends and acquaintances of his then in company with him, 'that villain! Who lieth so richly entombed here he (said he) poisoned my great grandfather the famous Sir Nicholas Throckmorton.' It is like you never heard of the odd sort of charge Sir Nicholas gave his daughter Raleigh when he was dying at Leicester House. I know not indeed whether she had any opportunity to comply with it. But, whether she had or no, I conceive that what my great ancestor said his daughter Raleigh should do, was intended to all his posterity, and consequently that I myself am as much concerned to obey it as she was. Let the will of the dead therefore, gentlemen be fulfilled, at these words he got upon the monument, and with all the contempt, fury and indignation which could possibly be expressed in such an action let go most heartily and plentifully on Leicester's face and tomb. God I hope will forgive me (said he) for profaning his house, (wherein this detested coarse deserves not to lie) for my obedience to command of my ancestor and this compliment, thou wretch I will always remember to pay thee whenever I come to Warwick. F. P.

A Genealogical and Historical Account of the Throckmorton Family, pg. 181-182.

The cause of his death is by no means beyond suspicion. I must admit that, of all the biographies I have written, the circumstances surrounding this one are the most compelling due to the coincidence with Edward Courtenay's lost letters. If Nicholas was murdered, no one would have left incriminating evidence such as correspondence, witness statements, or written statements. Moreover, if a scrap of evidence was in fact overlooked at the time, time can obliterate any infinitesimal piece of information that resides in a cold, dark, climate-controlled archive in the basement of a university, college, or private collection. I was unable to locate it, however.

Based on the correspondence I reviewed to, from, and about Leicester and Throckmorton, there is insufficient evidence to continue to suspect that Throckmorton was poisoned; however, the fact that Leicester left Throck-morton at his home before returning to London does not help to provide a conclusive and definitive answer. The statement 'Sir Nicholas to sit and occupy his lordship's place' may imply that someone intended to poison Leicester, but Nicholas was the unfortunate recipient when Leicester left for London at the queen's request.

At least for the time being, I must apologize to my readers because, according to surviving documents, this compelling aspect of his life remains unanswered.

His will was dated February 5, 1570.

Fig. 21. Throckmorton, Charles W. *A Genealogical and Historical Account of the Throckmorton Family*, pg. 159.

CHAPTER 5: THE LEGEND OF THROCKMORTON

This chapter is dedicated to a poem whose authorship has been and likely always will be a matter of debate, unless an obscure document surfaces that conclusively identifies the author.

Edward Partiericle, Esq., of Ely, provided the Reverend Francis Peck with the copy that is frequently distributed. It has been reported that Mr. Partiericle discovered the family heirloom among his father's documents. Catherine, daughter of Sir Arthur Throckmorton, son and successor of Sir Nicholas Throckmorton, was his grandfather's paternal grandmother.

Mr. Peck described the condition of the original manuscript as dreadful, 'Wrote in very bad ink, in many places now almost worn out and obliterated, and transcribed at first, as appears by the frequent mistakes in it, from a very faulty copy by two persons who could neither of them make it out.'

In 1762, Mr. Peck undertook the monumental task of transcribing the poem as a literal copy at first, but then realized it was impossible and 'took certain liberties' to make it legible and give it meaning and measure. This copy is now preserved in the British Library's *Additional Manuscript Collection* #5841. It appears that the original document has disappeared.

Mr. Cole, the Rector of Bletchley in Buckinghamshire, who interacted with members of the Throckmorton family and reviewed a 1678 collection of manuscripts containing the poem, was an additional source for *The Legend of Sir Nicholas Throckmorton*. Mr. Peck's transcription was based on this copy.

I discovered a version of '*The Life and Death of Sir Nicholas Throckmorton*' in the Earl of Oxford's collection located at the British Library (*Harleian Manuscript Collection*, #6353), but the date is missing.

The primary point of contention was whether the author was Nicholas himself, an actual relative of Sir Nicholas, or an Elizabethan poet who assumed the character as a poetic vehicle. Nevertheless, it is reasonable to infer that the author was a nephew of Sir Nicholas and that he or she knew something about the family, despite a few extremely rare errors. It contains valuable information about the life of Sir Nicholas Throckmorton, regardless of its origin.

From approximately 1750 to 1890, historians frequently debated these errors and their authors, and most, if not all, of these debates are beyond the scope of this work. This is the copy that Mr. Peck transcribed.

Certainly, another source for contention could be; 'Sir Henry Wotton, diplomat and poet (uncle of Sir Thomas Wotton)' is cited on page 181 of *A Genealogical and Historical Account of the Throckmorton Family.*

The mass of Throckmorton's original papers came into the possession of Sir Henry Wotton, diplomatist and poet (uncle of Sir Thomas Wotton, 2nd Baron Wotton who m. Sir Nicholas' granddaughter, Mary Throckmorton) who bequeathed them to Charles I, but the bequest did not take effect. After many vicissitudes the papers passed into the possession of Francis Seymour Conway, first Marques of Hertford, (1719-1794), whose grandson the 3rd Marques of Hertford made them over to the public record office, on the recommendation of John Wilson Croker, before 1842 (*Notes & Queries, 3rd series*, IV, 455).

A portrait of Sir Nicholas painted when he was 49 is at Coughton, an engraving by Vertue is dated 1747. A poem giving his life was first printed by Francis Peck in 1742, the best version of the poem is that transcribed by William Cole and now in the British Museum. *Additional MSS.*, 5841, another is in Harl. MSS., 6353.

My publisher and I have had numerous discussions regarding the modernization of a number of the texts I frequently include in my works to conform to current acceptable phonological standards. In the following circumstance, I must concur with them in the following poem. I have chosen to 'tidy up' the wording to make it much simpler to read without modifying the rhyme scheme. However, as it will be read, not every word in the poem rhymes.

Please keep in mind that the accompanying poem has been translated numerous times over the centuries, resulting in numerous variants. Despite the fact that I chose to work with one of the older translations, I imagine this one could be added to the plethora available.

1. In bed I lay, forecasting how to live,
Devising means by credit to arise;
Then haughty heart against base estate did strive,
And I supposed the meaner sort unwise;
With every man does frame his proper lot,
The poorest soul is still the simplest sot.

2. Dislodging thoughts, and falling to my rest,
Morpheus scarce had muffled up mine eye,
But in a dream a man his steps addressed
Anerst my bed: whom when I did spy,
Wan were my looks, appalled with sudden fear:
Yet, as he spoke, I laid a listening ear,

3. And heard him say, who know not, warning need;
Young years are prone in slippery ways to slide.
Attend my words, and let them stand in stead
Of beaten path young hare-brained heads to guide.
Thou hope's, by hap, some favor for to find;
But all in vain: thou sails' against the wind.

4. I see for thee it is not to attempt
Those lucky chances others doe achieve,
For Fortune long gone has quite exempt
Thee from the rest she meant for to relieve,
And rolled thee in a register with those
Whose chief joys consist in deepest woes.

5. In deepest woes thy dreary doleful days
Shall droop away, though life doe still endure;
Whose wished end thy forward fate delays
Because it were the salve of all thy cure.
But, since the heavens ordain so from on high,
Thou then shall live when say thou would die.

6. Aghast I stared; my hair did stand upright;
For all the space he held me by the arm:
The sentence hard, but stranger seemed the sight;
Till by his words I knew he meant no harm.
Abandon dread (quote he); for good I came:
Assure thyself; since I thy Uncle am.

7. Who's past the straights best knows the thorough-fare:
Who wades the ford, can better strangers teach:
The fencer best to break a thrust declares;
Who saw the thief can best of all impeach.
Then blameless I who bear the Circe's cup
Whose poison sweet first made me thereof sup.

8. The monster kept in labyrinth slew all,
Save only him who had the clew of third.
Thou cannot pass one year without a fall,
Unless thou takes that council which I bid.
A warning may show thee to set thy feet
That in the end thou need not them to fleet.

9. Attentive ear lend to me a space;
The marking mind the profit bears away:
Forbear thy sleep to hear discourse a race
Of him who ran, although he ran astray.
And all the world my life and facts that knew,
Shall witness bare how my report is true.

10. A brother fourth, and far from hope of land,
By parents' hest, I served as a page
To Richmond's duke, and waited, still at hand,
For fear of blows, which happened in his rage.
In France with him I lived most carelessly,
And learned the tongue, though' nothing readily.

11. But let me show what crooked chance befell
For me to taste amidst my childish years,
Attainders came; a woeful tale to tell,
And needs must now rehearse the same with tears,
How break-neck Wolfe, that once sucks sweet of prey,
Could never leave until his dying day.

12. For, after that resolved stood the King.
To take a new, and leave his wedded wife;
My uncle was a mean to work the thing
By Reynold Poole, who brewed all the strife,
And then at Rome did work the contrary:
Which drove the King at home to tyranny.

13. He marking how that Poole, and others mow,
Did hinder him from getting a divorce,
Of Roman church then made an overthrow,
And had of such a small or no remorse.
Straight by his laws he banish out the Pope;
And prelates wore for tippet Tyborn rope.

14. When Exeter and Poole had lost their heads,
Who thought it much that change should spring of lust;
Then ladies scorned to die in downed beds;
And people feigned so far as well they durst.
But where the prince doth reign by cruelty,
There subjects fawn, and fall to flattery.

15. Thus were great peers brought to the chopping feast,
With diverse more, whose blood would make a stream.
Yet not content, he sent to have the rest
To execute his bloody stratagem;
But wiser they; who, since their friends sped ill,
Thought better sure themselves to save than spill.

16. Yet, for contempt, they all did penance pay:
Amongst which crew my uncle Michael one;
Who lost his lands and all for making stay.
But, by good hap, he was not all alone.
And then he found that friendly company
Is greatest help to man in misery.

17. My father's foes clapped him through cankered hate
In Tower fast, and gaped to joint his neck.
They were in hope for to obtain a mate
Who heretofore had labored for a check.
Yea, Grevills grieved him ill without a cause,
Who hurt not them, nor yet the Prince's laws.

18. Then flatterers, that fawned for to be fed,
Festoons appeared, as dolphins in a shower,
Who lye unknown, with close dissembling head,
Till fortune hides her merry looks, and lower.
Adversity shows gold exchanged for dross,
And makes them see their love is laid to loss.

19. Our friends were hurt, our foes were in their ruff:
Fear to offend made many seem so coy:
When prince displeased had taken a thing in snuff,
There were that ran the wounded to destroy.
Yet manly mind the sinking held by chin,
Though currish crews sought means to keep them in.

20. Thus every thing did run against the hair;
Our name disgraced, and we, but witless boys,
Did deem it hard such crosses then to bare;
Our minds more fit to deal with childish toys.
But troubles are of perfect wit the schools:
And life at will feeds men as fat as fools.

21. Then care and I were linked in youthful prime;
My streams of joys were stopped with the damn of prince's wrath;
I, fatherless a time,
Had friends but few, and master less became:
This latter loss was cause that old grief's grew,
As scars, scant healed, by every wrench renew.

22. Our sun eclipsed a long time did not shine;
No joys approached near to Coughton House:
My sisters they did nothing else but whine;
My mother looked much like a drowned mouse.
No butter then would stick upon our bread:
We all did fear the loss of father's head.

23. While flocking foes to work our bane were bent;
While thunder claps of angry Jove did last;
Then to Lord Parr my mother saw me sent:
So with her brother I was safely placed.
Of alms he kept me in extremity,
Who did misdoubt a worse calamity.

24. Quite void of hope, and drowned in despair,
We saw no cause which once might make us glad;
But signs enough that we should still impair,
And want no cross whereby to make us sad.
Yet, when we thought our state would never mend,
Unlooked for, our sorrows had an end.

25. If patients, when that they are brought most low,
Find present death or present remedy;
If ebbing streams begin again to flow:
Then so it is with man in misery.
The stormy hail, which patters thick on tile,
Doth never last the going of a mile.

26. For when the King's fifth wife had lost her head,
Yet he misliked the life to live alone,
And, once resolved the sixth time for to wed,
He sought outright to make his choice of one.
That choice was chance right happy for us all:
It bred our bliss, and rid us quite from thrall.

27. Oh lucky looks that fawned on Katharine Parr!
A woman rare, her like but seldom seen.
To Borough first, next unto Latimer
She widow was; and then became a Queen.
My mother prayed her niece with watery eyes,
To rid both her, and hers, from endless cries.

28. She, willing of herself to do us good,
Sought out the means her uncle's life to save;
And, when the King was in the pleasing mood,
She humbly then her suit began to crave.
With wooing times denials disagree,
She spoke, and sped: my Father was set free.

29. And, as the ship that stuck fast in ground
Doth rise with the flood, and floated out apace,
So we, that once in deepest dumps were drowned,
In court began to show a cheerful face.
This was the spring of all our budding joys
Which laughed to scorn the winter of annoys.

30. The frost did thaw which nip our growth with cold;
The heat of sun did make us bud again;
The wind and waves our course which did with-hold
Did drive us to the wished port amine.
The prince's wrath was pacified and gone;
His favor grew; which caused us spring anon.

31. Lo! then my brethren, Clement, George, and I,
Did seek, as youth doe still, in court to be.
Each other state, as base, we did defy,
Compared with court, the nurse of dignity.
Tis truly said, no fishing to the sea's;
No serving to a King's—if you can please.

32. If vintners use at first to sell good wine;
If nothing sweeps so clean as newest broom;
If naughty cloth at first seems smooth and fine;
Then so it is with every new-come groom,
Whose pains at first by double forwardness
Doth hide the blot of faulty slothfulness.

33. Those samples taught us, at our entrance in,
That doing well should be our chief defense:
And so we thought some favor for to win
By meek demeanor, and by diligence.
We wished to please, we feared to offend;
We saw the prince's wrath brought heavy end.

34. We took great pains, when kindled hope did flame
From youthful breasts, swollen with ambition.
We labored much for to advance our name,
And daily gaped to get promotion.
We served in hope, and hoped not in vain;
The King's good will for guerdon we did gain;

35. Whose wrath is worse than death, by man's account:
For whom the prince mislikes, them most men hate;
And whom he fancies, he doth make to mount:
And none alive shall have so happy state.
Thrice happy she that made us happy then!
For we did rise as well as other men.

36. First in the court my brother Clement served:
A fee he had the Queen her cup to bring.
And some supposed that I right well deserved,
When sewer they saw me chose unto the King.
My brother George in youth, by valor rare,
A pension got, and gallant halberd bare.

37. Now when our joys were newly set a broach,
The King did loathe to live so lazily;
Wherefore he was thus bold as to encroach
The borders of his proved enemy.
He knew Frenchmen used leagues of amity
As cloaks, to hide some coined treachery.

38. Their truces daily made, but never kept,
Were proofs and patterns of dishonesty.
By mocking of the King his wrath they heap,
That never meant to put up injury.
Ill angering of a wasp, or waspish King;
For ill abide where they bestow their sting.

39. And sure for this the faithless French did pay
A just reward of fained flattery.
How oft were they to Englishmen a prey!
Still losing goods, and towns, by infamy.
But I will only tell how that our Liege,
In royal person, Boulogne did besiege.

40. With whom there marched a troop of English train,
Whose forward minds, not bridled by mistrust,
But pricked forth for honor or for gain,
Headlong themselves to thousand perils thrust.
There three of us did serve in royal band:
The fourth did wait upon Northumberland.

41. And, when our camp to pitch their tents was bent.
The rattling shot did fly about our ears.
The bullets thick, as messengers, were sent,
To plant within our hearts some flying fears.
They played it hard. For why? the French blood rose
That in despite we lodged so near their nose.

42. Our army, first, was forced to defend
The painful pioneers, who trenches made;
Which once dispatched, a double gain did lend:
A shield from foes, and from the sun a shade.
Next after that a mount was raised in haste
Where all the greatest ordinance was placed.

43. Lo! then the battery began with speed!
On either side was sending still of shot,
No sparing one another's blood to shed,
While war doth last, or skirmishes be hot.
Few Frenchmen peeped or looked us in the face
But felt our shafts let flying strait apace.

44. Our culverins such knocking peals address,
Our bombards from the mount did never cease:
Our sackers, double, canons, and the rest,
Break down their walls; and we did still increase.
As fish for water, so they gapped for aid:
But all relief, by force of foes, was stayed.

45. When that a month we had besieged the town;
When victuals, men, and powder waxed scant;
When all their forts were well nigh beaten down;
When no supply came to relieve their want:
Then all agreed them and their town to yield:
For they doe hate to fight a pitched field.

46. They called a parley: whereof this was the end;
That they with bag and baggage might depart,
But when the King did thereto condescend,
It grieved the greedy soldiers to the heart.
Yet so the King obtained the victory:
Renowned of his foes for clemency.

47. He safe returned, and left a garrison
To fence the town, with battery weakened.
Amongst which crew my brother George was one,
Who all the siege two hundred soldiers led.
His warlike heart desired there to stay;
Till Frenchmen caught his body for a prey.

48. Our country-men, now flesh, did leap for joy;
Per force they held the town that they had won,
Maugre the French, that sought them to annoy;
But all in vain; for little harm was done.
The Dolphin, Rhine grave, and the Lord of Baize,
Did oft assail; and commonly did lease.

49. Naught makes man so bold as good success;
For George, that scraped in siege, did venture far:
He pricked forth his prance to the press
Of Frenchmen's camp, whereas he took a scar;
And when he saw himself amongst his foes,
It was truce boot to bid him lay on blows.

50. Two more were taken with him in self-same plight,
Who thought, belike, for to subdue an host:
But such as venture rashly for to fight,
Come all too soon, as they did, to their cost.
Their courage now was cooled; their haste made waste:
As prisoners they in dungeon dark were caste.

51. Then leisure and occasion bid them write
Some mournful verse to wail their evil hap:
And Englishmen, their damage to requite
In skirmishing, the next day, at a clap,
Took seven-score captives of the French away:
Such usuries their luck was then to pay.

52. In treaties came, which did conclude a peace,
When Boulogne had spoke English for a year.
Eight hundred thousand crowns was her release:
And captives thought their ransom very dear:
If in eight years their fine they did not bring,
Their town should rest as subject to our King.

53. A thousand pounds our brother George redeemed:
Yet then an hundred pounds and he were wide.
With golden weights they prized him, as it seemed,
For that he was unto the King allied.
They knew he Captain was; they learnt his name:
Yea all, and more, was known by flying Fame.

54. The King delivered Frenchmen two or three,
By such exchange our brother to discharge.
He found in prison pain; but once set free
Did much commend the life that lives at large.
Home he returned, and many welcomes had:
Safely to see him here his friends were glad.

55. When first in Presence-Chamber he was come
The King said, Welcome, George, unto our grace;
I know thou loved the alarm of a drum;
I see the marks of manhood in thy face.
He, humbly kneeling, thanked his Majesty,
That he had got him set at liberty.

56. And often after that the King would jest,
And call him Cousin, in a merry mood,
Because therefore the Frenchmen had asset
His fine so high: which turned him to good.
His foes did say in serving he was free,
And for reward the Prince gave land in fee.

57. Then none of us did unrewarded go:
I had a gift yearly worth fifty pound.
Which I recite, because thou should know,
I have received benefits to drowned.
Besides I had a stipend for my life,
Who shortly left the Court, and took a wife.

58. And now, because the King and Queen did use
By friendly signs their liking to display,
What men our company would then refuse?
Our betters then with us did seek to stay.
For lo! it is a path to dignity
With Caesar's 'friends to be in amity.

59. Then Pembroke, and his Wife, who sister was
Unto the Queen, their kinsfolk friend much;
And Parr, their brother, did them both surpass:
Who, for to pleasure us, did never grudge.
Now when these called us Cousin at each word,
The other peers would friendly speech afford.

60. In many suites their help did us avail;
Few things, or none, that time with us sped ill.
Our ship new caulked began to bear a sail;
And we had wind and weather at our will.
All men gave us faire words of courtesy,
A hound that dry-foot hunts prosperity.

61. This was the time that we acquaintance got
Throughout the realm, of such as bore the sway.
The beams of shining sun were very hot,
Whose warmth began at setting to decay.
Which setting sudden was: Death did surprise
Our King, yea then when most wee looked to rise.

62. This warlike King, borne sure to victory,
Did never dangerous battle undertake,
But he did triumph on his enemy;
Whose name once known did make his foes to quake.
The King in France, the Queen at Flodden Field,
Want both; at once Frenchmen and Scotts did yield.

63. When cruel Atropos had stopped his breath:
When he interred lay in Windsor town:
Then was our edge abated by his death,
We anchor cast: our sails were pulled down:
We feared a storm; which vanished in the air:
The clouds consumed, the sky proved very fair.

64. King Edward, crowned in his infancy,
All Popish laws and rites did straight withstand.
Those days did rule the mighty Tres-Viri,
Protector, Pembroke, and Northumberland.
But, since I dare not touch the Common-Weal,
Yet with myself I may be bold to deal.

65. My sovereign lost, the Queen I did attend
The time that mourning widow she did rest;
And while she married was, unto her end
I willingly obeyed her Highnesses' hest;
Who me esteemed, and thought my service good:
Whereas in truth to small effect it stood.

66. Her Husband fourth was uncle to the King;
Lord Seymour, High by office Admiral:
In praise of whom loud peals I ought to ring;
For he was hardy, wise, and liberal.
His climbing high disdained by his peers
Was thought the cause he lived not out his years.

67. Her house was termed a second Court of right,
Because there knocked still nobility.
He spared no cost his ladle to delight,
Or to maintain her Princely Royalty.
Elizabeth, there sojourning a time,
Gave fruitful hope, through blossoms bloom in prime.

68. For, as this Lady was a Princesses born,
So she in princely virtues did excel.
Humble she was, and no degrees would scorn:
To talk with poorest souls she liked well.
The sweetest violets bud near the ground:
The greatest states in lowliness abound.

69. If some of us, that waited near the Queen,
Did ought for her, she passed in thankfulness.
I wondered at her answers, which have been
So futile placed, with speedy readiness.
She was disposed to mirth in company:
Yet still regarding civil modesty.

70. Virtue from her ran swiftly, like a stream;
To all her friends great joy the same did bring.
Her Latin poesie, Semper Eadem:
In English, thus: A Woman, yet no Changeling.
Into a needless praise why do I rush?
The proverb says, Good wine craves not a bush.

71. Virtue, go vaunt thyself, and grant me leave
To show thee, how the Queen, past middle age,
Which barren was before, did then conceive,
And bare a child; but laid her life to gage.
I wish my friends in time they would foresee,
Lest, all too late, themselves examples be.

72. But, when my Queen lay buried in her grave,
To Musselborough Field I mourning went.
The gladsome victory to us God gave.
Home with those tidings I, post-haste, was sent.
When joy full message was dispatch and done,
Beyond desert, a recompense I won.

73. For Somerset Protector did vouchsafe
My service small by writing to commend.
That I employed was, my foes did chase;
It grieved them to the guts that he should send
Me to the King, whose Grace did straight agree,
That I in Privy-Chamber one should be.

74. Then some, like angry steeds, at mouth did foam,
To miss the cushion, when I got reward;
But the Admiral, my spokesman, was at home,
Who stayed, his Nephew's safety to regard.
He was, at all essays, my perfect friend,
And patron too, unto his dying end.

75. When men surmised that he would mount on high,
And seek the second time aloft to match:
Ambitious hearts did sheer him then too nigh:
Off went his head: they made a quick dispatch.
But ever since I thought him sure a beast
Who causeless labored to defile his nest.

76. Thus guiltless he, through malice, went to pot;
Not answering for himself, nor knowing cause.
It was Cromwell's hap, and sure his rightful lot,
To make, and suffer, by his proper laws.
He framed Perillus' bull, therein to fry:
A whip he made which caused himself to cry,

77. That he deserved to drink as he did brew.
Thus Draco's statute yet by cruelty
Faultless condemned him whose want I rue,
Because he shielded me from injury.
Well, in their service while that I did stay
I wooed, I wan, I ware my wife away.

78. Oft since I thought, that nature well did frame
That he, who laughs his neighbor's house on fire,
Shall sigh to see his own consume with flame:
A just reward for so unjust ire.
Herein now let me warn, and thou shall see
A wonder of the world, if ought may be.

79. Howe Somerset, who then by equity
Protector was, and uncle to the King,
Of treason quit, yet dyed for felony.
Who thought not this a lamentable thing?
A pattern rare of singularity,
And matchless! left to all posterity.

80. Howe many rascals for more vile offence,
Yea foolish thieves, their clergy do not crave,
And pardon seek of course, before and since!
I think the wits of England then did rave.
What right of law allow, life to save,
The Duke and all his friends forgot to have.

81. Ye lawyers! which in office he had placed,
Or did support, were surely then to blame;
As guilty of his death, you all disgraced
May now of right go shroud your heads with shame.
Too far unlike the men of latter time,
Whose cunning gloss can shadow every crime.

82. That country, friends, by ignorance of right,
That lawyers blinded by oblivion,
That such as knew, should it conceal of spite,
Or stained be by vile corruption,
That all advantage given be must forego:
The case was hard, and yet the truth we know.

83. But learned, and mark the cause. This Duke did bring.
His only brother to destruction;
Wherefore our God, who hated much that thing,
Did justly send on him confusion.
And, that no lets might rise through policy,
He turned man's wit to mere simplicity.

84. Lest in a labyrinth I rush unawares,
I leave to run astray, and sound retreat.
Hark in the Court with me how each thing fares,
Who now about the King became so great,
That I above the rest wan special grace
Whereby it was hoped I should advance our race.

85. For lo! the King's affection was such,
That he would jest with me most merrily;
And, though there at my betters still did crutch,
Yet nevertheless he use my company.
He, wearied much with Lords, and others no,
Alone with me into some place would go.

86. Let Sydney, Neville, and the rest that were
In Privy-Chamber then but tell a truth,
If they have scene his liking anywhere
Such as to me, who never felt his wroth.
I lived in so great favor, that my could
Was well nigh joined then with what I would.

87. And on a time, when knighted I should be,
The King said, Kneel. Yet then I went my way;
But straight forth himself ran, and spied me,
Behind a chest, in lobby where I lay;
And there, against my will, he dubbed me Knight:
Which was an eye-sore unto some men's sight.

88. When to the King my wife was showed, new brought
To Court (who for the nonce was meanly clad):
He told her, That I was a husband naught,
Because he saw her courtly robes so bad.
But she excused the fault with poverty
Which me enforced to keep her beggarly.

89. And I replied, for her, It was no way
To bear the merchant's stock upon her back;
Unless I knew some means it to repay,
And us to save from ruin and from wrack.
He answered, Dost thou want, and blush to crave?
Of right the tongue-tied man should nothing have.

90. But we are well contented for to give
Something of profit, which thou shall spy,
Whereby thou shall be able for to live,
If not before some farther help we die.
Rightly of us thou never shall complain,
Of travail ill rewarded for its pain.

91. My friends had me take time, while time there was;
And while the iron was hot to strike the stroke.
The bargeman must not let the tide over pass;
To proffer pig each man doth open his poke.
They said, While Maye doth last, make choice of May;
Lest, when thou wouldst, she womanly say, Nay.

92. Lessons late learned are freshest in the mind:
I put in your against death to get some store.
I feared lest Fortune should be held behind;
Wherefore I caught her by the lock before.
For Paulers-Pury I did speak, and speed:
'Twas granted me, for to relieve my need.

93. Now, something gained, I, licensed to absent
Myself a space, a progress rode
Unto my friends: with me my wife there went:
And with my Father we a while abode.
To me he showed good countenance openly:
But yet alone he checked me bitterly.

94. He thumped me on the breast, and thus began:
Sir Knight! Sir knave! a foolish boy you are:
And yet thou think thyself a goodly man!
Why should thou scorn thy Father's daily fare?
Or send me word when I should see the here?
As who should say, I should provide good cheer.

95. Too base for thee thou thought thy Father's food.
But since it is so, I tell thee in good soothe
My carter's meat I think is far too good
For such a one that brings so dainty tooth.
I see thou grow into disdain of me:
Wherefore know this, I careless am of thee.

96. These taunting terms did trouble much my mind.
But I did sound the cause of all this grief.
The sore once seen, a plaster I, did find:
And after that my stay was very brief.
He thought to him some injurie was done,
That I was Knight before his eldest son.

97. To Court my eldest Brother then and I
Did come; yet would I no man should disdain
That by my means he knighted home did he:
Whereby my Father pleased was again.
My brother John too, let it no man scorn,
By furtherance mine, King Edward's man was sworn

98. When all of us at years: when two made Knights:
When five of us had been of Parliament:
All forward in the world: when all these sights
Our Father saw; then summoned hence he went.
No boot to strive when Death lists hence to call;
Who is no sparing judge: but visits all.

99. Whose want though somewhat I bewailed with tears
The miss of him yet did I not discern:
My loss I could not see through youthful years.
But all too late at length this I did learn,
That he who sees his father lade in grave,
May leave to look so sure a staff to have!

100. I could not mourn a night. My joys did flow:
The King me fancied daily more and more.
For as his years so did my favor grow:
Which caused me look more stately than of your.
We see the friendly countenance of a King
To foolish paradise doth many bring.

101. I careless wax of the inferior sort:
Nobility I now did much esteem.
For why? Myself began to bear a port,
And I, as then, mere madness did it deem,
To leave the head, and sue unto the foot:
Because that proof doth shew it is little boot.

102. I drew no water but at fountain top;
There sought I liking only to attain:
To bear me up I craved no other prop:
Whom to withstand my foes did work in vain.
For my defense I had so sure a shield,
That malice, raised in rage, with shame did yield.

103. When some with false reports did me accuse,
And yet could not enforce his Majesty
His settled fancy thereby to refuse:
In childish cradle of security
I rocked myself asleep; devoid of care;
For why? I was the King's familiar.

104. In scornful guise I spate in Fortune's face:
A banner of defiance I displayed;
And underfoot I trod her royal mace,
As one who then should never need her aide.
I bid her take revenge by cankered spite;
For I contemned her power and all her might.

105. And sure I judged Fortune was far unable
To fall with me a trip that stood so fast:
Methought I sat too safe within my saddle
By jerking or by plunging to be caste.
Some by authority might me reprove,
And seek for to unhorse: but not remove.

106. When on Northumberland the King again frown,
For the Protector's death, and he it viewed;
Straightaways he sought at once to pull me down:
He thought I was the man his bane that brewed.
Of all alive he most misdoubted me,
For that the King and I did still agree.

107. He much disliked our secret conference,
The privy whisperings that the King did use;
He thought they little made for his defense,
And that, alone, the King I did abuse with tales.
But sure of me he did misdeem,
Who thought I drew not yoked in his team.

108. When such would seek to hurt, but could not harm
When as myself was placed in pillory
Of pleasures, not too cold, nor yet too warm;
When, entered on the grace of dignity,
Hope tickled me to sit in Honor's chair:
When I did build me towers in the air,

109. When on the top of all prosperity,
I solace took in arbor of delight:
Then lo! my mirth was changed to misery;
And I a pattern made of Fortune's spite.
My King, my joys, at once Death took away:
And I enforced Queen Mary's dump to play.

110. This King to others was a lamp of light,
Whose fame of right must want an ending day!
A foe to none! a friend to every wight;
The sky did gape to catch his soul for prey.
For age he might deserve a riper end:
Death calls the best, and leaves the worst to mend.

111. Mourning from Greenwich I did straight depart
To London, to an house which bore our name.
My brethren guessed, by my heavy heart,
The King was dead: and I confessed the same.
The hushing of his death I did unfold:
Their meaning to proclaim Queen Jane I told .

112. And though I liked not the religion
Which all her life Queen Mary had professed,
Yet in my mind that wicked motion
Bight heirs for to displace I did detest.
Causeless to proffer any injurie
I meant it not, but sought for remedy.

113. Wherefore from four of us the news was sent,
Howe that her brother he was dead and gone.
In post her goldsmith then from London went,
By whom the message was dispatched annon.
She asked if we knew it certainly?
Who said, Sir Nicholas knew it verily.

114. The author bred the errand's great mistrust:
She feared a train to lead her to a trap.
She said, If Robert had been there, she durst
Have gaged her life, and hazarded the hap.
Her letters made, she knew not what to do:
She sent them out, but not subscribed thereto.

115. When first the Queen was crowned, I lived well;
But Spaniards came, and Wyatt quickly rose;
Who only meant outlandish force to quell:
To him adherent men did me suppose.
When he had played his woeful tragedy;
Then next ensued my bitter comedy.

116. Who tastes no sweet cannot discern the sour:
The bond-child can but little say for ease:
Who sees but frowns, knows not if Fortune lower
Who knows no earth, cannot dispraise the seas.
But he whose rest exchanged is for war
May boldly say, that peace exceeded far.

117. Then woe to me! whose happiness was past!
With whom the world was turned upside down.
My calm was gone; on rocks my ship was caste:
For favor late, all things on me did frown:
A metamorphosis that seemed strange,
My pleasure with such perils to exchange.

118. Lo! too fond fancies, erst which pleased my will,
Were swallowed and consumed in seas of care.
I plunged on ground of grief: I gorged my fill
Of homely food, and yet my daily fare.
Who, for a moment of felicity,
What man was ever so plunged in misery.

119. Instead of Court, which comfort lately bred,
A close restraint bridled my liberty;
And I, examined, was to Tower led:
A prisoner there, I wanted company.
I missed my courtly mates, and all alone
I was murdered up in dampish walls of stone.

120. Thence, traitor like, I'm brought through every street,
With bills conducted to the Common-Hall.
In passing I with friends and foes did meet:
The one did fear, the other hoped, my fall.
Ill luck! when all did hate, or pity me.
But mark what doleful sight I chanced to see!

121. My Wife, my Mother, and my Brethren there
Were come to see me then with watery eyes:
Mistrustful love the worst doth always fear;
Whom when I saw so passionate in cry's,
Their plaints and mourning noise I more did rue
Than loss of life, which might on me ensue.

122. Because the Chronicle doth shew at large
My accusation, and acquittal both,
I mean thereby to ease me of that charge,
Lest that my being tedious thou dost loath.
Yet read it, when thou has convenient leisure:
Perhaps my passed pain shall bring thee pleasure.

123. There shalt thou view a president most rife,
How I, arraigned of treason, was set free
By jurors' verdict, not to lose my life:
The only a per se of my degree: I mean, that was but of Gentility:
Yet few have escaped of Nobility.

124. The plunge once past, then was I back again
To Tower led; where I remained a year,
And heard that me once more they would arraign:
Which sure, I thought, would touch me very near.
But, since that passed laws of equity.
Amongst the rest I went at liberty.

125. When this course had my stomach overlaid,
I guessed straight what should the second be:
The fagot I did fear; and therefore stayed
No long time here: to France I hied me.
And there I found what it is to be a guest
Abroad, and what to live at home at rest.

126. When I, who first exiled myself through fear,
Had so continued full two years and more,
And knew with patience crosses for to bear;
When I waxed pliant unto Fortune's lore;
When with all evils I contented grew;
Then Fortune did begin to smile anew.

127. Then Hope did comfort me that things would mend,
For after night there dawned gladsome day.
Long is the course that never finds end:
Fortune falls if the hawk still misses the prey.
Base music it tis which changed not his note!
Poor miscreant he who always wears one coat!

128. Thus Hope, when cares did kill, did promise make
That sorrows mine, as all things else, should cease:
That from my legs those fetters I should shake,
And that my glory should thereby increase.
We see the sun doth no time show so clear
As after storms and clouds he doth appear.

129. For lo! the man who lent me law of late
To save my life, and put himself in danger,
Did then advancement get to mend his state;
And next did seek to appease the Prince's anger:
Whose heavy wrath he knew, was bent on knee:
But yet at length from that he set me free.

130. In time himself shall stand as much in need
To have some help; and then shall wish for me.
But sure his case I rue: my heart doth bleed
To think of that, which thou thyself shalt see:
How he by wrongful means, for doing right,
Shall justice have, devoid of mercy quite.

131. Yet then for my avail, (who hid my face
From Prince's sight,) my brother did not let
To sue, util she received me to her grace,
And said all former faults she did forget,
And eke forgive. So I returned again:
I mercy craved: I mercy did obtain.

132. I thus acknowledge, that beyond my reach
I intermeddled with the Prince's state,
My betters I did go about to teach:
To Spaniards I did bear a mortal hate.
My mind was bent to let their coming in:
I tell a truth: dissembling is a sin.

133. But herein I deserved most the blame;
The liking of a Queen I much withstood:
Her fancy to my mind I sought to frame:
I thought the cruel Spaniard meant no good.
But such as think to cast beyond the moon,
Like fools, are still deceived: and none so soon.

134. I warped the web of woe within my loom;
Whereof when I had made confession,
I did submit me to her Highnesses' doom,
And straight received absolution.
Her clemency enforced me her to count
My friend whose pity did my faults surmount.

135. And sure Queen Mary was most merciful,
Though nursed up in superstition,
Was ever English Prince so bountiful
To subjects? Mark her restitution,
Not of their blood alone, but of their lands,
Which then remained in her princely hands.

136. When I had had a breathing time of rest,
The Queen, unwilling with her husband's foe
To keep her peace, an any straight addressed
To France: among which crew I needs must go.
I better thought to do some service small
Abroad, than here at home doe none at all.

137. Virtue I thought was exercised in war:
Peace nursed Vice, a mother of Rebellion;
Yea idle Ease the manly mind doth mar
With civil sects that breed confusion.
This caused the man that succor sought by flight
To Frenchmen's realm, against them now to fight.

138. When we with Spaniards won St. Quintin's town,
And did enjoy the same to Frenchmen's foil;
There sickness me, with others, did cast down.
But I, whose health agreed not with their soil,
Unto my native land returned with speed,
And there myself cheered up: which was but need.

139. Then T, who was misliked of the time,
Obscurely sought to live; scant seen at all.
So far I was from seeking up to climb,
As that I thought it well to escape a fall.
Elizabeth I visited by stealth,
As one who wished her quietness with health.

140. Repairing oft to Hatfield, where she lay,
My duty not to slack, that I did owe:
The Queen fell very sick, as we heard say;
The troth whereof her sister sought to know.
That her none might of malice undermine,
A secret means herself did quickly find.

141. She said, since naught exceeds woman's fears,
Who still do dread some bait of subtitle:
Sir Nicholas, know, a ring my sister wears,
Enameled black; a pledge of loyalty;
The which the King of Spain in espousals gave:
If naught falls out amiss, it is this I crave.

142. But hark! open not your lips to anyone,
In hope it to obtain of courtesy,
Unless you know my sister first be gone:
For grudging minds will soon join treachery.
So shall thyself be safe, and I be sure.
Who takes no hurt shall need no care of cure.

143. Her dyeing day shall thee such credit get,
That all will forward be to pleasure thee,
And none at all shall seek thy suite to let.
But go, and come, and look here to find me.
Thence to the Court I galloped in post,
Where, when I came, the Queen gave up the ghost.

144. The ring received, my brethren, then who lay
In London town, with me to Hatfield went:
And as we rode, there met us on the way
An old acquaintance, Hope of advancement;
A sugared bait, that brought us to our bane:
But chiefly me, who there withal was taken.

145. I egged them on, with promise of reward:
I thought, if neither credit or some gain
Fell to their share, the world went very hard.
Yet reckoned I without mine host, in vain.
Who chickens count before the hen doth hatch,
Of all their brood have oft no better catch.

146. When to the Court I and my brethren came,
My news was stale; but yet she knew it true.
But see how crossly things began to frame!
The Cardinal dyed! whose death thy friends may rue.
For then Lord Grey and I were sent in hope
To find some writings to or from the Pope.

147. We found a note how many men were burned:
Small treasure there, for ought that we could see.
When we, from search of written scrolls, returned,
Chief-Butlership reserved was for me.
Excepting that, all offices were gone:
The fruits were pulled, and all the birds were down.

148. Now when I saw my latter reckoning fall
So short of that I made account before,
It troubled and did greatly me appall;
It shamed me with my friends: it grieved me sore.
But time, I thought, this blemish would outwear,
And where there was default, the same repair.

149. As flowing floods recourse unto the seas,
So Princes' gifts each day return again;
And I, who knew my Prince's mind to please,
O' the exchequer then was made a Chamberlain.
And when the Judge of Chester town was gone,
There placed was, with fee, my brother John.

150. With trifles then I pleasured my friends:
For things of value were bestowed at first.
Wherefore they made contentment of odd ends:
Small beer doth serve their turn who are athirst.
For me there hap a far unlucky chance;
Who straight was sent Ambassador to France.

151. And on St. Michael's Feast, while I did stay,
The French King kept a princely royalty;
And to his Court all leigers there that lay
Were brought, and feasted with solemnity.
First placed was the Pope's Ambassador;
And next the ledger of the Emperor.

152. Their liege Portugal with me did jar;
He stepped in to take the upper place
Of me; but that was like our feast to mar:
For I in fury struck him on the face.
I pulled him down, and told him, Verily
My Queen should never lose her sovereignty;

153. And since that place my Prince's was of right,
Nor he, nor yet his King should her embrace;
In whose behalf I challenged him to fight:
My stomach could not suffer such disgrace.
But by the King that quarrel was appeased;
I had the place; and so my mind was eased.

154. And when the time of my return drew near,
The number of the Protestants grew great;
But their increase the King began to fear;
And them with grievous punishments did threat.
Then rigor ruled, and banish was remorse,
Until they in arms did save themselves perforce.

155. And so the King lay then in Orleans;
Of whom I sought some audience to have:
For I had weighty things of importance:
Wherefore of him safe-conduct I did crave.
Since all his realm on hurly-burly was,
I thought alone I might not safely pass.

156. I had a day assigned me to come,
With sixteen hundred men of Paris town;
Who marched, like May-game soldiers, with a drum,
Bravely set out, like men of high renown.
Their purse was full; they had received their pay:
But they, and theirs, were to their foes a prey.

157. Or lo! the Admiral had notice got
How many men, what time, and eke which way
We came. That thing once known, he slackened not,
But hastened on, our journey for to stay,
With horsemen, well appointed for the war;
And, scarce eight hundred, he our sport did mar.

158. A bloody cruel massacre he made:
Scant one of sixteen hundred escaped alive.
The spoil was great; whereof his men were glad.
These blades were priests the simple nuns to shrive.
And first of all the horsemen towards me ran;
And changed my place into a serving man.

159. But see! beyond my hope my lucky hap!
They came to keep, who I supposed would kill;
And I, who deemed in itself taken in a trap,
Was safe: For me, or mine, no man might spill.
The Admiral to me did safeguard send:
Because my Queen, in truth, their chief friend.

160. Whilst I was stayed with him I made such shift
That I unknown wrote letters to the King,
And safely sent them forth by secret drift:
My prisoner state in piteous words wailing:
I craved that he would seek my liberty,
Or to my Queen he offered injurie.

161. And, after that a second skirmish fell,
Wherein the Protestants the better got.
The Admiral pursued the chance so well,
That still the spiteful Papist went to pot.
Tea then the Prince of Conde, who was loath
Idle to rest, from footmen's safeguard goeth.

162. When he was gone, who would not lose the spoil,
In came the Duke of Guise for rescue then.
When he perceived his friends were put to foil,
Unto the camp came he with all his men.
He ransacked all; and into every tent,
A searching for some hidden foes he went.

163. There, writing my mishap unto the Queen,
At length he found me, captive-like (for all
My crew was weaponless, as prisoners been),
And thus with bitter words on me did call:
Thou girded gown-man, with thy pen in hand,
Dost best deserve to die, of all the land.

164. Beyond the policies of Michaiavel
Thou didst the Councilors of France over reach;
Their doings thou did undermine with wile;
And what thou knew to rebels did impeach.
Thou notice gave; thou led us with a train,
To their good hap: and to thy endless pain.

165. The soldiers cried, never changing note,
It is shame to let the English devil live!
With greedy haste they ran to gore my throat;
I look that me of breath they would deprive.
But then the Duke, who knew the law of arms,
Did shield both me and mine from present harms.

166. No certain proof, but bare presumption,
Could me as guilty of that fact accuse.
Some, causeless, thought I sought effusion
Of blood; and that the King I did abuse.
Who to my Queen wrote great complaints of me:
Which all untruths I proved well to bee.

167. And when I thence returned without reward,
At home my foes their nest had feathered soft:
To foreign service men gave small regard.
And then my underlings were kept aloft.
They, who in absence-mine did profit get,
Supposed my presence surely them would let.

168. Wherefore they wrought that I might be employed
Abroad, in dwelling-place of daily dangers;
And by that means I little rest enjoyed,
And lesser safety found with trustless strangers.
To serve my Prince yet I was well content,
How oft, or wheresoever I was sent.

169. When open war between us and France began,
Chatillion the Admiral with us did join.
Newhaven town when worthy Warwick wan,
Then was I sent for to transport some coin,
And as Ambassador to treat of peace;
That deadly hate and bloody wars might cease.

170. First I conferred with the Admiral,
Who presently the battle made at Dreux;
But when I saw his side was like to fall,
I meant not to be taken, if I could adieu.
Unto a ladies lodge, where I did lye
The night before, for succor did I fly.

171. But to the Duke of Guise she me betrayed:
Who kept me prisoner close within a tower.
There I from escaping was with fetters stayed,
Until he knew I was Ambassador.
He then for anger at the mouth did foam;
Yet safely suffered me to retire home.

172. Moreover I was sent to Scotland twice.
No causeless war ensued my going first.
It was time, and just occasion, bad us rise
In arms: but soldiers that for war do thirst,
When I should come again did nothing grieve:
They said, I carried war within my sleeve.

173. They did me all the honor might be had:
Above they greeted mee with ordinance.
When to the gates I came, the soldiers glad
Did smile on me with cheerful countenance.
Some inkling they had heard before of war:
But when I came they thought it was not far.

174. And shortly after Drury proved it true:
He Edinburg Castle, and the town,
With force did take. He made his foes to rue
Their bragging boasts; who still were beaten down.
When peace did spring, and cruel war was past,
Then I obtained more quiet rest at last.

175. And living in the Court, the Queen would use,
In weightiest matters, my advice to crave.
And I to tell my mind durst not refuse,
But, look! what course I thought was best I gave.
If so it fell that I did disagree
With the Lords of Council, they would chafe at me.

176. Yet, afterwards, if any great demand
Or suite was made, whereto the Queen said, No:
If once a thing disliked she did command,
Into a common bye-word it did grow,
That weasel-face Throckmorton had been there.
So I, though guiltless, all the blame did bear.

177. And, when the Chancellor of the Dutch Land
Was dead, the Queen did promise me that place.
Wherefore, my things to order out of hand,
I rode from Court, and tarried too long space.
When I returned, I knew the office gone;
To Presence-Chamber I repaired anon.

178. And sure the Queen I may not rightly blame;
But I am bound to thank the gentleman
Who in my absence needs would beg the same:
By whom I lodge on pallet, as his maim.
His overthrow, for feigned flattery,
Shall wished be of my posterity.

179. And though he stands as doth the mighty oak,
Whose branches coverts are whole hoards to keep:
An arbor he for heat; for storms a cloak;
Yet may it be he shall not shroud a sheep.
The branches spreading broad men soonest lap:
On hills most often hits the thunder clap.

180. Hereafter, one of mine shall hope his harm,
And speak too soon the thing his heart would wish.
But wit too dearly bought his tongue shall charm;
Whose fault shall oft be laid in his dish.
And he shall know that cold and malice take
More suddenly than any they forsake.

181. Now to myself; of whom thou wonders so,
That I, who was a Courtier all my days,
And whom the Queen had known so long ago,
And whom she ready found at all assays,
Was never yet advanced in dignity;
Nor much enriched by prosperity.

182. Yet there have many Courtiers been of late,
Who, for small service, and in lesser time,
Have rose to wealth, and mended so their state,
As to the top of honor they could climb.
But Fortune was resolved on mee to frown:
She set me up; she best might keep me down.

183. Her means was this. A barre lay on my back
Which held me low, and cloyed my wings with lead.
False friends, as well as foes, brought me to wrack:
Or else I never could have hung the head.
My deeds were scanned, which spiteful eyes did note,
In hopes to spy some hole within my coat.

184. When last in arms the Northern Rebels rose;
When Norfolk's Duke committed was to Tower:
Then lo! was warped the web of all my woes;
And then approach my wretched luckless hour.
In prison put, not thinking of the same,
Where none might visit me that bare my name.

185. Six times the Council did examine me,
As one consenting to the practices
Of Rebels. But I cleared myself most free
From all their treasons, and their villainies.
I proved the Councilors knew as much as I:
For otherwise I had been sure to die.

186. My fault, if that I made a fault, was this:
I knew with pen one wooed a prisoned Queen.
To beat a dog small cause sufficient is:
A staff is easily found to wreak our teen.
He peaching scraped, and Council bare no blame:
It was I, who neither was, had all the shame.

187. Returned I was to prison back again;
Where, that I might not loathe to live alone,
Both pensive thoughts and hurtful sighs did reign;
Assisting still my broken heart to moan:
Nott for because I wanted liberty:
To me hard prisons were no novelty.

188. To have my foe nay judge was cause of grief;
For festered hate with envious eye doth look.
This something was: but yet the occasion chief
Why troubles these with ease I could not brook
Was this, that men should deem me of their train
Who traitors were unto my Sovereign.

189. What cankered hap had I, who from my youth
Had been esteemed of her Majestic!
Who long had known, and oft had tried, my troth,
Which never was stained by dishonesty.
I made no comp of life to do her good;
But no great danger to her standard stood.

190. For most assured service, wanting rest:
For faith, for loyalty, for duty done:
For honest heart, obedient to her best:
For which desert, is this requital done?
To be imprisoned, causeless, in the end?
To just minds such thanks how can thou send

191. But what can I suppose this doing is
My Queen, who favored me beyond desert?
Of whom my mind hath never thought amiss:
No, no! my foes have wrought the same by art.
And though my lot was framed by destiny,
Yet Hope thereto brought me by flattery.

192. With glaring eyes he brought me to the view
Of honor, credit, and excessive gain;
Of courtly dames, with sweet and heavenly hue;
Of haughty looks of pomp, which bears a train
Of rich attire embossed with beaten gold;
Of rare delights, of pleasures manifold.

193. These hidden hooks were they that did the feat:
These pleasant snares did egg me to the Court;
These enticing baits, as mice do wish to eat,
These me with hope of prey unaware did sport.
These open signs foretell the contrary:
The garland stands but for a mockery.

194. The Court Medusa is for face most fair;
Whose head the glittering tinsel doth attire:
Yet thence spring poisoned snakes, instead of hair:
Her ground unsure as is the quaking mire.
There did I find the shadows did beguile,
Led in by nattering Hope, by subtle while.

195. Desire to rise corrupt youth in prime:
She harbors swelling pride in all men's hearts:
The envious nest and mother of all crime:
Religion's foe; the mold of all my smarts.
She hatched in the brain such fantasies,
As daily turn to wicked practices.

196. Thou cursed Hope! which fawning did allure
Me still to feed on things of little trust!
Vain are thy shows! thy signals are unsure,
And like the winds that never continue just!
But vainer they who seem to credit thee,
Who art the ground of all uncertainty.

197. Were it not thou pretend better still,
We could content ourselves to live in thrall,
And take as well in wrath our wonted ill,
As they their sour who taste no sweet at all.
But whiles by thee we gape for to be served,
We hazard soonest to be hunger-starved.

198. Ah wretched Hope! thou mother of mishap!
Whichever turn the best into the worst!
Thy branches neither yield leaves, fruit, or sap,
But barren bark; and therefore still accurse!
Whose smiling cheer is mixed with most deceit,
Wherewith the fond are drawn into the bait.

199. Thou, Hope! doe seem to ravish with delight!
And yet thy drifts are nothing but delays!
Each due desert, and each apparent right,
Thou boldest back with dilatory pleas!
Therefore bewitched most of all are they,
Who with thy promises are led astray.

200. The harmless birds, that light on the lime,
In hope of life doth wrest above her force;
Whereby, at length, before her fixed time,
She yielded up her silly fainting course!
But were not Hope that fed her thoughts in vain,
She would not seek to hasten so her pain!

201. The fearful hare doth gird before the hound
Amine, in hope to escape the bloody chase!
The nimble doe through thick and thin doth bound
To save her life, yet quail in her race!
Thus trustless Hope procure things to strive
Above their reach, half dead and half alive!

202. What boots the fowl within the falcon's claws
To struggle much? he may not once resist.
What hopes the prey within the lion's paws?
To wish to live, or hope to be desist?
No help! For naught avails their hopes, I say,
Whose contraries do cut the same away.

203. For, as the hives which honey never hold;
Or as the fire which warm never a whit;
Or else as clothes which doth defend no cold;
Is Hope: which oft doth rather hurt, than hit.
Then, since I see the same so fruitless is;
Fie! fie! on Hope! farewell both he, and his.

204. Adieu! beguile full Hope! Come on Despair
Of worldly weal! thee I must entertain!
In every sphere appears the cloudy air:
The sky's above have bent themselves to rain.
Of right I must acquaint myself with Care:
My lodge! my friend! my servant! and my fare.

205. Since I am thought a traitor unto Her
Who me, belike, condemned to the same:
How could she else have kept me prisoner
Unless she thought I did deserve some blame?
And since it is so, O Death! fling out thy dart!
This corrosive consumes me to the heart!

206. If thou with quick dispatch wilt not make haste,
By fatal clap to rid my wretched life;
Yet restless thoughts my body so shall waste
That soaking sighs shall shortly end the strife.
And I the port of rest shall gain at last
There safe to sit in spite of Fortune's blast.

207. In prison I had not continued long
But I might see my happy hour draw near:
An hour to end at once both grief and wrong;
And when I knew my short abiding here,
That sorrow me remediless would kill,
With fainting hand I wrote my woeful will.

208. And first of Care, my old and fastest friend,
This one and last request I needs would crave,
Whereto no Nay, but he must condescend
To undertake the charge that I him gave:
I willed he should perform my obsequies;
And then begin to dole my miseries.

209. To Care I first bequeath my worldly haps:
My solitary, melancholic moods:
My doleful thoughts, which hinder quiet napes,
These are the chiefs parcel of my goods.
My heavy head, which was a shop of wares
Fraught still with quaint concepts, and daily cares:

210. My throbbing heart, with scalding sighs half worn;
My frowning looks, procured by inward grief;
My carcass lean, with pensiveness forlorn;
My flesh, consuming clean without relief:
These, bound in conscience, I to thee restore,
Of whom the same I did receive before.

211. My hollow eyes, my pale and shriveled skin,
My grey-grown hairs amidst my youthful prime,
My aching bones, and all that is therein,
Give them whom grief makes old before their time.
My ill-luck, lo! I do bequeath it whole
Unto my foe; for whom it is too good a dole.

212. My honest heart, from villain most free,
All my good parts of body or of mind,
I do command to be entombed with me:
For which the world hath little use behind.
My tongue, which closely sorrow did conceal,
I wish them who in vain their woe reveal.

213. My lightness I return to woman kind,
The workers of our woe, from whence it came;
Wherewith all manly virtues from our mind
Are quite exiled, or blemished with the same.
And, where all mourners' weeds of black have been:
My friends! instead of black, mourn ye in green!

214. Thou Care! alone, shall bring me to my grave.
And, since my parentage it is not base,
Prepare one banner of my arms to have,
Pertaining to my most unlucky race.
What anomie it is that I may bear,
Behold! a perfect blaze ensued here.

215. A glittering field of riche alluring gold,
Where Fortune blind doth vaunt her whirling wheel,
On base pointe sable she a wretch do hold;
And in contempt, she spumes him with her heel.
Whose naked limbs portend a naked troth:
Although his place shows misery and wroth.

216. And so, when this unlooked for prisonment,
A cooling card in midst of jollity,
Had quenched all hope of high preferment
With running clouds of sudden misery:
When Care, who like this soil, had taken such root,
That him to move it was but little boot;

217. When I had, in my will, resolved to die:
Then, lo! my Wife so earnestly did sue,
That I at length was set at liberty,
With help of Middlemore and Killigrew:
Who both were of the Privy-Chamber then;
Yet heretofore had been my waiting-men.

218. Love then infringed all dutiful obeisance:
My wife abased me to mine enemy,
Humbly entreating my deliverance:
Yet I commanded her the contrary.
I would not yield, although I were too weak:
The sturdiest oak doth never bend but break.

219. But thus he proudly answered then my wife:
Although your husband, Madame, be the man,
Who by my help would naught in all his life
Vouchsafe to take: yet, do he all he can,
He shall be now beholden unto me:
And by my means his freedom you shall see.

220. That he should be a means me free to set,
Assure myself my grief it was not small.
With feigned cheerful face yet did I jet,
And looked as one that was not grieved at all.
When Death of breath deprived Lord Treasurer.
Then I with him was joined a mourner.

221. When, as to Paules we waited on the hearse,
Instead of mourning talk to mourning gown,
Each did begin old grudges to rehearse:
Both weary of the other's holding down.
Our hearts through private conference did relent:
To bury wrongs forecast both were content.

222. When it was perceived that we began to agree;
Then, lo! both Lords and many others sought
That we would change our state to amity:
Where to we yielded both. Yet this I thought;
Whose believes a foe late reconciled
Is for the most part spitefully beguiled.

223. Now this atonement was but newly made,
When cruel cat with captive mouse can play:
A certain rule that joys began to fade,
And that the silly mouse should be a prey.
Or Fortune dandled me within her lap,
Whom most she sought to speed with fatal clap.

224. She gave out friendly speech, that I should be
Of Privy-Councill, and Vice-Chamberlain:
But she meant, by the sequel you may see,
That all her sleeves were cyphers set in vain.
Her ireful hate, that me with force suppress,
Was then disposed in scornful guise to jest.

225. And she with crosse mishaps so settled Care,
Who daily wasted both my lunges and heart;
That flesh was fallen, and bones were all most bare,
Which promise made with speed to end my smart.
And when it was known that long I could not live;
No soul would spare sweet friendly words to give.

226. Was ever man so bound to Sovereign
As I to mine, who in extremity
Did send both doctors for to ease my pain,
A comfort great to cure my curiosity!
But physick came in vain, when I was killed!
Too late to keep when all the milk is spilled.

227. So did I yield to happy Death his fee;
Who in my life did seek to bear some sway:
 But never could from worldly cares be free,
Until buried in a quiet grave I lay.
The swelling barns are not so full of corns,
As great estates are set with prickling thorns.

228. Wherefore, silt burned child may well his friend
Beware, lest he be scorched in flaming fire,
I wish thou should thine errors late amend,
And from those dangerous thoughts myself retire.
Diogenes lived safely in his cell;
And thou, in Littleton, may safely dwell.

229. Recount my Life by years, by-months, by hours;
Seek out each dram and scruple of true joy,
My sweets laid out untold; my bitter sours
Will poise each good with ounces of annoy.
In this account I give thee now alone:
My stint is paste; and I must needs be gone.

FINIS.

Nichols, *The Legend of Sir Nicholas Throckmorton*, pg. 1-58.

Appendix: Ancient Statutes and New Orders for the Town and Castle of Berwick on 30 September, 1560

Ancient Statutes of the town and Castle of Berwick.

1. Soldiers not having taken the oath to forfeit their wages.
2. Full returns of retinues to be made.
3. Traitors and conspirators to be punished as such.
4. Stealers and receivers of the queen's ordnance and stores to suffer death.
5. Intercommuning with the Scots and encouraging desertion to be taken as treason.
6. Persons indicted for felony or treason to be put into bail during the queen's pleasure.
7. Annoying Scots or other aliens having the queen's safe conduct to be punishable.
8. Affrays at any of the gates or the watch hill to be punished with death.
9. Any going from the walls after the watchword is given to suffer death.
10. Sentinels suffering searchers to pass between them and the battlements without first giving the watchword to be imprisoned and fined.
11. Soldiers absent without license to lose double wages.
12. Soldiers doing duty as scourers to be responsible for any horses lost.

13. Clerks of the watch are to see the watch of the walls truly guarded.
14. The clerks are to appoint soldiers to watch and ward indifferently without affection.
15. The clerks are to withdraw pleas to the queen's hindrance.
16. Soldiers withstanding the tipped staff to be punished.
17. The yeoman porters to give diligent attendance at the gates.
18. If they shut not the gates and wickets duly, and deliver not up the keys, they are to suffer death, and the master to be imprisoned during the queen's pleasure.
19. They shall not suffer Scots or other aliens to enter the town without license.
20. Taking bribes at the gates shall be punished with a fine of fourfold the bribe.
21. The gates shall be shut at every alarm, and all carts with fodder, straw, etc to be searched under pain of death.
22. Counterfeiting the keys of the gates and storehouses punishable with death.
23. Prisoners to be ransomed openly, that the captain may not lose his thirds, under of forfeiture of goods.
24. Prisoners not to be led or to go into the streets with- out guard.
25. No soldier to use any vile occupation, as fishing.
26. Every soldier to wear a jacket of the queen's colors, white and green.
27. No soldier to use dice or cards for money except within the twenty days of Christmas, or else at any of the gates of the town, or within the watch-houses, market-place, or tollbooth, under pain of three days imprisonment, and the stakes to be forfeited to the queen's bridge at Berwick.
28. No dogs to be kept over the feast of the Exaltation of the Holy Cross next coming, no greyhounds or spaniels to be in the streets except they be "handled or led in leashes or lyans;" for the third offence both master and dog shall be put out of the town. No dogs shall be in the streets at night.
29. The great ordnance to be safely kept.
30. No person to be retained to the ordnance "till he be halberd by the captain."
31. Watchers neglecting to give warning of every ship and person coming within sight to have their heads struck off at the market cross.

32. Embezzling the ordnance stores to be punished with death.
33. Horsemen and archers to have horses and all furniture of their own without borrowing.
34. No soldier to steal any weapons upon pain of imprisonment and banishment.
35. No livery or cognizance to be worn but the queen's.
36. No soldier to be in the streets without a bill or axe.
37. No soldier to mow any grass in the bounds.
38. The quartermasters of booty, etc. to do their duty.
39. Soldiers "hosteying" upon the queen's enemies, and not defensibly arrayed, to have but child's part of booty, and to lose their horse and arms.
40. No enterprise to be made upon the enemy unless the captain first be made privy to it.
41. Searchers not diligently doing their duty to be put out of wages.
42. Every watcher found asleep, for the third offence, or warning his fellow who is asleep of the approach of the searchers, for the second offence, as well the sleeper as the escrier, both to be put over where they made the said default, and set in baskets, and a can of drink in their hands, and there he or they to tarry unto the time the rope be cut, and so to redeem themselves.
43. Whoso has the rule of the watch-bell, if he come not to the church and strike a general larum as cause shall require, shall suffer death.
44. No Scottish born person to be of the garrison on pain of death.
45. The scout-watch to do their duty.
46. The constables to do their duty.
47. Soldiers of the relief to be attendant upon the captain.
48. No soldier to come on the town wall suspiciously by night without the watchword.
49. No Englishman may lead a stranger on the walls under pain of loss of goods and banishment, and if by night to be taken as a traitor.
50. None may go over the town walls, or measure the depth or breadth thereof deceitfully, or cast any stores or filth into the ditches.

Signed by the queen the last October 2nd

New orders issued to Berwick:

New orders for the Town of Berwick and the garrison of the same;
to be observed until the fortifications are fully finished
and a garrison established there.

1. The ancient order to stand, saving where it contains any article contrary to these.
2. The church being new desolated, shall be repaired, and the governor and officers shall attend divine service on holidays and Sundays.
3. Services are to be held on Wednesdays and Fridays, so that every soldier may attend at least once in fourteen or twenty-one days.
4. Sermons shall be preached at least once every month, when all who can be spared from their duty are to attend under pain of forfeiting three days' wages.
5. List of particular councilors of Berwick.
6. Forms of oaths to be administered to the governor. Marshal, treasurer, porter, clerk ofvthe check, captains and common soldiers.
7. No soldier to have any freehold in the town or exercise any handicraft, save that of maker of instruments of war.
8. No soldier to take double wages, except for task work on the fortifications.
9. Fornication forbidden under pain of banishment.
10. Twenty days imprisonment and loss of pay for making frays and combats.
11. Combats for trials of titles prohibited upon pain of banishment and loss of pay.
12. Martineers to be esteemed as rebels.
13. None to play at dice by night except he be of the council, under pain of four days imprisonment.
14. No person shall walk abroad after 10 o'clock in the summer and 8 in the winter, or whistle, sing, or shout after the said hours.
15. Not more than a twentieth part of the garrison to be absent at the same time.
16. None to be absent above forty days in the year, save for sickness.
17. Captains to be appointed by the governor.

18. No soldier to be discharged without the consent of the governor.
19. Neither shall gunners of great ordnance be discharged, but as before.
20. Touching the order of the pay.
21. Stuff and instruments of surgeons to be viewed.
22. N o soldier on being discharged is to take away useful amour.
23. Pensioners to be reduced to fifty-six and no more.
24. The governor and council to distribute the bands into quarters of the town.
25. Allowance of powder for the harquebusses for practiua
26. The eight constables to be reduced to four.
27. Soldiers to watch and ward after the ancient manner.
28. A perfect muster of the bands to be held every quarter, all to be suitably equipped and none under 16 years of age.
29. No flesh to be eaten on the fast days, on pain of four to six days imprisonment; and if by a soldier, he shall forfeit a month's pay or twenty days imprisonment "on bread and water
30. The governor and council may make further necessary rules.
With additions by Cecil and dated by him: 29 September 1560

Bibliography

Primary Sources

Almack, Richard. *Papers Relating to Proceedings in the County of Kent, A.D. 1642–A.D. 1646*. Camden Society, 1854.

Bayley, John Esq. F.S.A. *The History and Antiquities of the Tower of London*. In two volumes. London England, T. Cadell, 1821–25.

Burke, S. Hubert. *Historical Portraits of the Tudor Dynasty and the Reformation Period*. London, 1883.

Calendar of State Papers, Foreign Series, of the Reign of Elizabeth.

> *V.2. 1559–1560*. London, 1865.
>
> *V.3. 1560–1561*. London, 1865.
>
> *V.4. 1561–1562*. London, 1866.
>
> *V.5. 1562*. London, 1867.
>
> *V.6. 1563*. London, 1869.
>
> *V.7. 1564–1565*. London, 1870.
>
> *V.8. 1566–1568*. London, 1871.
>
> *V.9. 1569–1571*. London, 1874.

Camden, William. *The History of the Most Renowned and Victorious Princess Elizabeth*. London, 1675.

Castelnau, Michael de. *Memoirs of the Reigns of Francis II and Charles IX of France*. London, 1724.

Digges, Dudley. *Compleat Ambassador*. France, 1655.

Edward VI. *Writings of Edward the Sixth, William Hugh, Queen Catherine Parr, Anne Askew, Lady Jane Grey, Hamilton, and Balnaves.* London, 1831.

Emlyn, Sollom. *Complete Collection of State-Trials and Proceedings for High-Treason and other Crimes and Misdemeanours. V1.* London, 1742.

Forbes, Dr. Patrick. *A Full View of the Public Transactions in the Reign of Q. Elizabeth.* In Two volumes. London, 1740.

Foster, Joseph. *Alumni Oronienses: The Members of the University of Oxford. 1500–1714. V.4.* London, 1891.

Gairdner, James. *Letters and Papers Foreign and Domestic, of the Reign of Henry VIII. V. 18–Part 1 and 2.* London, 1901, 1905.

Garencieres, Ophilus. *The True Prophecies or Prognostications of Michael Nostradamus.* London, 1672.

Hamilton, William Douglas. *A Chronicle of England, during the Reigns of the Tudors, from A.D. 1485 to 1559. By Charles Wriothesley, Windsor Herald.* London, 1877.

Heylyn, Peter. *Ecclesia Restaurata, or The History of the Reformation of the Church of England. An Appendex to the former book touching the Interposings made in Behalf of the Lady Jane Gray.* London: H. Twyford, 1661.

Holinshed, Raphael. *The First and Second Volumes of Chronicles, Comprising the Description and History of England, Ireland and Scotland.* London: Henry Denham, 1587.

Keith, Robert. *History of the Affairs of Church and State in Scotland.* Edinburgh, 1844.

Lee, Sidney. *Dictionary of National Biography.* Vol. LVI, Teach-Tollet. New York, 1898.

Leycesters Common-wealth: Conceived, Spoken and Published with Most Earnest Protestation of all Dutiful Goodwill and Affection. London(?), 1641.

Miscellaneous State Papers from 1501 to 1726. Two volumes. London. 1778.

Nichols, John Gough. *The Chronicle of Queen Jane and of Two Years of Queen Mary and especially of the Rebellion of Sir Thomas Wyat.* Camden Society, 1850.

The Legend of Sir Nicholas Throckmorton. London, 1874.

Schiern, Fredewrik. *Life of James Hepburn, Earl of Bothwell.* Edinburgh, 1880.

Scott, George. *The Memoires of Sir James Melvil of Hal-Hill.* London, 1683.

Strype, John. *Ecclesiastical memorials: relating chiefly to religion, and its reformation, under the reigns of King Henry VIII. King Edward VI. And Queen Mary the First: with the appendixes containing the original papers, records, etc. In seven volumes.* London, 1721.

Historical Memorials, Ecclesiastical and Civil, of Events Under the Reign of Queen Mary I. XX.

Throckmorton, Charles Wickliffe. *A Genealogical and Historical Account of the Throckmorton Family.* Old Dominion Press, Richmond VA, 1930.

Tytler, Patrick Fraser. *History of Scotland.* Edinburgh, 1845.

Wotton, Thomas. *The English Baronetage; Containing a Genealogical and Historical Account of all the English Baronets. V.2.* London, 1741.

Secondary Sources

Acts of the Privy Council of England. Vol. I., A.D. 1542–1547.

Anderson, Walter. *The History of France during the Reigns of Francis II and Charles IX. V.2.* London, 1769.

Annals of the reformation and establishment of religion, and other various occurrences in the Church of England. Compiled out of papers of the state, etc. London, 1824.

Bacon, Francis. *The History of the Reigns of Henry the Seventh, Henry the Eighth, Edward the Sixth and Queen Mary.* London, 1676.

Bain, Joseph. *The Hamilton Papers. Letters and Papers Illustrating the Political Relations of England and Scotland. V.2, 1543–1590.* Edinburgh, 1892.

Bernard, John Peter. *A General Dictionary, Historical and Critical in Which a New and Accurate Translation. V.3.* London, 1735. (Biographical accounts).

Borthwick, Robert. *History of the Princes de Conde in the XVI and XVII Centuries. V. 1.* London, 1872.

Brewer, J. S. *Calendar of the Carew manuscripts, preserved in the archi-episcopal library at Lambeth. In six volumes.* London, 1867–1873.

Calendar of State Papers, Domestic Series, of the Reigns of Edward VI, Mary, Elizabeth, 1547–1580. London, 1856.

Calendar of State Papers, Domestic Series, of the Reign of Elizabeth, 1566–1579. London, 1871.

Calendar of State Papers, Domestic Series, of the Reign of Elizabeth, 1601–1601, with Addenda, 1547–1565. London, 1870.

Calendar of State Papers, Foreign Series, of the Reign of Elizabeth, 1559–1560. London, 1865.

Calendar of State Papers, Foreign Series, of the Reign of Mary, 1553–1558. London, 1861.

Calendar of State Papers, Relating to Scotland. Vol. II The Scottish Series of the Reign of Queen Elizabeth, 1589–1603. London, 1858.

Campbell, Hugh. *The Case of Mary Queen of Scots and of Elizabeth Queen of England. Legally, Briefly, and Historically Stated.* London, 1825.

Carte, Thomas. *A General History of England. V3.* London, 1752.

Coombe. *Anderson's Historical and Chronological Deduction of the Origin of Commerce.* Dublin, 1750.

Caulfield, James. *The Court of Queen Elizabeth.* London, 1814.

Dasent, John Roche. *Acts of the Privy Council of England.* London, 1890.

Decrue, Francis. *Anne Duc de Montmorency, Connetable et Pair de France.* Paris, 1889.

Diary of Henry Machyn, Citizen and Merchant Taylor of London from A.D. 1550 to A.D. , The. 1563. London 1848.

Drake. *Secret Memoirs of Robert Dudley, Earl of Leicester, Prime Minister and Favourite of Queen Elizabeth.* London, 1706.

Fleming, David. *Mary Queen of Scots. From her Birth to her Flight into England.* London, 1898.

Foster, Joseph. *London Marriage Licenses, 1521–1869.* London, 1887.

Froude, James A. *The Reign of Mary Tudor.* London, 1910.

Hayward, John. *Annals of the First Fours Years of the Reign of Queen Elizabeth.* London, 1840.

Haviland, John. *The History of the Life and Death of Mary Stuart, Queen of Scotland.* Church-Yard, 1624.

Hungerford, John. *The English Catholics in the Reign of Queen Elizabeth.* London, 1920.

Hume, David. *The History of England.* London, 1742.

Jardine, D. *Criminal trials. The Library of Entertaining Knowledge, Volume I.* London, 1832.

Lesley, John. *The History of Scotland, from the Death of King James I in the year MCCCCXXXVI, to the Year MDLXI.* Edinburgh, 1830.

Letters and Papers Foreign and Domestic, of the Reign of Henry VIII. 19 Volumes total-all reviewed. Published in London.

Letters of Mary, Queen of Scots, Now First Published from the Originals. Two Volumes. London, 1844.

Life of Queen Elizabeth. The. London, 1905.

Life of the Learned Sir Thomas Smith, Kt., D.C.L. Oxford, 1820.

Locke, Gladys Edson. *Queen Elizabeth: Various Scenes and Events in the Life of Her Majesty.* Boston, 1918.

Maclean, John Esq. *The Life and Times of Sir Peter Carew, Kt.* Bell and Daldy, London 1857.

Markham, Clements R. *Sir. King Edward VI, an appreciation, attempted by Sir Clements R. Markham, K. C. B. With sixteen portraits.* London, 1907.

Medows, Philip. *Oberservations Concerning the Dominion and Sovereignty of the Seas.* Savoy, 1689.

Melville, Sir James. *Memoirs of his Own Life.* Edinburgh, 1827.

Merriman, Roger Bigelow. *Life and Letters of Thomas Cromwell.* Oxford, 1902.

Miscellany of the Maitland Club Consisting of Original Papers and Other Documents of Scotland. Glasgow, 1847.

Miscellaneous State Papers from 1501 to 1726. Two volumes. London. 1778.

Mumby, Frank. *The Girlhood of Queen Elizabeth. A narrative in Contemporary Letters.* Boston, 1909.

Naunton, Robert. *Fragmenta Regalia, of Observations on the Late Queen Elizabeth, Her times and Favourites.* 1642.

Nichols, John Gough. *Literary remains of King Edward the Sixth. Edited from his autograph manuscripts, with historical notes and a biographical memoir.* Two Volumes. New York, 1964.

Parliaments and Councils of England, Chronologically Arranged from the Reign of William I to the Revolution in 1688. London, 1839.

Raven, John. *The Parliamentary History of England from the Earliest Period to the Year 1803. Volume 1, 1066–1625.* London, 1806.

Ridpath, George. *The Border–History of England and Scotland.* London, 1766.

Rapin, Thoyras. *The History of England as Well Ecclesiastical as Civil.* London, 1732.

Robertson, William. *The History of Scotland during the Reigns of Queen Mary and of King James VI. The Works of William Robertson.* London, 1794.

Sharp, Cuthbert. *Memorials of the Rebellion of 1569.* London, 1810. Great detail and accounts of that rebellion.

Shaw, William. *The Knights of England. A Complete Record from the Earliest Time to the Present Day.* V. 2. London, 1906.

Sims, Richard. *A Manual for the Genealogist, Topographer, Antiquary, and Legal Professor.* London, 1861.

Stanclift, Henry Clay. *Queen Elizabeth and the French Protestants in the Years 1559 and 1560.* Leipzig–Reudnitz. 1982.

Strickland, Agnes. *Lives of the Queens of Scotland and English Princesses.* New York, 1851.

Star-Chamber Cases. Shewing What Cavses Properly Belong to the Cognizance of the Covrt. London, 1630.

Strype, John. *Ecclesiastical memorials, relating chiefly to religion, and the reformation of it, and the emergencies of the Church of England, under King Henry VIII. King Edward VI. and Queen Mary I.* London, 1822.

Thorpe, Markham John. *Calendar of state papers relating to Scotland, preserved in the State Paper Department of Her Majesty's Public Record Office.* Two volumes. London, 1858.

True Chronicle Historie of the Whole Life and Death of Thomas Lord Cromwell. London, 1602.

Tytler, Patrick Fraser. *England under the Reigns of Edward VI and Mary with the contemporary history of Europe illustrated in a series of original letters never before printed.* In Two Volumes. London. 1839.

Van Dyke, Paul. *Thomas Cromwell.* 1904.

Wright, Thomas. *Queen Elizabeth and Her Times, a Series of Original Letters.* In two volumes. London, 1838.

Image Sources

Bouchot, Henri. *Les Portraits aux Crayons.* Paris. 1884.

Caldwell-Marsh, Anne. *The Protestant Reformation in France.* London, 1847. Portrait of the Battle of Dreux.

Chamberlain, Arthur. *Hans Holbein the Younger.* London, 1913. Portraits of Thomas Wyatt the Younger and Peter Carew.

Cust, Lionel. *The National Portrait Gallery.* London, 1901. Portraits of Cecil, Leicester and Suffolk–(Henry Grey).

Davey, Richard. *The Nine Days Queen, Lady Jane Grey and her Times.* London, 1909. Portrait of Lady Jane.

Hume, Martin. *Two English Queens and Philip.* London, 1908. Portrait of Philip II.

Law, Ernest. *The Royal Gallery of Hampton Court.* London, 1898. Portratis of King Henry VIII and Elizabeth I.

Pollard, A. F. *Henry VIII.* London, 1902. Portrait of Lord Fitzroy.

Powell, Frederick. *History of England: From the accession of Henry VIII to the Revolution of 1689. Part II.* London, 1908. Battle of Pinkey.

Yorston's Popular History of the World, Ancient, Mediaeval and Modern. Yorston and Co., New York. 8 volumes in total. 1884. Portraits of Henry Guise, Prince of Conde and The Calvinists. This is an absolutely wonderful multi-volume work encompassing portraits over a millennium.

Young, G. F. *The Medici, with Portraits and Illustrations.* London, 1913. Portraits of Catherine and Henry II.

INDEX

Surrey, Earl of, 8
Southwell, Sir Richard, 17, 41
Syon, 20, 27
Syon Abbey, 20

T

Temple Bar, 37, 160, 164
Thames River, 22, 35
Thomas, William, 39, 58-61
Thomworth, John, 133
Throckmorton, Andrew, 10
Throckmorton, Arthur, 167
Throckmorton, Lady anne, 30
Throckmorton, George, 7, 8, 11, 12, 18, 24
Throckmorton, Francis, 159
Throckmorton, Job, 24
Throckmorton, John, 39, 82, 159
Throckmorton, Sir Nicholas, 1-3, 10, 12, 13,
   21, 23, 32, 34, 35, 39, 41, 44, 51, 58, 74, 75,
   78, 79, 88, 97, 116, 127, 135, 141, 146, 158-
   165, 167, 168, 207
Throckmorton, Robert, 7
Tournon, Cardinal, 79
Tower Hill, 19, 32, 37-40
Tower of London, 18, 26, 29-31, 33-37, 39,
   42, 45-47, 61, 64, 72, 79, 158
Tower Wharf, 35
Trail, Robert, 127
Treaty of Edinburgh, 96
Treaties of Greenwich, 13

U

Underhill, Edward, 30

V

Vaughan, Cuthbert, 49-51, 61

Vaux, Anne Katherine, 7
Vaux, Sir Nicholas, 7
Venice, 83, 84, 90

W

Wales, 7, 10, 104
Walsingham, Sir Francis, 162, 163
Warner, Sir Edward, 32, 57, 61
Warwick, Earl of, 107, 114, 121
Warwickshire, 5, 7, 11, 138
Westminster, 24, 32, 36, 38, 39, 88, 163
Westminster Abbey, 32
Westmoreland, Earl of, 32, 157
Westward Forest, 158
White, Sir Thomas, 41
Whitehall, 24
William, King, 7
Wilton, Lord Gray of, 29
Winchester, Bishop of, 32
Windsor Castle, 158, 159
Wingfield Manor House, 157
Winkfield, 158
Wolsey, Cardinal Thomas, 8
Workington, 156
Wotton, Sir Henry, 3, 168
Wotton, Sir Thomas, 3, 168
Wyatt the Younger, Sir Thomas, 21, 34-
   37, 39-41, 45-53, 55-58, 60, 61, 64-66,
   68-70, 72, 73, 78, 81, 188
Wyatt's rebellion, 37, 39, 45, 58, 65, 78, 81

Y

Yarmouth, 29
Yorkshire, 11, 12, 15

Printed in the United States
by Baker & Taylor Publisher Services